D1426503

The First Empires

The Making of the Past

The First Empires

by Nicholas Postgate

Advisory Board for The Making of the Past

Series Editor Graham Speake
Managing Editor Giles Lewis
Picture Editors Hilary Kay, Andrew Lawson
Design Keith Russell
Visual Aids Dick Barnard, Roger Gorringe
Production Andrew Ivett

Frontispiece: one side of a 10-foot-high stele erected by King Ur-Nammu to commemorate the building of the temple and ziggurrat at Ur. In the second register Ur-Nammu, in the rounded hat, pours an offering to the god Nanna (on the right) and to Ningal, his wife, and below he is seen with workman's tools over his shoulder preparing to play his symbolic part in the work (c. 2100 BC).

ISBN 0 7290 0042 7

Elsevier · Phaidon – an imprint of Phaidon Press Ltd,
Littlegate House, St Ebbe's Street, Oxford

Planned and produced by Elsevier International Projects Ltd, Oxford,

Origination by Art Color Offset, Rome, Italy

Filmset by Keyspools Ltd, Golborne, England

Printed by Brepols Ltd, Turnhout, Belgium

Contents

Maps

Preface to the series

This book is a volume in the Making of the Past, a series describing the early history of the world as revealed by archaeology and related disciplines. The series is written by experts under the guidance of a distinguished panel of advisers and is designed for the layman, for young people, the student, the armchair traveler and the tourist. Its subject is a new history – the making of a new past, uncovered and reconstructed in recent years by skilled specialists. Since many of the authors of these volumes are themselves practicing archaeologists, leaders in a rapidly changing field, the series is completely authoritative and up-to-date. Each volume covers a specific period and region of the world and combines a detailed survey of the modern archaeology and sites of the area with an account of the early explorers, travelers, and archaeologists concerned with it. Later chapters of each book are devoted to a reconstruction in text and pictures of the newly revealed cultures and civilizations that make up the new history of the area.

Published titles

The Egyptian Kingdoms
The Aegean Civilizations
The Spread of Islam
The Emergence of Greece
Barbarian Europe
Biblical Lands
The New World
Man before History
The Greek World
The Rise of Civilization

Future titles

The Roman World
Ancient Japan
The Iranian Revival
Ancient China
Rome and Byzantium
Prehistoric Europe
Indian Asia
The Kingdoms of Africa

Introduction

The valley of the Tigris and Euphrates and the Nile valley are often described as the twin cradles of civilization in the Near East, and it is true that the cultural traditions inherited and adapted from the Levant by Greece and Rome derive from these two centers. But although the birth may have been roughly simultaneous, Egypt and Mesopotamia were very far from identical twins. Compared with the monolithic phenomenon of Egypt – one ruler, one river, one language and one people – Mesopotamia harbored a bewildering confusion of races and dynasties. When history dawns in the south of modern Iraq, about 3000 BC, we find the Sumerians in residence: of unknown origin and with a language which has defied all attempts to relate it to any other, although Basque, Hungarian and Chinese have all been tried. With them in the south, and upstream along the Euphrates, were Akkadians, once, we suspect, nomads in the Arabian desert like the Bedouin of today, and speaking, like them, a Semitic language. For throughout history the settled lands fought a fruitless war along their southwest frontiers against the infiltration of such tribes – first the Akkadians, ancestors of the Assyrians and Babylonians, then Amorites, Aramaeans, and finally Arabs, their languages all members of the Semitic group. In time these all became absorbed into the settled community; nor were they the only new arrivals: in the northeast were the ever-present, fierce, and – according to their opponents – barbarous mountain peoples. Although usually content to assert their independence, on two occasions at least they overran and themselves ruled the south – the Gutians (c. 2150 BC) and the Kassites (c. 1500–1150 BC). Immediately to the east of Sumer there lay also the land of Elam with the city of Susa, which, though politically and culturally overshadowed by their neighbors, jealously preserved their individuality during the whole 3,000 years of their coexistence.

Internal politics were quite as complex. During the early centuries the leadership was shared between any of a dozen city-states, and even the dynasties of Akkad and Ur, whose armies marched to the Mediterranean and whose kings were remembered in legend, lasted no more than a century or two. It was only under the Amorite dynasty of Hammurapi that Babylon emerged as a political and cultural metropolis, and she only maintained this position for 1,500 years as a result of the economic depression of the south which had sapped the vigor of potential rivals. One of the main forces for change was the insecurity of the irrigation systems fed by the Tigris and Euphrates, but even in northern Mesopotamia, where agriculture relied on rainfall alone, the political scene was constantly shifting. On the Assyrian plains with their mountain backdrop the earliest identifiable population is Hurrian – with another unrelated language; on the Turkish plateau an Indo-European language called Hittite had made its appearance by 1800 BC; and Semitic tribes pressed up continually from the desert. Unpredictably, the destiny of Mesopotamia belonged with the small trading city of Assur on the Tigris, from which the Assyrian empire grew, rather like the Roman, until it ruled from Egypt to the Caspian Sea, and established a pattern of empire which was consummated by Alexander.

Of course the geography which exposed Mesopotamia to all these comings and goings worked in the opposite direction too. Although her close commercial ties both east and west guaranteed interaction with her neighbors, her most important export was unquestionably the system of cuneiform writing. The one factor which held the different peoples of Mesopotamia together as a unity was their shared tradition of scribal craft, which conserved down the centuries the memories of its earliest exponents. Mesopotamian influence in the Levant was especially strong, and it was cuneiform – not the equally venerable Egyptian writing system – that was adopted by the literate Near East, so that even the pharaoh, writing to his Palestinian or Anatolian correspondents, made use of cuneiform. With the script there went other Mesopotamian skills and sciences. Greek mathematics and astronomy owe a still-unreckoned debt to Babylonian scholars, and the Mesopotamian diviners, or readers of omens, were famed throughout the ancient world. Recent discoveries have proved that cuneiform was in use in Syria as early as the reign of Sargon (c. 2300 BC), and it is no surprise therefore to find that the Book of Genesis retells stories written down in Sumerian before the days of Abraham.

Less than a century and a half have passed since the Mesopotamian world was no more than a shadowy memory of Greek historians and the Assyrian kings were no more than awesome names from the Old Testament. Today we know that for perhaps as much as 2,500 years before this, the Tigris and Euphrates valley had harbored a society whose literacy had made it a center of scholarship and technology for the whole of the Near East, and the originator of methods of business and government administration which persist to the present day. Thanks to the durability of the clay tablets on which they wrote, the Mesopotamian scribes have left us not only their literary compositions and accounts of military triumphs, but also the most trivial details of their daily life. The archaeologist has thus an incomparable opportunity to reconstruct with the collaboration of the specialist in ancient languages the structure and development of the society which created this first literate urban civilization.

Chronological Table

BC	IRAN	SUMER & BABYLON	ASSYRIA	LEVANT	ANATOLIA
3000	JAMDAT NASR PERIOD	JAMDAT NASR PERIOD	JAMDAT NASR PERIOD		
2900	Proto-Elamite script	ED I			
2800		Hegemony of Kish			
2700		ED II			
2600	Sumerian conquests	En-mebaragesi ED III			
2500	DYNASTY OF AWAN	Royal Cemetery of Ur			
2400		Eannatum of Lagash	Sumerian culture at Assur	Hegemony of Ebla	
2300	Akkadian domination	AKKAD DYNASTY Sargon Naram-Sin	AKKADIAN CONQUESTS	AKKADIAN CONQUESTS	AKKADIAN CONQUESTS
2200		GUTIANS			
2100	Sumerian domination	UR III DYNASTY Shulgi	Sumerian domination	Sumerian domination	
2000	OLD ELAMITE KINGDOM	AMORITE & HURRIAN STATES ESTABLISHED ISIN	OLD ASSYRIAN KINGDOM AMORITE & HURRIAN STATES ESTABLISHED	Trade between Assur and Kanesh AMORITE & HURRIAN STATES ESTABLISHED	AMORITE & HURRIAN STATES ESTABLISHED
1900		LARSA Rim-Sin	MARI Yasmah-addu	marches to sea	
1800		OLD BABYLONIAN PERIOD Hammurapi	Samsi-addu Zimri-Lim sacks Mari	KINGDOMS OF QATNA YAMHAD ALALAKH	HITTITE OLD KINGDOM Hattusilis I
1700					
1600		Ammi-saduqa Samsu-ditana			Mursilis I sacks Babylon
1500		KASSITE DYNASTY	Mitannian domination Nuzi	MITANNIAN EMPIRE Saushtatar	HITTITE EMPIRE
1400	Babylonian conquest	Kurigalzu II	MIDDLE ASSYRIAN EMPIRE Assur-uballit I	"AMARNA AGE" Tushratta	Suppiluliumas Muwatallis
1300	CLASSICAL ELAMITE PERIOD	Kashtiliash	Adad-nirari I Shalmaneser I	Assyrian domination Egyptian-Hittite balance of power	Hattusilis III
1200	Shutruk-nahhunte	Babylon taken invades Babylon	Tukulti-ninurta I	INVASION OF "SEA PEOPLES"	INVASION OF "SEA PEOPLES"
1100		SECOND DYNASTY OF ISIN	Tiglath-pileser I	marches to sea	
1000		ARAMAEAN INVASIONS	ARAMAEAN INVASIONS	ARAMAEAN INVASIONS Solomon	
900		CHALDAEAN TRIBES	Assur-nasir-apli II Shalmaneser III	ARAMAEAN AND NEO-HITTITE STATES	KINGDOMS OF URARTU
800	Urartian influence Elam allied with Babylon Scythians		Adad-nirari III Tiglath-pileser III	Battle of Qarqar Damascus taken	Sarduris III
700	Assyria conquers Elam	Marduk-apla-iddina NEO-BABYLONIAN	Sargon II Sennacherib Esarhaddon Assur-ban-apli	Samaria taken Jerusalem taken Egypt annexed	PHRYGIA LYDIA Rusas Midas Gyges
600	Cyaxares Cyrus II	Nabopolassar Nebuchadnezzar II Nabonidus Babylon taken	FALL OF ASSYRIA	Jerusalem sacked	Croesus
500					

PERSIAN EMPIRE

1. Civilization in Context

Typical scene in the marshes of southern Iraq: reed houses, and in the foreground some newly woven reed mats.

Although the two great civilizations of the ancient Near East, Egypt and Mesopotamia, are both founded on irrigation, there could hardly exist a greater contrast. To see the cities of pharaonic Egypt today it is almost enough to sail up the River Nile and visit the sites as they are passed on each bank. Of the major historical centers of Sumer and Akkad not one is now in sight of either Tigris or Euphrates, and yet once Kish, Nippur, Uruk and Ur (to name but four) lay on major channels of the Euphrates, and from this one fact derived much of their character and importance. It is one of the fundamental ingredients of Mesopotamian civilization that even now is perhaps not fully appreciated, that the great rivers which brought the country's life-giving water were not only liable to flood disastrously or run low at seasons inconvenient to the farmer, but might alter their courses so radically that within a few generations a once flourishing city might find itself nothing but a venerated ruin isolated in the desert. Characteristically this happened at times when central authority for the control of canals and the maintenance of weirs was lacking, and since it is precisely during such troubled times that our written sources fail us, we cannot pinpoint in time any single radical change of course until the 19th century. Nevertheless, the accounts of boat trips by men and gods up and down the waterways of Sumer show that in those days a major course of the Euphrates united the great cities of Nippur, Shuruppak, Larsa, Uruk and Ur, and since in the deep alluvial soil of southern Iraq, crisscrossed by small irrigation channels, transport is predominantly by water, it is easy to see that a correct appreciation of the history and civilization of our area is impossible without a good understanding of the ways and wanderings of the two great rivers after which Mesopotamia takes its name.

Both Tigris and Euphrates – the modern Arabic Dijle and Firat are closer than our Classical forms to the Sumerian names Idiglat and Buranun – rise in ancient Urartu near Lake Van. Flowing in opposite directions they emerge from the Anatolian plateau through steep gorges and then make their way to meet in the flat alluvial plain south of modern Baghdad, before they disperse into the head of the Arabian Gulf. Modern usage applies the term Mesopotamia to the entire area thus enclosed (except the high Turkish mountains), and it is useful to have a single term to cover the homeland of the civilizations of Sumer, Akkad, Babylonia and Assyria. However, this should not obscure from us the differences in climate and physical environment which distinguish one part of the area from another. Thus in southern Iraq it is a

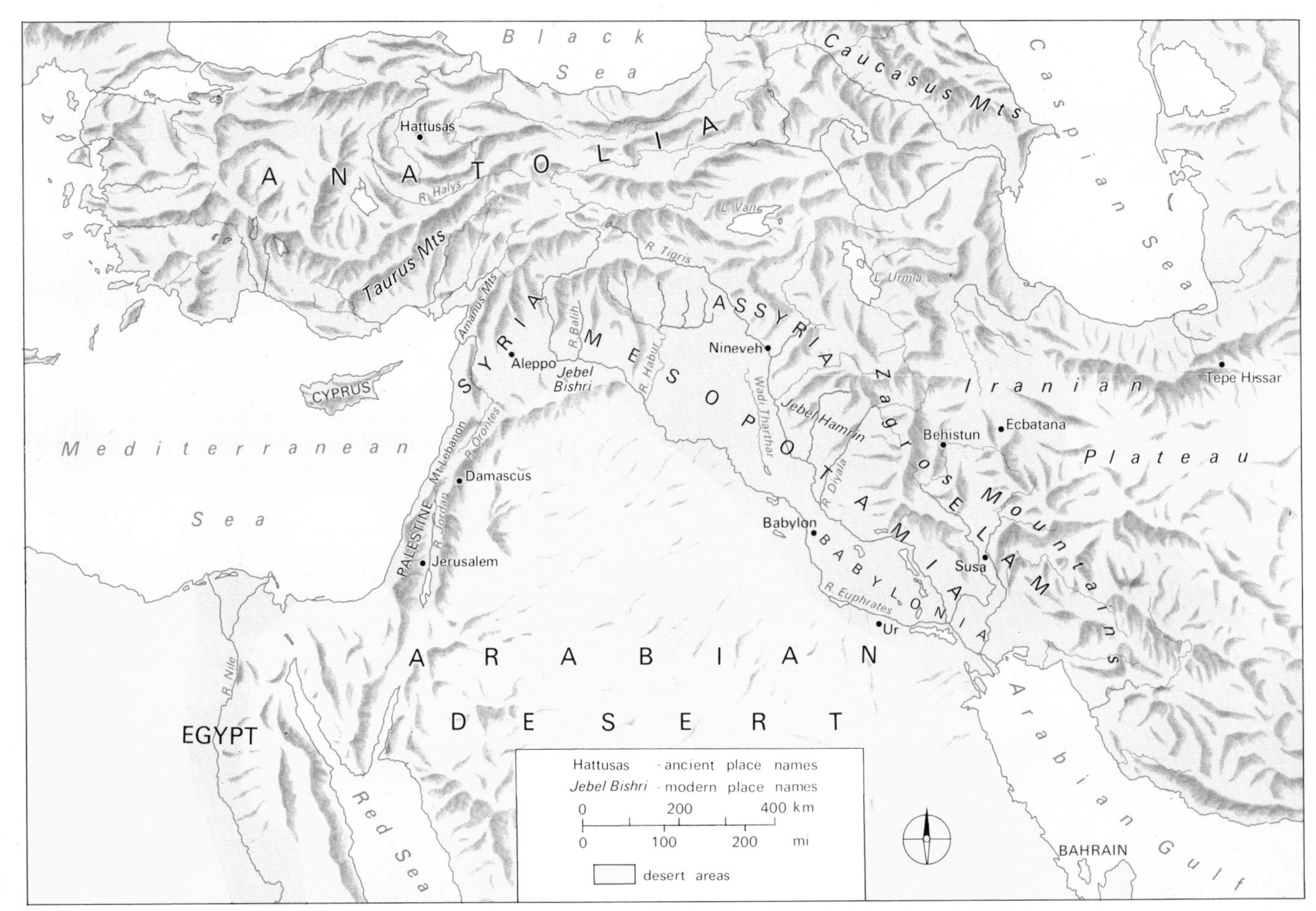

The Near East.

geographical fact of life that, in contrast to the north, agriculture cannot succeed without irrigation, and it is evident that during the prehistoric Ubaid period considerable strides had been made in the science of directing the waters of the two rivers onto the fields as and when they were needed. Evidently the occupation of the alluvium coincided with the disposition of the water channels, although in any given area it would be hard to say whether the existence of a canal had attracted settlers, or the growth of settlement had necessitated a canal. Another reason why the major clusters of towns and villages must have hugged the line of the rivers and their offshoots has already been alluded to: the need for communication. For virtually the only natural resource Sumer had to offer was an infinite supply of mud: mud for brick walls, clay for pottery and even for inscribed tablets. This meant that all stones and metals, and any timber except the soft trunks of palm trees, had to be imported, and even at the dawn of history it is clear that boats had long reached a stage at which they could serve as the chief means of transport in this land of waterways.

We do not wish to give the impression that Sumer was nothing but fields intersected by canals, a sort of ancient Holland. Dense thickets could grow up along the canals themselves, where the deposition of silt in floodtime combined with the earth thrown up by workmen clearing the canal bed to form levees which were too high for irrigation, and in these thickets might lurk wild boar, wild cats or even lions, a perpetual threat to livestock. Where the waters of a canal eventually flowed out into low-lying ground, swamps or even lakes were formed, and these joined up with the salt waters of the Gulf to make huge marshes as exist today, abounding in fish and water fowl, and providing one of the staple commodities of life, the reed. For in the absence of wood not only baskets and mats can be woven from reeds and grasses, but even boats and houses, and of course we should not forget that it was the reed which also provided the stylus with which the scribe impressed his signs on the damp clay. Finally, a great proportion of the land lay beyond the reach of water, and here, even between the two rivers, there stretched desert, broken only by sand dunes or the vestiges of earlier habitation. The natural setting of Sumerian civilization thus emerges as very far from a continuum: although no natural eminences existed to constitute obvious strategic sites for a town, there must have been convergences of natural and man-made circumstances which favored the growth of a city in one place rather than another. Associated with these cities, with their commercial and political attractions, were clusters of villages or even

Arab boys crossing their local canal in a *guffa*, modern representative of the bitumen-coated basket.

towns, but between the irrigated surrounds of one city and the next there could easily stretch open spaces of uncultivated and uncultivable land, which could only be the subject of dispute for strategic, not economic, reasons.

The nomads. It is, however, these open spaces which introduced to Mesopotamian civilization one of its main ingredients. The interaction of the urbanized settled population with the nomadic tribes which constantly pressed on its western borders and frequently penetrated between the cities is a recurring phenomenon without which we cannot hope to understand the history of the area. Just as the city-states of Greece developed independently largely because of the natural barriers which separated them, so the desert spaces between the cities of Sumer enabled them each to pursue its own course; but this same barrier did not afford the same degree of military protection as did the mountains and seas of ancient Greece, and at all times it was a virtual impossibility to exclude the nomads from the rich grazing in the deserts east of the Tigris and between the two rivers – even when, as under Shulgi of Ur, a wall was built against them at great expense.

History knows three major waves of nomadic penetration into Mesopotamia: the Arabs, already attested in the 7th century BC and earlier from Assyrian historical

Two age-old forms of water transport: the reed basket and the inflated sheepskin (relief of Sennacherib from Nineveh). British Museum.

records, remained on the fringes of our area for as much as 13 centuries before erupting in the most decisive of all such movements. They were preceded by the Aramaeans, who flooded into the settled areas of the Near East around 1000 BC, and created a cultural continuum from Persia to Egypt under the successive empires of the Assyrians, Neo-Babylonians, and Persians, based on a common language and the use of their alphabetic script. The first securely attested incursions are those of the Amorites, whose period of maximum penetration lies some 1,000 years earlier; before them, however, it is a fair assumption that there came into Mesopotamia after the same pattern Akkadian-speaking nomadic groups: their language is of the Semitic family, like Arabic, Aramaean and Amorite, and although there is no magical connection between Semitic languages and a nomadic way of life, simple human geography makes it probable that the Akkadians too were once intruders from the western deserts. Perhaps they were preceded by yet earlier waves, but if so we shall never detect them, since the nomad will not figure in a purely archaeological record, having no imperishable material culture from which his presence can be deduced.

Although we can point to certain periods when nomadic infiltration suddenly swelled into an invasion, it would be a mistake to envisage the desert lands as empty in the intervals. There will always have been the last remnants of an earlier wave or the precursors of a new one, to herd the sheep of the townsmen or mount raids on their property. This continual exposure to the nomad had a variety of consequences which were crucial to Mesopotamian history. One concerns foreign relations. There had to be a relatively stable agricultural populace to create the food surpluses needed for the maintenance of the big cities, but farming communities are characteristically not the most outward-looking. As we shall see, the big organizations within the city – palace and temple – did maintain foreign relations for the purpose of diplomacy and trade, but without doubt it was the nomadic component in society which kept the strongest links with the outside world, specifically to the west, and whose horizons extended naturally beyond the confines of the two great rivers.

Abraham in the Bible moves from Ur of the Chaldees, in the far south of Sumer, up the Euphrates to Nahur, somewhere on the headwaters of the River Habur, and then southwest to Palestine, in an itinerary entirely plausible in the context of the early second millennium BC. Throughout history we see that the nomadic tribes spilled out from their desert homes wherever there were desirable lands for the taking, not only eastwards, but north into Upper Mesopotamia and Syria, and westward into Palestine. The consequences of this are particularly evident on political history. A. L. Oppenheim observed that "assemblages" larger than the city "became effective only when and where certain nonsedentary elements of the population attempted to create suprasegmental power structures into which they coerced those engaged in agricultural pursuits whose interests were basically parochial," and that "evidence suggests that all the politically active and aggressive kings were probably of nonurban extraction, whatever their specific linguistic backgrounds may have been." This is easy to understand: it is obvious that the ambitions of a political leader who had retained tribal connections throughout the Near East would hardly be bounded by the limits that climate had imposed on the settled areas of southern Mesopotamia, and if we may judge from later parallels, the town-dweller lacked entirely the warlike ideals and social structures which gave the nomad the strongest incentives towards military domination.

In contrast to their role in the political development of Mesopotamia, the impact of the nomads on cultural life was negligible. The wandering life does not conduce to the accumulation of goods, and the successive waves of nomads generally adapted very quickly to the old-established cultures of the cities, even if the assimilation of their social life was a longer process. It is true that Akkadian eventually became the major literary language of Mesopotamia and that in the first millennium BC it was in turn displaced by the alphabetic script and Aramaean language introduced from the west, but this is more a reflection of the ethnic and linguistic history of the area than of any cultural changes. The example of the Amorites is instructive: Hammurapi of Babylon came of Amorite stock, and claimed the same ancestors as his contemporary Samsi-Addu who ruled in northern Mesopotamia. Both kings wrote, and doubtless also spoke, in the Babylonian dialect of Akkadian, and the Amorite language itself is known to us only through personal names.

Hammurapi was the promulgator of the famous code of laws, certainly one of the abiding monuments of ancient Mesopotamia, and yet a couple of centuries before him the Amorites are described with great scorn in Sumerian literature as the barbarian outsiders who "do not know houses," "do not know grain," "dig up truffles in the desert" – as do the Bedouin to this day – and eat uncooked meat and do not bury their dead. Their subsequent assimilation is such that although the last kings of Hammurapi's dynasty still bear Amorite names, once this

Above: modern nomads using the traditional tent: the roof of black goat-hair is made from their own flocks. Inside, the ground is strewn with mats and rugs, and a hanging separates the women's quarters.

Opposite: a good year for the desert nomad: truffles like this can be an important addition to the Bedouin's menu.

Below: the Assyrian army in the field shown in a cross-section of the tents. On the left a warrior refreshes himself while his bed is prepared, and in the next tent a butcher flays a sheep (relief of Assur-ban-apli from Nineveh). Vorderasiatisches Museum, Berlin.

dynasty came to an end the Amorites are never again encountered in Mesopotamia (although an Amorite kingdom survived in Syria). The fact is that Mesopotamian civilization was a force stronger than its component parts. Although it might be revitalized by the advent of a new population with new language, ideals or even religion, it is only the imposition of an entirely alien civilization – Hellenistic or Iranian – that breaks the continuum.

The businessman. The hard core of this tradition was of course the city. It was the city which harbored the temples and served as the repository for written traditions and as the funnel through which the skills of the metalworker, jeweler or sculptor could survive the recurrent periods of anarchy. But above all, the city was the milieu of the businessman. While he sometimes worked as an employee or contractor for temple or palace, more often than not the successful merchant was an independent agent with his investments widely spread at home and abroad. As well as lending and borrowing from his fellow citizens, he certainly had connections outside the city: he might lend to needy farmers in the lean months before the harvest, and often enough this debt would never be repaid; in an almost irreversible process the farmer had to pledge his land to find the interest and in due course became a tenant to the merchant who now owned the land himself.

Another investment was in sheep and goats: a flock will normally grow of its own accord, and standard agreements existed between the owner and the shepherd who grazed the animals. Generally the sheep owner asked of the shepherd a fixed annual rate of growth, and secured his employee's interest in the welfare of the flocks by allowing him to keep for himself anything in excess of this quota.

Equally integral to the make-up of Mesopotamia was its extensive foreign trade, whether the merchants were operating over long distances or just between one city and the next. Every country has its trade links with the rest of the world, but Mesopotamia was more dependent on them than most. In particular she needed the raw materials for the industries in which her craftsmen excelled, and this required constant intercourse with the east, rich in woods, stones and minerals, whether overland or by sea, through the Arabian Gulf. Westwards there was the lure of the rich markets of the Mediterranean coast, and from before history merchants from Mesopotamia must have been making their way up along the Euphrates or across the northern plains to reach Syria and the seaports with their wares. As we shall see, there was even a phase when the enterprising merchant houses of Assur ran a lucrative trade in tin with the inner regions of Anatolia, and the traveling merchants of Sumer, Akkad and Babylon outdistanced the victorious armies of their kings in every direction, often hazarding their goods and even their lives. In the law code of Hammurapi provision is made for the ransom of a merchant who has been captured and enslaved in a foreign land – if necessary by the use of temple or palace funds – and it was no unique event when at the same date two merchants wrote piteously to the wife of the head of the Amorite community at Sippar to complain that "the enemy captured us above Ekallatum [a city north of Assur], and we are being held in the palace at Kakmum." The measure of government support accorded to Mesopotamians pursuing their business abroad reflects the importance of their activities to the whole society, and state interest in trade emerges even more clearly a few centuries later, when the Hittite king Tudkhalias IV found it necessary to include in his treaty with the Syrian states a clause forbidding them to let Assyrian merchants within their borders.

Trade was certainly not a simple one-way affair. While Mesopotamia had to supply her own needs, the existence of a prosperous merchant class was probably due in large measure to the quality of her craftsmanship which created the demand for her products. One of the major exports was textiles, and there is ample evidence for the careful selection and grading of local wools, and even for breeding experiments. At other times the merchants were acting as middlemen along one of the great trade routes of Asia, as when the Assyrians organized the donkey caravans which carried the tin from further east to the Anatolian markets. One reason why the traders of Mesopotamia could operate so far and wide was that they profited from the advantages of writing. This not only eased the lot of the traveling merchant, who could write back for fresh supplies without making the journey in person, but it made possible the establishment of permanent merchant colonies far from home. More crucial still, it facilitated refined accounting procedures and we encounter disconcertingly "modern" flexible and sophisticated commercial transactions.

To equip and finance a trading caravan or fleet of ships was an undertaking requiring considerable capital investment. This was often supplied, directly or indirectly, by the palace or a rich temple, but funds might also be raised from wealthy private businessmen or a consortium formed for the purpose, and an agent was usually hired and contracted to bring back a specified proportion of the capital outlay. When such a partnership was initiated the stake of each partner had to be legally documented, and in all cases a sealed tablet was prepared constituting the contract between the traveling agent and the principals, in which the division of profit and loss was defined. At some periods it is true that the organization of commerce was created a state monopoly, or became such as a result of depression in the private sector, but even when a business venture was undertaken by the palace or a temple, semi-independent contractors were used for preference, and the whole affair was conducted along commercial lines. This was the case under the Ur III kings, when every smallest detail of the state administration was set down in writing, on a tablet sealed by the responsible official, and before long the written document became not merely a valuable adjunct but actually an indispensable component of Mesopotamian urban society, such that it is stated outright in the code of Hammurapi (c. 1800 BC) that even a marriage contract was invalid in the absence of a legally correct sealed tablet.

The scribe. Clearly, then, one of the most important members of our society was the scribe. To the ordinary person it was the scribe who wrote letters and drew up the every-day legal documents by which they lent and borrowed, bought and sold, while the complex temple and palace administrations relied on the scribal class to maintain their archives. It may be that at some dates literacy was a relatively widespread accomplishment, but in general the complexities of the cuneiform writing system ensured that long training was required to become a fully fledged scribe. No doubt the profession carried with it considerable prestige: King Shulgi is lauded in literary texts for his scribal prowess, and Assur-ban-apli some 1,400 years later could read and was proud of the fact. These were the exceptions; more characteristic are the occasions when a correspondent of the king adds a postscript intended only for the eyes of the scribe who will read out the tablet.

Schools were certainly organized by the temples, but they did not have a monopoly. At Ur Woolley found a house which may well have belonged to a schoolmaster, since it had been altered to accommodate pupils and writing exercises were found scattered inside. A yet more evocative "school" of the Old Babylonian period formed part of the great royal palace of Mari, where two rooms between the king's apartments and the officials' quarters were fitted out with rows of mud-brick benches, and school exercises were found on the floor. The largest collection of these "exercise tablets" comes from Nippur, where a very flourishing center of the scribal craft persisted. Many of the tablets were unmistakably the work of apprentices or even absolute beginners. Others reveal the methods of instruction. These are divided into two columns, with the teacher's "fair copy" on the left. The pupil wrote his version in the right-hand column, and this side was erased and reused. Sometimes the pupil's half had been erased so often that it was finally cut off, and the left-hand half preserved on its own. Another method of instruction was to write the fair copy on one side of a rounded tablet, leaving the other face for the pupil: in this case of course he would not be able to copy the signs directly, but had to turn the tablet over each time he needed to check with the original.

The basis of instruction was provided by the long lists of signs and words we call "lexical texts." Some of these lists can be traced back to the earliest known phase of cuneiform writing. Originally in Sumerian, Akkadian translations were added over the years, and we have thus an invaluable series of specialist glossaries listing in the two languages plants, animals, tools, foods etc. The Sumerians were great classifiers, and their lists encompass all the natural phenomena of their world as well as man-made objects and concepts. Much of the scribe's early training consisted of learning such lists by heart, but in the later years he might progress to more specialist subjects. There were mathematical problems and land-surveying exercises, and even music seems to have been included in the syllabus. In the Old Babylonian period all advanced school-work was in Sumerian, and the curriculum covered a whole range of texts. Particularly popular were short proverbs, either singly or in collections. Many are hopelessly obscure to us after 4,000 years, but some are timeless: "Friendship lasts a day, kinship lasts forever" or "A scribe whose hand moves as fast as the mouth, that's the scribe for you." Other favorites were hymns in praise of the kings, letters written to and by the kings of the last Sumerian dynasty (the Ur III kings) which seem to be genuine historical documents, and the "disputes." These very typical Sumerian compositions describe a verbal contest between rivals; sometimes the rivals are just two schoolboys, but we also meet disputes between personified concepts like "Winter and Summer," "Cattle and Cereals" or "The Hoe and the Plow."

The scribe as accountant: spoil from a captured city is noted down (relief of Tiglath-pileser III, Nimrud). British Museum.

For us however the most fascinating products of the Old Babylonian schools are the Sumerian myths and epics. The myths tell their stories of the gods of Sumer with a revealing mixture of primitive religion and deliberate etiological invention aimed at explaining the world around us. Like most peoples, the Sumerians cast their gods in a human mold, and some of the epics, which recount the exploits of kings during the heroic age of Sumer – Lugalbanda, Enmerkar or Gilgamesh – also include in the action gods and goddesses, and myth and epic alike display a matter-of-fact attitude towards the divine world reminiscent of the Homeric poems. One of these myths gives us the earliest known account of the great flood – the ancestor of Noah's Flood in Biblical tradition. After describing the creation of the world and mankind, together with the five antediluvian cities of Eridu, Bad-Tibira, Larak, Sippar and Shuruppak, the poem tells of the sending of the flood by a decision of the gods and the warning of Enki, god of wisdom, to Ziusudra, the Mesopotamian Noah. Then we read "after the flood had swept across the land for seven days and seven nights, and the violent wind had tossed the great boat on the high waters, the sun came out and brought daylight to heaven and earth. Ziusudra pierced an opening in the great boat and the sun with his rays came into the great boat."

Above: a copy of the 11th tablet of the Epic of Gilgamesh, in which the story of the Flood is told. British Museum.

Opposite: cylinder seal depicting gods and their attributes: Shamash rises between Ishtar (with wings) and Ea (with water and fish). British Museum.

Later traditions. As we shall see, this same myth crops up again much later in a different guise, but outside the Old Babylonian period we really know very little of the world of the scribe. Certainly successive dynasties must have encouraged scribal craft, since apart from the purely practical requirements of their administration the kings depended on the scribes in another field, and that was as the repository of tradition. The Mesopotamian was very conscious of the longevity of his civilization, and documents like the Sumerian or Assyrian King List illustrate this feeling. Time and again an Assyrian king will describe how when rebuilding a temple he came across the foundation documents of an earlier king, and treated them with the respect enjoined on him by the inscription itself. Grubbing in the ruins of ancient Sippar, the late Babylonian King Nabonidus came across half the head of a statue of the great King Sargon, and in a long inscription he tells how he had his craftsmen restore the other half, while account tablets listing the offerings made before the statue of Sargon show that due respect was indeed accorded.

Assur-ban-apli, the last great Assyrian king, was also a patron of letters. The great library of cuneiform tablets collected or written for him was found in his palace at Nineveh, and formed the backbone of our acquaintance with Mesopotamian literature for several decades, while even today his library serves as our guide to cuneiform written traditions down the 1,000 or more years which had elapsed since the disappearance of Sumerian as a living language. Assur-ban-apli's exact motives are unclear: sometimes it is stated that a tablet was copied "for my own perusal," and it is tempting to think that he may have been inspired by a sincere academic enthusiasm for tablets for tablets' sake, but we also meet more often the pragmatic explanation that he was assembling the manuals and reference works needed by the priests and omen readers in their work of looking after the physical and spiritual well-being of the king, his court and the army. So a tablet listing literary compositions states in its colophon (the equivalent of our title page, but coming at the end) that "The wisdom of Ea [god of incantations], the craft of the lamentation priest, the secrets of the seers, which are suited to appease the heart of the great gods, I have written down on tablets according to the originals of Assyria and Babylonia, checked them and deposited them in the library of Ezida, the temple of Nabu in Nineveh."

While the bulk of Assur-ban-apli's library consisted of omen tablets and other generally religious texts, it also included lexical lists, and a few specifically literary compositions. To judge from their infrequency, these may have been considered unimportant, but they are nonetheless of absorbing interest to us. Pride of place must go to the Epic of Gilgamesh: even before the end of the Old Babylonian period the various Sumerian tales about this great hero had been woven together with the story of the Flood to make a single great epic, occupying several tablets and written in vivid Akkadian. The version from the Nineveh library is on 12 tablets, the language has become much more formal, and each episode is expanded. This may serve as a rule for the great majority of texts in

the scribal repertoire: beginning with a Sumerian original, the first Akkadian version was written down in the Old Babylonian period, new texts being added all the time as Akkadian gradually eased out the older language. There followed generation after generation of copying, re-editing and compiling, which reached its zenith in Assur-ban-apli's library, but it is hardly surprising that much of the life has gone out of the texts by the end of the process.

The scribes of Assur-ban-apli's day were still copying out proverbs used well over 1,000 years earlier by pupils in the schools of Babylonia, and the inspiration and often the very words of prayers, hymns and similar compositions were virtually frozen with the fall of the Hammurapi dynasty. After this time scarcely a single significant addition was made to the scribal literary corpus, if we except the historical inscriptions which were in any case only rarely recopied. In view of the conservatism of the scribes of Babylonia and Assyria, it is interesting that among the "literary" cuneiform texts found outside Mesopotamia proper there is a bias towards precisely those compositions which appeal most to our tastes: Megiddo in Palestine yielded a piece of the Epic of Gilgamesh, and from as far afield as El Amarna in Egypt come parts of the legend of Adapa and of the myth of "Nergal and Ereshkigal." At Boğazköy, the Hittite capital, fragments of legends have been found about the kings of Akkad, Sargon and Naram-Sin, and here too were copies of the Epic of Gilgamesh together with translations into Hittite.

The temple and the priests. The essence of Mesopotamian urban society was the temple. It was the expression of the "community spirit," whether it served a city, a town or only a village. The temple owed its existence to the community, and its fortunes rose and fell accordingly. Esagila, the temple of Marduk, chief god of Babylon, must have begun from humble origins in a small town, and grown in size and wealth as Babylon became in turn a provincial city, the capital of a small independent state, and eventually the metropolis of a great empire. On the other hand, gods whose cities declined tended to disappear themselves: the worship of the god Sud seems to have died along with his city of Shuruppak, and even the major goddess of birth, Ninhursag, scarcely survived the desertion of her city of Kesh. There were of course the occasional exceptions: the most important of these is the god Enki (Akkadian: Ea) whose chief shrine was at Eridu. Although during most of the historical period Eridu was a ruin, he never lost his special position in the Mesopotamian pantheon as god of wisdom, sweet waters and incantations.

Each city acknowledged one chief deity, but not to the exclusion of others. Quite apart from the chief deity's spouse, children and menials, each of whom might have a temple, or more often a single shrine, there would be other entirely independent establishments. At Girsu in the Early Dynastic period the temple of Bau, Ningirsu's wife, was run by the ruler's wife as an entirely separate institution, and later at the same city we detect another reflection of political events in a deliberate effort to provide in Girsu itself individual shrines for all the gods representing the different townships within the state of Lagash. For in the early days of Sumer when the cities coexisted on terms of approximate equality, their pantheons retained their separate identities, even though the gods and goddesses visited each other's cities, both in myth and by actual ritual boat trips. In time, however, the cities were absorbed into larger units, and by a dual process each subject city had a temple for its god at the capital, while many of the local deities were assimilated by their more powerful neighbors and are scarcely heard of again. In course of time this process of syncretism left a "short list" of some eight major gods, with their wives, who achieved general recognition throughout Mesopotamia. So when Sargon (721–705 BC) built his new capital at Khorsabad, there were included in the palace enclosure temples for Ea, Sin, Shamash, Nabu, Adad and Ninurta, together with their wives, while lesser deities had temples in the outer town. One notable absentee from this list is Assur, chief god of Assyria, but this is because he had just the one shrine at Assur itself, like Marduk at Babylon, and the other gods came there to acknowledge his supremacy: the ritual banquet held on the occasion of their visit lists as many as 246 gods and goddesses, and shows that though the local cults may have been overshadowed by the predominance of the "great gods," they were by no means quite forgotten.

One consequence of the process of coalition is that the local associations of each god give way gradually to a greater emphasis on his or her "speciality." In a different way from the deified concepts like "Fire" or "Drought," the great gods developed their own special attributes, and it was for this that Sargon needed them all within his palace. The storm god Adad would be appealed to in a shortage of rain, and Shamash, the sun god, was patron of divination by omen, as well as of justice. Ea was god of incantations against disease, and Nabu had taken over from the Sumerian goddess Nisaba as god of writing, so that his city Borsippa was a recognized center of scribal craft, and his temples served to accommodate a city's main library.

The temple and society. Although important temples soon accumulated lands and other possessions which made them as self-sufficient as a medieval monastery, in origin they were the creation of the secular community, and it was recognized that a temple had obligations towards that community. The temple's reserves of wealth, built up by good husbandry and from the contributions of its congregation, were often made available to the faithful, whether as capital for a business venture or merely as a short-term loan – sometimes even free of interest – to tide a needy farmer over the difficult months before the harvest. The law code of Hammurapi recognizes this social duty of the temple by prescribing that if the family of a merchant who is in captivity abroad are unable to raise a ransom themselves, the temple should do so. Another public service of the temple was to provide a home for all those with no one else to support them: orphans, foundlings and the offspring of religious prostitution all

The Temple Oval at Khafajah: before its construction the ground was dug to a depth of more than 20 feet. The inner oval encloses the temple proper, and the priest's residence is accommodated between the inner and outer walls. After Darby.

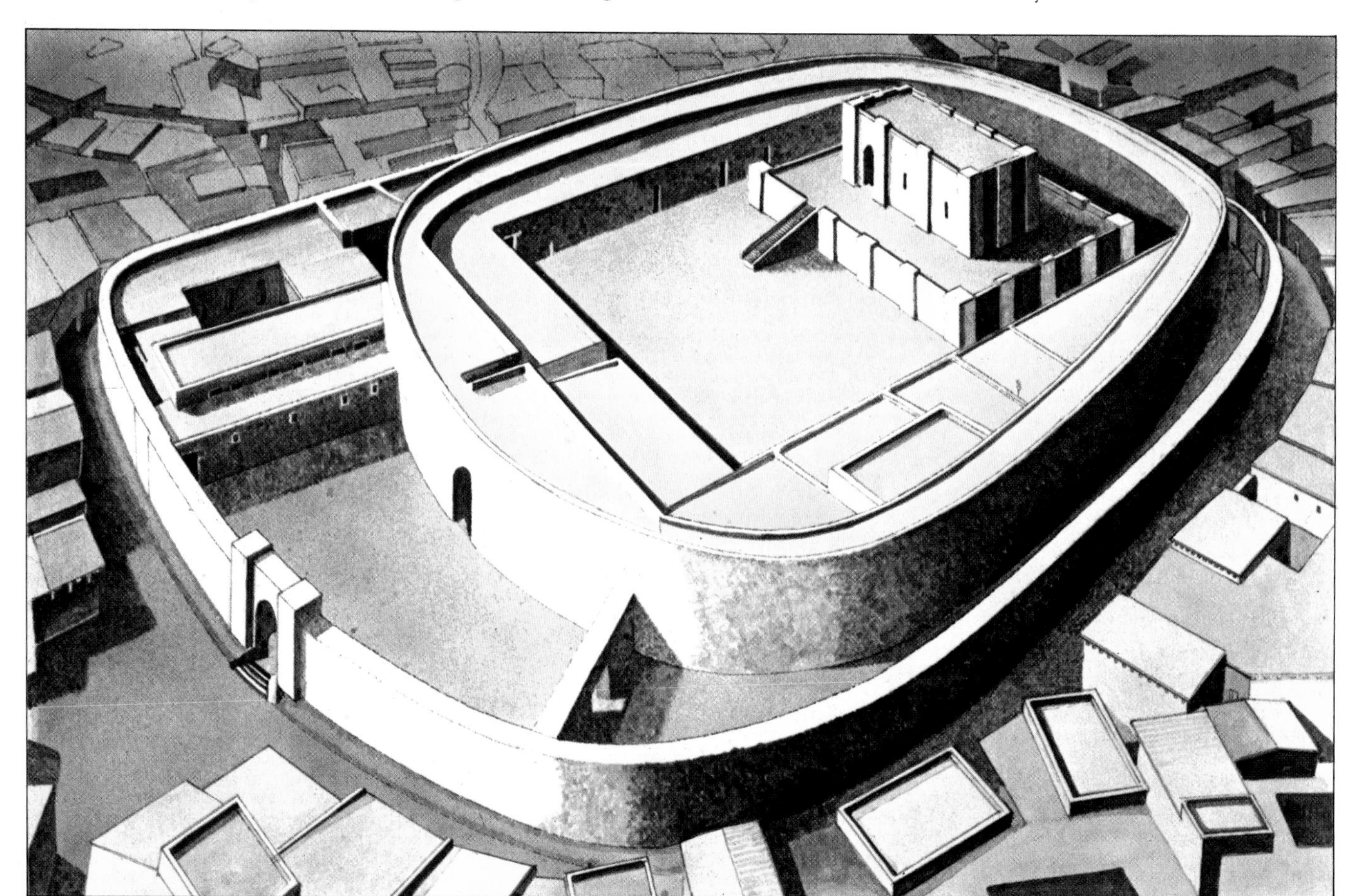

found their way into the household of the god, and in times of famine parents might lighten their burden and save a child's life by dedicating it to a temple. As in other times and places, a child might even be presented to a god in fulfillment of a vow, and the additions to the temple personnel ranged from batches of prisoners-of-war allocated by a victorious king, to members of his own family, such as his daughter at the temple of the moon god in Ur.

One curious phenomenon virtually restricted to the Old Babylonian period (say, 2000–1500 BC) may have a sociological explanation, although no very convincing one has yet been put forward: various temples, like that of Marduk in Babylon but, *par excellence*, the Shamash (sun god) temple in Sippar, had associated with them a class of priestess called *naditum*, a name which refers to the fact that they did not bear children. These ladies, some of whom were well connected – e.g. Hammurapi's own sister and daughter – lived together in a "cloister" attached to the temple. They were not idle, but some of them at least pursued an active business life, managing country and town properties as well as running the affairs of the cloister. Since they had severed themselves from the predominant patriarchal household system, a priestess was allowed by her family a share of the paternal estate equal to that of a son; this share usually reverted on her death to the male members, but her father had the right to give her an entirely free hand with her property, and then a *naditum* might adopt a daughter from among the younger members of her order, who could inherit her property and would look after her in her old age. It is sad to have to report, although perhaps not unexpected, that we have more than one lawsuit in which a *naditum*'s brothers try to reclaim, unjustly, property which had passed out of their grasp in this way.

Annexed to the great temple of the moon god Nanna (or Sin in Akkadian) at Ur was a building which resembled the "cloister" in some respects, but had an entirely different function. This was the *gipar* in which resided the *en* or high priestess of Nanna. The first holder of this office known to us is the daughter of Sargon of Akkad, Enheduanna, and the last, daughter of Nabonidus, was appointed almost 2,000 years later in a restored *gipar* on the original site. Other great gods, such as the sun god of Larsa, had female high priestesses, called *en*, and they are sometimes expressly described as the "wife" of the god. Only one held office in one city at one time, but lesser deities might have a rather similar priestess, who also lived in a house attached to the temple. The priestesses' residences were taboo, and this was evidently to prevent them mixing with men under normal circumstances; the prohibition against sexual intercourse is the reason why in the legend of the birth of Sargon of Akkad his mother, who was an *en*-priestess, had to place him, like Moses, in a reed basket on the river, from which he was rescued by a gardener.

In the Old Babylonian version of the flood story the

Limestone plaque showing Enheduanna, high priestess of Nanna at Ur, attending a libation ceremony in front of the ziggurrat (on left); found at Ur by Woolley. Pennsylvania.

taboo is explained as a means of keeping the birthrate down, but in fact it is virtually certain that all these priestesses were chosen to act as the partner of the god in a cultic enactment of sexual intercourse which goes back to primitive fertility rites. Who exactly took the part of the god in these cases is uncertain, although the obvious presumption must be that it was the high priest; a similar ritual is known from the Inanna (Ishtar) temple at Uruk, where the king (or once his son) was the *en* of the goddess, and references in the texts to the king as her "spouse" make it clear that the kings took part in person in ritual sexual intercourse in the temple, doubtless with a priestess representing Inanna. In this ritual the king was held to represent the god Dumuzi (Tammuz), himself originally human according to myth. When the participation of the king died out, about the time of Hammurapi, the Tammuz cult also seems to have lost its earlier status, and it is virtually absent from post-Sumerian literature. It did however survive, together with the worship of Inanna/Ishtar, goddess of love and war, and it is closely related to the belief in the "dying god" known further west as Adonis. Indeed recent discoveries have brought yet closer parallelism, since we now know from a Sumerian myth that Dumuzi is condemned to spend half the year in the underworld while his sister substitutes for him during the other half, a motif echoed by the Demeter and Persephone myth.

Apart from these fertility rites, the Mesopotamian priesthood appears remarkably empty of what we might consider religious feeling, but this must in large measure be a consequence of the nature of our sources. The temple scribes were required to keep a tally of the establishment's daily transactions, not to record the emotions of the servants of the gods. Nevertheless, the "high priest" was acting primarily as a steward or major-domo for the deity's household. He was responsible for the proper administration of the estates, and for seeing that his god or goddess was correctly fed and clothed: for one thing emerging clearly from the temple records which have come down to us is that the greatest attention was given to the adornment of the statues of the god and his wife, and to furnishing their table twice daily with their meal or "regular offering," which we must suppose was usually redistributed among the temple personnel after the gods had taken their fill. The office of priest was often passed down from father to son, and there is no reason to suppose that it demanded any special religious qualities, although there may have been some physical requirements. The high priest of a major temple was at all dates an important person: at Umma and Isin in the Early Dynastic period the priest was indeed the secular ruler of the city-state as well, and, on the other hand, the king of Assyria always held the title of high priest of Assur in person. The potential influence of the priesthood, especially in Babylonia, is reflected in the control that even strong kings tried to exert on them: in Neo-Babylonian times the kings could not appoint the priests themselves, but they installed royal officials as overseers in an obvious bid to curb the power of the temples.

The lesser members of the temple staff are a colorless group at this distance of time. Apart from certain specialists like the singers and the lamentation priests, they seem to have differed little from the junior employees of any comparable secular establishment. In Babylonia indeed most if not all of the junior posts were open to all and sundry, since they could be bought and sold like any other commodity. The office of "temple butcher" or "temple brewer" carried with it a variety of perquisites, and in the Old Babylonian period already we find the most menial appointments like "courtyard sweeper" or "door keeper" being sold off like shares in a company. This practice survived, not to say flourished, down into Seleucid times, and so we hear that a certain Nanaya-iddin has sold his right to the office of temple brewer in the temples of Uruk for one twelfth of a day daily from the 1st to the 30th of the month, for $\frac{5}{6}$ mina of silver in Antiochus staters.

Magic and omens. Quite separate from the regular staff of the temple household were the members of two professions which we might ourselves class as priests, but were for their contemporaries more scientific experts: the "incantation priests" and the "omen priests." Incantations were the spells recited as part of a magic ritual against evil; the rituals were very varied, and they could be applied to almost any situation. The most obvious occasion for the use of incantations was in the presence of illness: the various diseases were conceived of as kinds of demon,

Opposite: impression of a Neo-Assyrian seal showing priestly figures with bells or buckets saluting the sacred tree over which hovers Assur in his "winged disc"; the priests have fish-skins draped over them like cloaks. Pierpont Morgan Library.

Below: this statuette from the Temple of Ishtar at Mari shows "Ur-Nanshe, the singer," cross-legged on his basketwork stool; although he looks like a lady, he has a man's name, and there is ample evidence that temple singers could be eunuchs or in other respects of dubious masculinity. Damascus.

which had to be persuaded to leave the sick person. One of the essential preliminaries of such a ritual was to identify the relevant demon – since otherwise it could not be addressed – and hence we read this description of the Lamashtu, who attacks the newborn: "Anum created her, Ea brought her up; Enlil decreed for her the face of a dog; her hands are slender, but her fingers are long; her claws are longer, and her elbows are stained." These lines belong to a tradition in which the evil influence is identified by giving a "potted history." One such is the toothache charm, which runs: "After Anum had made the sky, the sky had made the earth, the earth had made the rivers, the rivers had made the canals, the canals had made the mud, the mud had made the worm, the worm came weeping before Shamash and shed tears before Ea: 'What will you give me for my food?' 'I will give you the ripe fig.' 'What is the ripe fig to me [the worm replies]? I will drink among the teeth; place me on the gums, and I will consume the blood of the teeth and destroy the marrow of the gums'." Sometimes there was a possibility that the evil influence came from an unappeased ghost; then the exorcist listed the "one who lies in the desert and is not covered with earth, or one who fell from a palm tree, or one who drowned in a boat . . ."

In order to give his spells validity, the exorcist had to carry out the prescribed rituals. He himself would don special magician's clothing, such as an "awesome red cloak," or a garment which covered his head, giving him the guise of a fish or an animal. In his hand he might hold a staff, or a palm leaf, or a ritual bucket, and sometimes an image or other symbol of the gods invoked to assist in the ceremonies. There were various means of symbolizing the banning of the evil influence: one method identified the sick person with an animal which is killed as a substitute, sacrificing "the flesh of this piglet for his flesh, the blood of this piglet for his blood." Purification by fire was particularly efficacious, and a typical incantation runs: "Just as this onion, which [the exorcist] peels and throws into the fire, will never be planted in a vegetable patch, will never take root in the ground, will never put up a sprout and see the sun, and will never be served at the table of a god or a king – so may the illness which afflicts my body, my flesh and my veins, be peeled off like this onion and consumed in the flames, and may the curse depart from me that I may see light."

Not all incantations are for casting out illness. A charm could be recited to keep any evil influences away from contemplated actions, and indeed we meet spells for good luck on a journey, success in love and so on. Special rituals were enacted when a house was built, and apotropaic figurines were made and buried under the floors, especially by the doorways. Similar, though more elaborate, precautions were taken for the protection of a temple or palace, and the same intention, to ward off evil, lies behind the great stone beasts which guarded the gateways of Assyrian public buildings; although their size is unique, these figures, known as "favorable genies," are only giant versions of lions and other apotropaic figures already known in Sumerian and Old Babylonian temples.

Omens. With the science of divination or omen reading the Mesopotamian had another weapon by which to forestall evil. Evil foreseen could be avoided, and the results of any intended action could be checked in advance by the use of divination. Various techniques were in use: the observation of unsolicited portents – astronomical events, unnatural births, animal behavior, etc. – made possible the prediction of the future, but even more useful were the omens which could be solicited on a particular question by the diviner himself. In this category were omens derived from the configuration of smoke, of oil poured on water, or of arrows thrown on the ground – compare the modern tea leaves – but the divinatory technique *par excellence* was extispicy: the observation of the entrails of a sheep or other animal. The most used organs were the lungs, the heart and the liver, and a major part of the diviner's profession was to learn the different processes on each, with their special names like "gate of the palace," "pathway," "plain," or "river." Not only from Mesopotamia itself, but from Syria, Anatolia and

Clay model of a sheep's liver divided into sections annotated for the use of the diviner (Old Babylonian period). British Museum.

Shell inlay pieces from Mari show a ram being sacrificed (Early Dynastic III period, c. 2400 BC). Damascus.

even from as far as Etruria – where the practice perhaps came with other Anatolian influences – there have survived models of the organs which show either the names of the different parts, like a three-dimensional diagram, or the appearance of the organ of a particular animal on a single occasion. A set of model livers of this type from the palace at Mari are among the oldest written witnesses to the reading of omens, and they show that the practice was in full swing already in the time of Sargon and Naram-Sin of Akkad, since these kings are the subjects of some of the omens.

Such "historical omens," which do contain reliable historical traditions, are in the minority. In general the procedure was that, if on a given occasion a sign was followed by an event like a military defeat or a drought, the fallacy of *post hoc ergo propter hoc* was applied, and a connection was divined between the two. On the basis of countless observations with ensuing events, the diviners compiled collections of possible omens with their significance, whether in the public or private world: ". . . if the finger [of the liver] is like a cow's tongue, his eunuchs will murder the king; . . . if the finger is half formed like a goat's head, and its upper half is split, the man's personal god will leave him for another . . ." The effort devoted to the recording of all types of omen seems to the modern skeptic quite disproportionate: some of the series in Assur-ban-apli's library comprise more than 50 large tablets, and omen texts preponderate over all other types.

The procedure of extispicy was probably quite straightforward. The diviner addressed the gods, whose answer was to be read in the animal, with a short prayer; usually these were Adad, god of divination, and Shamash, who as god of justice was held to deliver the final "yes" or "no" to the question put. The animal was then sacrificed and its entrails examined, and if the entrails were favorable and the god answered "yes," all was well; otherwise the procedure could be repeated until a favorable result was achieved. Private persons would consult the omens before any important decision, and the king was expected to do the same in affairs of state. Esarhaddon consults the omens before deciding about the betrothal of his daughter to the Scythian king, and from Gudea to Nabonidus no temple was built without first obtaining a favorable omen. Military decisions were equally subject to confirmation, and there is ample evidence that on any major expedition the army was accompanied by an omen priest. In Old Babylonian times, indeed, he acted as a general, and the ruler of the little state of Karana (Tell Al-Rimah), Aqba-hammu, was himself a diviner, member of a profession which traced its origin to the antediluvian king of Sippar, Enmeduranki.

The king. The institution of monarchy was the least static component of the Mesopotamian scene, and it is correspondingly difficult to describe in generalizations. While it is fair to say that, as at most times and places, the monarch was leader of his people in war, religion and law, books have been written about the nature of Mesopotamian kingship, and no consensus reached. According to the philosophy of the time, the success of a country in dominating another reflected equivalent events in the heavenly sphere: Hammurapi's prologue to his laws states that "Anum, king of the gods, and Enlil, lord of heaven and earth, assigned the government of the peoples to Marduk" – i.e. Babylon dominates Mesopotamia – and when the Sumerian poet lamented the destruction of Akkad, he ascribed it to the sins of Naram-Sin which had angered Ishtar and caused her to leave the city without her tutelary protection. On the individual plane the same principles applied. Hammurapi attributes his possession of the kingship to his selection by Marduk, even though he was in fact the son of the previous king; but if a usurper succeeded in imposing his rule, it would be accepted that his personal god had found favor with the national deity, and the *de facto* events on earth would lead to a formal reorganization of the pantheon. In fact, there resulted a divine right of kings, based solely on reality. Once, when the king of Isin had temporarily vacated his throne to escape the consequence of a bad omen, and a substitute had been placed in his stead, the king himself died (from swallowing hot porridge, we are told), and the substitute, a gardener called Enlil-bani, finding himself on the throne, remained there for 24 years (c. 1860–1837 BC).

While the king enjoyed the favor of the gods he had to meet his obligations towards them and towards his flock – the king is often called the "shepherd" of his people. His prime obligation was the service of his national or city god. At Assur the king was himself high priest; he was crowned king in the Assur Temple with an elaborate ritual during which the high dignitaries of state laid down their staffs before him, and after a military campaign a "letter" or long report would be addressed to Assur to inform him of the result. When a disastrous drought occurred it was the king himself who wrote around to all his governors to organize a public lamentation and plea for rain to the weather god Adad. At Babylon the religious duties of the king were yet more strict. No king was recognized as the king of Babylon until he had "grasped the hands of Bel [= Marduk]" in an annual ceremony forming part of the New Year celebrations in the Marduk Temple. These celebrations were also the occasion of the reciting of the "Epic of Creation," a poem in praise of Marduk incorporating the myth of his victory over Tiamat, a dragon figure personifying the forces of evil. Of all the grave charges leveled against the enigmatic last king of Babylon, Nabonidus, the primary ones were that he had exalted Sin, the moon god, above the national god Marduk, and that by his absence in Arabia he had failed for ten years to "grasp the hands of Bel" and had thus deprived the land of its major religious festival.

Whatever the final character of the New Year festival at Babylon, it must have developed from a traditional ritual going back to the city's early days when even the minor cities of Sumer and Akkad boasted their own pantheon and very often a local dynasty as well. Whether these rulers were unequivocal "priest-kings" like the *en* of Inanna at Uruk, including Gilgamesh and Enmerkar, or bore less exclusively religious titles such as *ensi*, we may be sure that their relationship to the city god was directed more to the continuance of fertility and prosperity within the state than to the success of the army on the battlefield. The military ideal came into prominence under the Akkadian empire, when the king (*lugal*) – a secular title hitherto without religious connotations – did his best to suppress local dynasties and either assumed or neglected their religious functions. Whether there is any connection with the claims of divinity apparently made by certain kings, notably Naram-Sin and Shulgi, it is impossible to say; this can only have resulted from personal hubris or some specific religious function, but in either case the concept of the king as a god never took deep root in Mesopotamia and, although debated, it remains an enigma.

"King of justice." In the nature of government the king was inevitably the fountainhead of justice. Most claim in their own inscriptions to be "king of justice," and the common view is expressed in the first line of a late (c. 700 BC) political pamphlet which declares, in the phrasing of an omen text, that "If a king attends not to justice, his people will be scattered and his land devastated." Naturally, the king could not handle all cases; even in a famous murder trial taken before the king in Old Babylonian times, the decision is referred by him to the Assembly of Nippur, and since local institutions were generally vital, most cases could be settled, whether in a village or a town quarter, by the "mayor" and elders. If a satisfactory result was not reached, then the case might be considered by the royal judges, by other officials or by a city assembly. Nevertheless, even in the days of the Assyrian empire a citizen could still stand in the assembly and appeal directly to the king – "unto Caesar" – and the royal correspondence shows us that this right was honored.

The king's role as chief judge was duly rationalized in religious terms, by considering him the agent of and answerable to the sun god Shamash, who, with his all-seeing eye, was also the god of justice. In reality, however, the king's exercise of justice was felt more as a social than a religious obligation. In Babylonia and Assyria the monarchy inherited a strong link with a nomadic past when the sheikh was accessible to all members of the tribe and expected to act as an impartial arbiter. Hammurapi announces that he was given the kingship "that justice might shine forth in the land, that the evil and dishonest might be confounded, and that the strong might not

The king in state. Assyrian King Sargon (721–705 BC) rides out in his chariot, complete with sunshade and attendants holding fly whisks (relief from Khorsabad). Louvre.

oppress the weak." Indeed, it seems that the principles of strict commercial law were often sacrificed to the ideal of social justice.

In a tradition stretching back at least as far as Entemena of Lagash (c. 2400 BC), the king periodically proclaimed a general amnesty on commercial debts, thus enabling all those languishing in debt slavery to return free men to their houses. This kind of *seisachtheia* persists into the last days of the Assyrian empire, and in Old Babylonian times, when debt slavery itself was less common, it extended to the cancellation of all financial obligations including debts to the royal administration ("the palace") itself, and arrears of taxation. A recently discovered appeal to the king from these years even discloses details of the procedure: its author writes "When my lord the king raised up the golden torch for the city of Sippar and so put into force the amnesty for the god Shamash who loves him, . . . the judges examined the cases of the citizens of Sippar and read the tablets of purchase for fields, houses and orchards, and saw that those tablets which were rendered null and void by the edict were smashed, but I brought mine to the Assembly and they were examined, passed and sealed by the officials" – alas something slipped, and later his tablets were also smashed together with his rights, and so the writer concludes "May my lord the king judge for me in the case of the smashing of tablets without the permission of the judges or the man concerned, and so let all Sippar see that my lord will not permit the weak to be surrendered to the strong."

Another device by which the kings sought to prevent the economic exploitation of the poor was price fixing. One king of Eshnunna (Tell Asmar) fixed the prices of grain, oils, lard, bitumen, wool, salt, copper, and the fees for hiring boats and carts and animals, as well as agricultural wages. Sometimes this was done by a separate proclamation, but on this occasion the price list was incorporated into a code of laws. The king's duty to promote justice was carried out as much by such measures for economic stability as by the civil and criminal laws which constitute the greater part of both these Eshnunna laws and the more extensive code of Hammurapi. It is characteristic that Ur-Nammu, founder of the Ur III dynasty and author of the earliest law code yet discovered, prided himself, as we read in the prologue to that very code, on his efforts to restore the sea trade with the Arabian Gulf, and on having standardized weights throughout his dominions. Hammurapi's own code was written after his kingdom had reached its fullest extent, and it seems clear that one of the major incentives to compose a new law code – and they are not specially frequent – was the administrative need to impose uniformity across newly conquered territories.

"Great king, king of the world." If hitherto we have concentrated on the religious and judicial relations between the king and his people, it is because they remained fairly constant throughout the historical period. As a ruling autocrat, however, the position of the king seems to have become more extreme as time went on and the size of his dominions grew. Traditionally the ideal of kingship as military leadership was represented by the near-legendary figure of Sargon of Akkad, and it is no chance that Sargon of Assyria adopted the same name, but during the first millennium BC the Assyrian kings in particular approached the type of Oriental despotism which was so abhorrent to the Greeks. In the great palaces of Nineveh and Babylon the king became more and more isolated from his subjects, surrounded as he was by courtiers and eunuchs – who also controlled the often extensive harem. Letters show that some at least of the kings were very active in the daily administration of their empire, but by sheer necessity the main volume of the work of government was handled by an efficient civil service based on a pyramid of officials from the provincial governor downwards. As a safeguard against the ever-present temptations lying in the path of the governors, the king also maintained a network of his own agents, forerunners of the Persian "eyes of the king," who could report directly to him any signs of disaffection or intrigue. An efficient system of "royal roads" facilitated control of the enormous tracts involved, and many of the administrative techniques developed during this first "world empire" were undoubtedly passed down to the Persians, and perhaps still further.

Of course it was as the "wolf coming down on the fold" that the memory of the Assyrian kings impressed itself most deeply on their contemporaries, and this is not an entirely false image. The Assyrian army was the most efficient fighting machine the world had encountered, and although it was no more bloodthirsty than many of its opponents, the Assyrians glorified the arts of war and the hunt in gory detail, whether in words or pictures. The army's shock troops were the horse-drawn chariots, and the administrative records from Kalhu and Nineveh bear witness to the ceaseless efforts devoted to keeping the numbers of both horses and chariots up to strength. Without men, though, neither was of any use: the chariotry and cavalry were mostly Assyrians proper, serving in the army in fulfillment of their "national service" to which their families were originally bound by the ownership of land.

Under very exceptional circumstances – as when Shalmaneser III raised 120,000 men to march against Damascus – all able-bodied men might be called up, but this practice could seriously disrupt the agriculture on which the Assyrian economy relied, and as time passed a force of professional "auxiliaries" was recruited from certain non-agricultural Aramaean tribes and organized as a standing infantry which did most routine border work and dealt with smaller trouble spots. For a major campaign, however, the cavalry and chariots were mustered towards the beginning of summer in one of the great palaces built for this purpose, and then as often as not the king himself would take the head of his troops in person, accompanied by his battle standards and the personal guard which "does not leave his side in war or peace." It was as the commander of his army that the king was at his most regal. The king was expected to display personal valor, and the laudatory epithets of the royal inscriptions lay stress on his bravery and on the fear he inspired in his enemies. This is epitomized by the royal seal itself, which shows the king in hand-to-hand conflict with the lion, to this day the royal beast.

Writing and Seals

VISUAL STORY

The system of cuneiform writing is at once the core of Mesopotamian civilization, and its most important influence on the surrounding world. Its origins can be followed back to about 3100 BC, when pictographs and numerals scratched on clay tablets are found at Uruk. Subsequently the signs were simplified and formed of wedge-shaped ("cuneiform") strokes impressed with the end of a reed into wet clay. The system was adopted in Elam and Syria, and later used to write Hittite, Hurrian, Urartian, etc. Alphabets imitating cuneiform were also invented for Ugaritic and Old Persian.

One of the conveniences of writing on clay is that it serves like sealing-wax to take the impression of a seal, and indeed clay sealings for the identification of merchandise may have come before writing itself. Herodotus tells us that Babylonians had their seals constantly with them, and to authenticate a document it was sufficient to roll the seal on the wet clay of the tablet or envelope before witnesses. In time the simpler Aramaic alphabetic system of writing superseded cuneiform, and waxed boards or scrolls replaced clay; the last cuneiform text known dates to the 1st century BC.

Development of Cuneiform

Above: one of the handsome Assyrian library tablets found at Koyunjik by Layard: this is a "lexical" text giving Sumerian legal words and phrases (in the left-hand column) and their Akkadian translation on the right. At the bottom of the left-hand column is the colophon (or "title page"). 8th century BC. British Museum.

Opposite: two mathematical tablets from Old Babylonian levels at Tell Harmal and Tell Dhibai (c. 1850 BC): that on the left is an exercise for the aspiring surveyor, based on a right-angled "Pythagorean" triangle with sides 45 : 60 : 75 (i.e. 3 : 4 : 5), and depends for its solution on the Euclidean principle that "In a right-angled triangle, if a perpendicular is drawn from the right angle to the hypotenuse, the triangles on each side of it are similar to the whole triangle and to one another." Baghdad.

Above right: an early administrative tablet from Jamdat Nasr (c. 2900 BC), listing areas of fields and crops. It is shown with the beginning of the text top left, but at this early date the tablet should possibly be rotated 90 degrees clockwise, and read from the top right. British Museum.

Below right: this chart shows how a few of the cuneiform signs developed from the original incised drawings of recognizable objects to formalized groups of impressed strokes in later years. Note that early in the process the pictograms were turned on their sides.

THE EVOLUTION OF THE CUNEIFORM SIGNS

PICTOGRAMS ÚRUK UPRIGHT	c. 3100 BC TURNED 90° TO LEFT	JEMDET NASR c. 2800 BC	'CLASSICAL' SUMERIAN c. 2400 BC LINEAR	CUNEIFORM	OLD-AKKADIAN c. 2200 BC	OLD-ASSYRIAN c. 1900 BC	OLD-BABYLONIAN c. 1700 BC	NEO-ASSYRIAN c. 700 BC	NEO-BABYLONIAN c. 600 BC	Picture	Meaning
										NECK + HEAD	HEAD FRONT
										NECK+HEAD + BEARD or TEETH	MOUTH NOSE TOOTH VOICE SPEAK WORD
										SHROUDED BODY (?)	MAN
										SITTING BIRD	BIRD
										BULL'S HEAD	OX
										STAR	SKY HEAVEN-GOD GOD
										STREAM of WATER	WATER SEED FATHER SON
										LAND-PLOT + TREES	ORCHARD GREENERY TO GROW TO WRITE

Seals and Sealing

Above left: after 2,000 years in which the cylinder seal was dominant, stamp seals made a comeback in Mesopotamia during the 8th and 7th centuries BC. This clay bulla, dated 716 BC, was sealed by an Assyrian official with his large elliptical seal (3·5 cm across), and shows the king standing before Adad(?) mounted on a bull and Ishtar on a lion. The cuneiform inscription records the delivery of 35 sheep. From the Northwest Palace at Nimrud.
Above: in order to authenticate a legal document, and prevent possible fraudulent alterations, the tablet would be enclosed in a clay "envelope" which was sealed, and often had the text repeated on it. This land-sale deed from Uruk has the witnesses' seals on the left side of the envelope (here removed from the inner tablet), and dates to the reign of Samsuiluna (c. 1750 BC). British Museum.
Left: four characteristic Jamdat Nasr period stamp seals, with their impressions (c. 2900 BC). Baghdad.
Opposite: although surveyors and architects could make use of clay tablets, we have – not surprisingly – no very convincing examples of Mesopotamian cartography. This world map was meant to illustrate a rather abstruse mythological treatise, and marks the "Salt Sea" as a circle, above it an area "where the sun is not seen"; inside the circle is an arc labeled "Mountains," below this the rectangular box is "Babylon," with a small circle marked "Assyria" just to its right; in the far south we have "Bit-lakin" and "the marshes". (Neo-Babylonian.) British Museum.

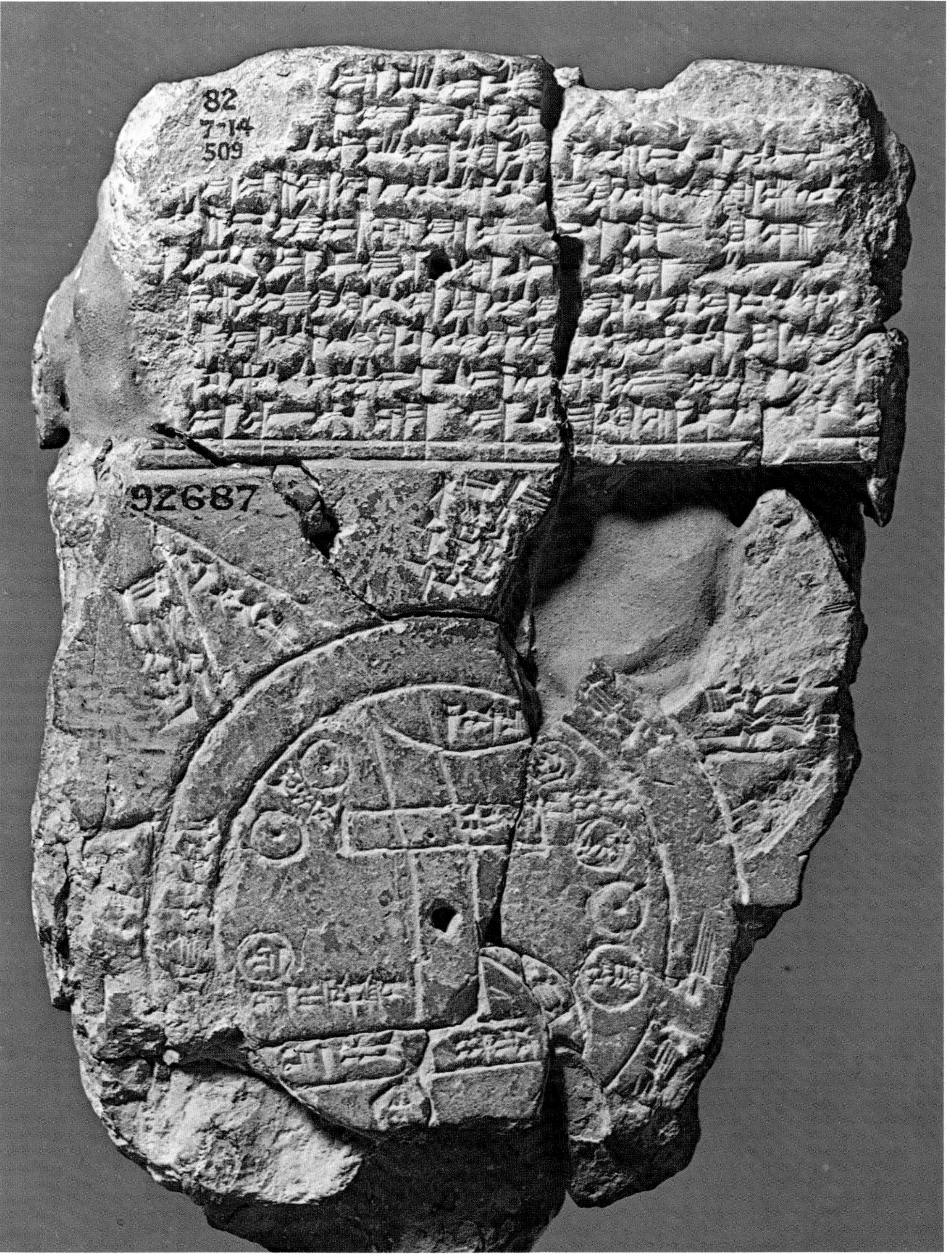
82
7-14
509
92687

Left: four early cylinder seals: center, two squat seals with typical Jamdat Nasr period designs; above and below, slender seals of the "Brocade" style (c. 2800 BC). Baghdad.

Below: Four Early Dynastic seals with their impressions: crossed animal contest scenes. Baghdad.

Above: despite the minute scale, the seal-cutter could achieve masterpieces of art. On this Assyrian seal a motif of 1,000 years earlier is readopted as the hero hoists the vanquished lion above his head; note how the drill has been used to point up the lion's paws. From the inscription we learn that the seal is dedicated to Nabu. British Museum.

Cuneiform in the West

Right: this treaty between Idrimi, king of Alalakh, and a certain Pillia, of Kizzuwadna, provides for the extradition of fugitive slaves from either country (found at Alalakh, Tell Açana on the Orontes; c. 1480 BC). British Museum.
Below right: on this tablet, which is distinctively non-Mesopotamian with the seal impressed in the center, is a treaty between Ugarit and the king of Carchemish, regulating the action to be taken should a merchant of one be killed in the other's territory, and specifying compensation. The seal is of Ini-Teshup, and bears his name in both cuneiform and "Hieroglyphic Hittite," as well as the name of his father, Shahurunuwa son of Sharri-kusukh. (From the Palace at Ugarit, c. 1250 BC).
Damascus.
Below: hitherto the earliest cuneiform in the west was in the Assyrian colony at Kanesh (c. 1850) with Alalakh and Boğazköy coming second. Now the tradition can be traced back to the time of Sargon of Akkad: here, at Tell Mardikh (ancient Ebla), south of Aleppo, large square lexical tablets and smaller economic records lie as they fell from the wooden shelves on which they had been stacked against the walls of the archive room. More than 15,000 tablets found here by Prof. Matthiae of the University of Rome in 1975 promise to give us a whole new chapter of Near Eastern history.

New Scripts and Methods

Left: the complexity of cuneiform yielded rapidly before the new alphabetic writing system from the west, and from Tiglath-pileser III onwards even the Assyrian royal administration made use of both. Here scribes record the slain and booty from one of Sennacherib's Babylonian campaigns: one holds a hinged writing board for cuneiform, the other a scroll on which he writes with pen and ink. British Museum.

Below left: Bar-rakib, king of the Aramaean state of Sam'al, sits before his scribe who holds a pen case and a writing board tucked under his arm. Bar-rakib, whose inscription in Aramaic appears above, was a vassal of Tiglath-pileser III and "ran beside the wheel of his chariot" (c. 730 BC). Vorderasiatisches Museum, Berlin.

Below: one of the most unexpected finds at Nimrud was a set of 16 ivory writing boards down a well in the Northwest Palace, where fragments of the more usual wooden boards were also found for the first time, still retaining traces of the wax (mixed with orpiment) on which the scribes wrote. This de luxe edition, whose hinges may well have been in gold, bears an inscription incised on the outer cover, telling us that "Sargon had the series [of astronomical omens called] *Enuma Anu Enlil* inscribed on an ivory writing board and deposited in his palace at Dur-Sharrukin." The interior of the panels is scratched to help the lost-wax filling to adhere (about 33 × 15 cm each). British Museum.

2. The Rediscovery of Ancient Mesopotamia

Sir Robert Ker Porter's view of Birs Nimrud (west face), painted in the 1830s when it was widely thought to be the "Tower of Babel." British Library.

When the western world first began to wonder about the ancient lands of Assyria and Babylonia, which it knew must have lain between the great rivers of the Bible, the Tigris and Euphrates, the first impression was one of desolation. Although the land itself was potentially fertile and as capable then of supporting intensive agriculture and a dense population as it had been in antiquity, the aspect of this depressed province of the decaying Ottoman empire seemed to bear out in every detail the thunderings of the Biblical prophets who had foretold for Nineveh that her people would be "scattered upon the mountains with no man to gather them," and for Babylon that it would "become ruin-heaps" and that "her cities are a desolation, a dry land, and a wilderness, a land wherein no man dwelleth." Even today every visitor to Iraq is struck by this character of desolation which hangs over the greatest of the ancient cities, and – like so many things – the contrast with the remains of other civilizations was best expressed by A. H. Layard, who wrote:

"The graceful column rising above the thick foliage of the myrtle, ilex, and oleander; the gradines of the amphitheatre covering a gentle slope, and overlooking the dark blue waters of a lake-like bay; the richly carved cornice or capital half hidden by the luxuriant herbage; are replaced by the stern shapeless mound rising like a hill from the scorched plain, the fragments of pottery, and the stupendous mass of brickwork occasionally laid bare by the winter rains . . . The scene around is worthy of the ruin he is contemplating; desolation meets desolation: a feeling of awe succeeds to wonder; for there is nothing to relieve the mind, to lead to hope, or to tell of what has gone by. These huge mounds of Assyria made a deeper impression upon me, gave rise to more serious thoughts and more earnest reflection, than the temples of Balbec and the theatres of Ionia."

An equally true description of a typical Sumerian site was given some 75 years later by R. C. Thompson for Eridu:

"The general appearance from the desert is of a flat, low mass of brown earth, with steep sides rising to nearly forty feet, the crest appearing to maintain an almost unbroken level, except that at the north are the remains of a lofty ziggurat, now whittled down by the rains to a sharp peak . . . But on approaching the mound one sees the rough lumps of limestone and sandstone which still buttress its sides, scattered about in disorder. The mound itself has practically become a basin; the interior, having for the most part consisted of buildings of unbaked brick, has melted into formless clay under the torrential rains which pour down during the winter. The temple tower . . . has conducted the rushing water down its slopes, which have easily gnawed channels both in the mass of disintegrating brickwork of the houses on the mound, and in the windborne sand which settles in every cranny and near every wall . . . From the ziggurat, as far as the eye can see there is naught but awful solitude . . ."

While the tumbled expanses of ruin which were once flourishing Sumerian cities like Ur or Warka, with their setting of salt and sand left to them by the changing watercourses, have a gauntness alien even to the grass-grown "huge mounds of Assyria," sites in the north and south of the country are alike in that they result equally from giant accumulations of the unbaked brick which is inseparable from the Mesopotamian scene. Babylon and the earlier capital cities of the south lay on alluvial soils, far from any convenient source of stone for building, and even in Assyria stone was generally reserved for decorative facades and the occasional application such as a quayside where it was desired to combat water erosion. Everything else, including the palaces of the kings and the temples of the gods, was built in the cheap and ubiquitous mud-brick. Brick can of course be baked, and for some purposes often was, but the fuel for baking was an expensive luxury and even though Nebuchadnezzar of Babylon may have hoped to assure his constructions immortality by the prodigious quantity of baked bricks prepared for his fortifications and palaces, ironically the superb quality of his brick defeated its own purpose since it has served successive generations as a convenient quarry for the finest building material in the country.

Nevertheless, the humble mud-brick has certain advantages of its own, apart from its cheapness. It is versatile and can easily be shaped or remodeled to suit a particular need, and it is a powerful insulator: the heat of summer and the intense winters are equally held at bay by mud-brick walls and a mud and reed roof, and this is no small consideration in the Mesopotamian climate. With the extremes of temperature and destructive rainstorms, the fabric of the mud-brick house soon begins to crack up, and even if it is carefully replastered annually, it is common for mud-brick architecture to be rebuilt at frequent intervals. The material is so cheap to make afresh that the old walls will be knocked in and form the basis of the new house, or else a family moves to another part of the village leaving the abandoned house to the mercy of the elements. Either way, each new house adds to the accumulation of successive layers of occupation, and so the settlement becomes a mound whose size is determined by the extent and longevity of its inhabitation.

Cities of the Bible. When Europeans first started to speculate on the possible site of the great Biblical cities like Nineveh and Babylon, it was inevitable that their attention should first have been drawn by the massive towers of brickwork which were still to be seen in the region of Baghdad, and were so much more striking than the low, pottery-strewn mounds which seemed scarcely to differ one from the other. Two in particular came in for comment: one, the ziggurrat of Aqar Quf very close to Baghdad, was conspicuous chiefly for its height, but the other, called Birs Nimrud, was further marked by the extraordinary lumps of vitrified brickwork lying around the foot of the tower, which gave witness to some immensely powerful heat which even today it is hard to account for. Small wonder that this impressive monument was "believed to represent the identical tower, which called down the divine vengeance, and was overthrown, according to an universal tradition, by the fires of heaven" – in other words, the Tower of Babel.

Ker Porter's view of the mounds of Nineveh. British Library.

Indeed there were good reasons for such a mistake: apart from the Bible itself the sources available to the scholars of the early 19th century were only fragments of the Greek historians, such as Herodotus, Strabo or Diodorus Siculus, and although they did indeed describe Babylon in their own ways, the accuracy of their various accounts and in particular of the dimensions attributed to the great capital allowed a considerable latitude of interpretation. Thus an English dilettante called J. S. Buckingham, who visited the ruins of Babylon in 1816, was able to adduce weighty arguments to show that the tower at Birs Nimrud (belonging to the Nabu Temple of Borsippa) was indeed the "Temple of Belus" described by the Classical writers, and that the ancient city stretched not merely from here to the great mounds which do belong to Babylon, a distance of some 10 miles, but for an equal distance beyond to the ziggurrat of Uhaimir which was hailed as one of the eastern towers of the great fortification wall – a wall which is reported by Herodotus as being 120 furlongs in length each side and having space on its summit for the driving of a four-horse chariot. In fact, Uhaimir is now known to belong to the entirely separate

and more ancient city of Kish.

In his observations Buckingham – who emerges from his own writings as a distinctly impetuous character – would have been well advised to follow more closely in the steps of his host at Baghdad, the prodigious Claudius Rich, whose achievements were matched only by his unfulfilled promise. At the time of Buckingham's visit Rich was firmly established as Resident of the East India Company at Baghdad, a post which he had held for nine years since he was appointed in 1807 at the age of 21. While he had rapidly made a name for himself there by his remarkable proficiency in Near Eastern languages and a great deal of self-possession which stood him in good stead with the local authorities, he had also found time to take a keen interest in the antiquities of the country. In addition to assembling a fine collection of Oriental manuscripts and other more ancient pieces, he was able to devote considerable effort to the examination of the ruins of Babylon, and the resulting "memoirs" far surpassed in accuracy and coverage any previous descriptions of the site. Rich's own observations on the spot show all the caution of the experienced – which was not always shared by the casual visitor or armchair scholar – and thus he was not misled like Buckingham by the undeniable resemblance of the Birs Nimrud ziggurrat to the Temple of Bel as described by the Greek authors, and wrote only with academic precision that "Had this been on the other side of the river, and nearer the ruins, no one could doubt of its being the remains of the Tower." Nor did Rich share Buckingham's error of believing that the many ancient and less ancient disused canal banks, which are encountered on the road

Medieval conception of the "Tower of Babel" is reflected in this 17th-century engraving by Olfert Dapper (1636–89).

from Babylon to Uhaimir, were "rows of houses or streets fallen to decay."

Rich also paid a visit to the north of Iraq in 1820 and described the ruins of Nineveh and Nimrud with equal attention, and although he himself met an early death in a cholera epidemic at Shiraz, the publication of his work made the educated world aware that under these deserted mounds must lie concealed the capitals of the ancient empires of Babylon and Assyria. Nonetheless the realization came slowly, and it was not until 1843 that Paul Emile Botta was sent to Mosul as French consul, with the very specific intention that he should investigate the remains of the Assyrian empire. He began his work opposite Mosul itself in the mound called Kouyunjik, but found little to meet his expectations. By good fortune, however, the locals directed his attention to a similar mound at Khorsabad, some 14 miles northeast of Mosul, where stones had from time to time been turned up. Here at the first stroke of the pick the soil yielded room upon room lined with the exquisitely carved slabs of the Assyrian King Sargon, and Botta was able to report enthusiastically to his supporters in the French Academy. Their response was exemplary: an artist was immediately dispatched to draw the newly found reliefs, arrangements were made for the Ottoman authorities to issue a *firman* permitting the continuation of the work, and funds were allocated which enabled Botta to carry on uncovering the vast palace complex into 1845.

Layard. In the meantime Botta's success had only served to whet the appetite of a young Englishman who had actually visited his work at Kouyunjik in 1843 and shared his enthusiasms. Austen Henry Layard, who in 1845 at the age of 28 was working at the embassy in Constantinople, had been knocking about the Near East since 1840, when he had parted in Persia from the traveling companion with whom he had originally planned an overland journey to Ceylon. Subsequently he had involved himself in an extraordinary series of escapades in the medieval world of the Bakhtiari tribesmen on the Persian-Ottoman frontier, turning up from time to time at Bushire on the Gulf or in Baghdad. During these years Layard had acquired, in addition to fluency in the local dialects and an intimate understanding of Oriental ways, an insight into the politics of the area which proved of considerable use to Her Majesty's Ambassador to the Sublime Porte in Constantinople, Sir Stratford Canning. Sent thither with a recommendation from Colonel Taylor, the current Resident of the East India Company at Baghdad, he had remained rather unofficially in the service of the ambassador until 1845, when the news of Botta's discoveries came through. His frustration must have been intense; years ago he had conceived the ambition of opening up the great Assyrian mounds, and now Botta, who generously allowed his friend to see his dispatches and drawings as they passed through the Ottoman capital, was writing to him "Come, I pray you, and let us have a little archaeological fun at Khorsabad."

Finally in the autumn of 1845 Sir Stratford Canning himself agreed to advance the funds for a preliminary investigation of the mound of Nimrud, and to send Layard off as his private agent. He needed no encouragement, and after riding in 12 days from Constantinople to Mosul, on 8 November Layard loaded a raft to sail down the Tigris to Nimrud, ostensibly accompanying a British resident called Henry Ross on one of his well-known hunting trips. This was only one of the various subterfuges which were imposed on all excavators in Mesopotamia during the last century. To this day the average person in any part of the world finds it hard to believe that archaeologists are not secretly after gold and buried treasure, and the natural suspicion and cupidity of the Ottoman officials never ceased to hover malevolently over the operations of Layard, and his colleagues and successors. Nor was the situation eased by inter-European rivalry: Layard himself wrote that "The enlightened and liberal spirit shown by M. Botta is unfortunately not generally shared," and it soon became apparent that the secrecy which had attended Layard's first archaeological exercise was well justified. The first day of excavations on the summit of the Nimrud mound had revealed large wall-slabs bearing cuneiform inscriptions at two different parts of the tell. By the time a week had passed and Layard was again in Mosul, he found the pasha well informed as to his activities, but, despite the efforts of some "who might have spared me any additional interruption without a sacrifice of their national character" (i.e. M. Rouet, Botta's successor), he was not actually forbidden to work and was able to send more men to take part in the excavations. Finally on 28 November his hopes were fully realized: in the southwestern palace there came to light slabs sculptured in relief with scenes of battle; today we know that these were made in the reign of Assur-nasir-apli II, and later transferred from the northwest palace to be reused in a new palace of Esarhaddon, but to Layard here at last was proof that Nimrud offered prizes as rich as those of Botta at Khorsabad.

It was symptomatic of the situation that the very same night brought orders from the pasha to suspend Layard's operations – with the characteristic excuse that he was disturbing the graves of good Muslims, graves, which, the pasha's officer admitted, had had to be created for the purpose by pillaging other, real, Muslim graves in the neighborhood. However, Layard had now justified the tentative operation with which he had been entrusted, and while he continued quietly uncovering slabs he was content to mark time while he awaited news of fresh funds and the benefit of a real *firman* from Constantinople. The

Opposite: Layard in his early days when he lived for long periods with a Bakhtiari tribe in conflict with the Persian authorities in the mountains of southwest Iran. British Library.

firman did indeed arrive, in May 1846, but funds were another problem. Canning seems to have been rather loath to relinquish his personal control of the operation by arranging for the government to provide the necessary funds, and hence we find Layard writing "I have received no instructions from Your Excellency on the subject of expenses. I have ventured to draw for 2,500 piastres, as you appear to wish me to continue the excavations. I have also had recourse, as far as I am able, to my private resources and shall continue to do so until I hear from you, in the hopes that, should the Government carry on the excavations, I shall be refunded." As it turned out this was a vain hope, and Layard's fears of the "hideous skeleton of Government generosity" were in the event quite justified. When the grant came it was for £2,000 only, of which no more than half was available for further work, and although Layard characteristically did his utmost to extract the maximum of results from the minimum expenditure, it was not without considerable disgust at the treatment he had received, both with regard to the inadequacy of the funds and the patronizing tone of the Foreign Office document engaging his services.

The excavation work continued primarily at Nimrud, where the two original palaces were joined by the Central Palace dating to Tiglath-pileser and others in the southeastern quarter of the mound. Work was carried on through 1846 and into the summer of 1847, when with the stub end of his funds Layard conducted brief investigations of Qalat Sherqat (Assur) and Kouyunjik. The terms of the government grant included the transport of sculptures back to Britain, and during the work three separate consignments of the best-preserved relief slabs from Nimrud were sent down the Tigris by raft to be shipped to England from Basrah. In May 1847 Layard determined to make an attempt to ship back one of the great winged bulls: Botta had sent some to Paris, but had sawn them up for transport, and despite the weight of the Nimrud figure which he selected, more than 10 tons, Layard succeeded in having one of Assur-nasir-apli's winged bulls dragged down to the Tigris and loaded it, and a monumental lion, onto a raft built for the purpose by craftsmen brought from Baghdad. Shortly after this he returned to London, via Italy and Paris where his results were warmly acclaimed, and in a remarkably short time he had completed his book *Nineveh and Its Remains* which brought him a well-deserved popular triumph. For in addition to displaying a surprisingly scholarly mastery of the historical background, Layard described both the problems of excavation and his incidental excursions in a forthright style which still makes gripping reading and underlines the quality of his achievement in carrying out the government's wishes in so wild a corner of the Near East. Once the book was out, and the sculptures and other antiquities were on display in London, it was clear that public opinion at least demanded further exacavations. And so, in 1849, although Layard's restlessness had already landed him back in Constantinople on the staff of the Turko-Persian frontier commission, he was sent back to Assyria with the sum of £3,000, which, although not princely, did at least enable him to set to work again in earnest.

Just before leaving on the previous occasion Layard had succeeded in locating sculptured slabs in the mound of Kouyunjik, which was of course the main palace mound

of Nineveh itself. Now he returned to the same spot, as well as his old diggings at Nimrud, and began to uncover room after room belonging to the great palace of Sennacherib. The slabs differed from those known at Nimrud and Khorsabad in that they portrayed the scenery of the royal conquests with minute detail. One slab in particular attracted attention: it showed the king himself seated in mountain terrain on a sumptuously carved throne while captives were brought before him; above the king's head was an inscription, most of which Layard was able to read correctly, saying "Sennacherib, king of Assyria, sat on his throne and the spoil of the city of Lakisu passed before him." Layard wrote: "Here, therefore, was the actual picture of the taking of Lachish, the city, as we know from the Bible, besieged by Sennacherib, when he sent his generals to demand tribute of Hezekiah, and which he had captured before their return; evidence of the most remarkable character to confirm the interpretation of the inscriptions, and to identify the king who caused them to be engraved with the Sennacherib of Scripture."

Another difference between Kouyunjik and the mounds of Nimrud and Khorsabad was less favorable. Here occupation had not ceased with the downfall of the Assyrian empire and the reliefs were buried under a thick later deposit. The result of this was that "the accumulation of earth above the ruins had become so considerable, frequently exceeding thirty feet, that the workmen . . . began to tunnel along the walls, sinking shafts at intervals to admit light and air . . . The subterraneous passages were narrow, and were propped up when necessary either by leaving columns of earth, as in mines, or by wooden beams. These long galleries, dimly lighted, lined with the remains of ancient art, broken urns projecting from the crumbling sides, and the wild Arab and hardy Nestorian wandering through their intricacies, or working in their dark recesses, were singularly picturesque." Picturesque or not, this is hardly an acceptable archaeological procedure, and in fairness it must be remembered that it was forced on Layard by the inadequacy of his funds. We cannot forbear to report on one of the consequences of this method of digging, as recounted by Layard's right-hand man, Hormuzd Rassam, in 1854: "One night while encamping on the mound of Kouyunjik, and I was fast asleep in my tent, there was a tremendous storm of hail and rain, and all of a sudden I felt myself going down a pit, with bed, tent, and everything else I possessed . . . It appeared that my tent had been pitched over one of the large tunnels dug at the time of Sir Henry Layard's excavations, which had been lost to the sight."

Opposite: Layard directs as one of the Nimrud winged bulls is lowered onto the wooden platform on which it was transported to the Tigris. The ropes broke when it was still 4 feet from the ground, but the bull mercifully remained intact. British Library.

Below: public interest in Layard's work is reflected in this engraving from the *Illustrated London News* showing a winged bull – perhaps the very same as that shown opposite – being winched up the steps of the British Museum, where it stands today. British Library.

The decipherment of cuneiform. It was during these burrowings in Sennacherib's palace that Layard made a find which, though less spectacular than the sculptures, was more far-reaching in its importance. This was the

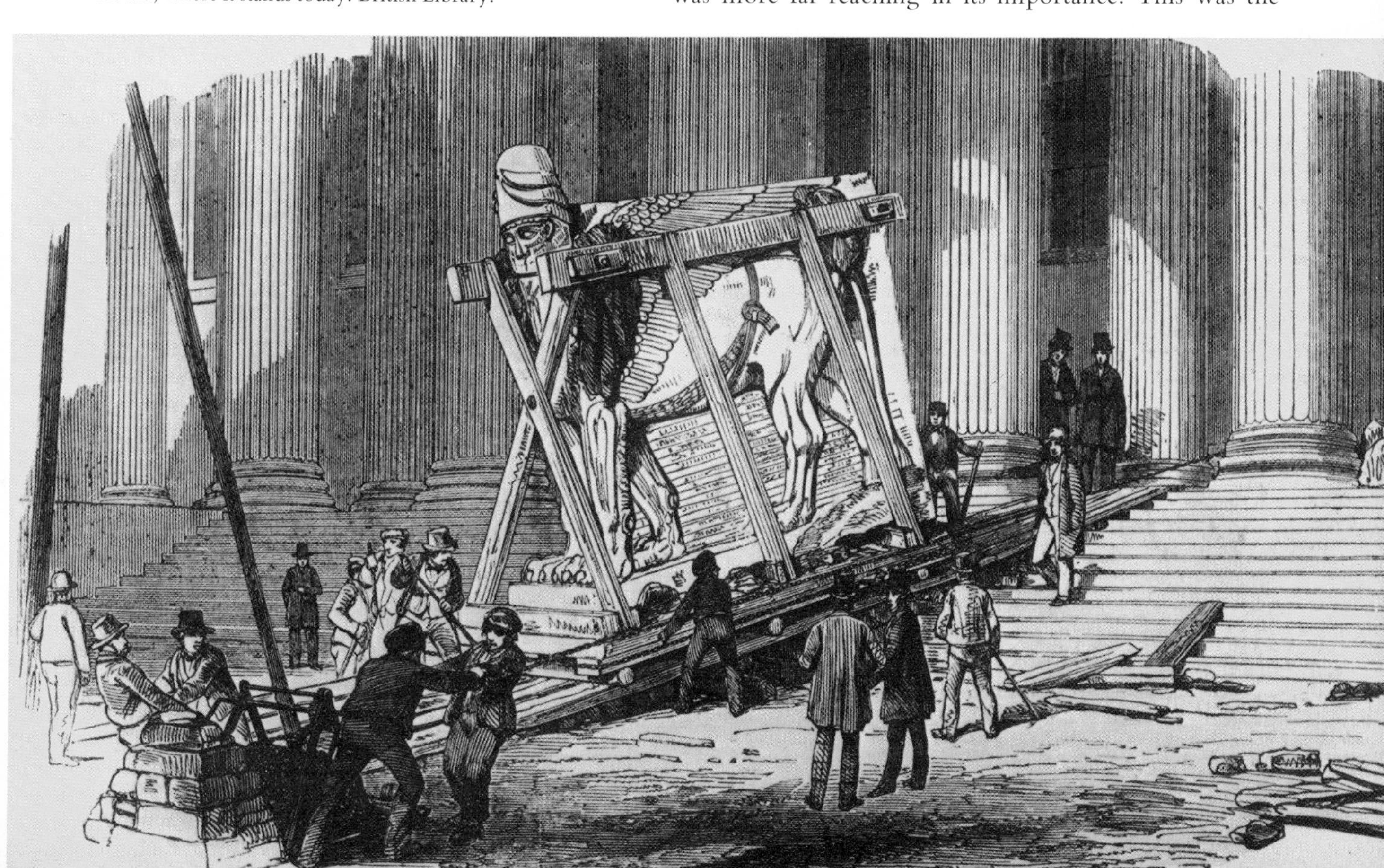

Layard sketching Sennacherib's reliefs at Kouyunjik; from this room came most of the cuneiform library found by Layard. British Library.

royal library of King Assur-ban-apli, a collection of clay tablets so large that certain rooms were entirely filled with them "to the height of a foot or more from the floor, . . . some entire, but the greater part broken into many fragments." Layard was fully aware of the significance of this discovery and rightly wrote that "We cannot overrate their value. They furnish us with materials for the complete decipherment of the cuneiform character, for restoring the language and history of Assyria, and for inquiring into the customs, sciences, and, we may perhaps even add, literature, of its people." Hitherto most of the cuneiform inscriptions which had found their way back to the museums of Europe had been short or longer historical texts on stones, bricks or the occasional clay cylinder. Now the great variety of the Kouyunjik library, in which Layard could easily detect word lists, royal decrees, legal documents and so on, promised a rich reward to any decipherer, and by the greatest fortune it so happened that such a decipherer was present at this very moment.

The Assyrian inscriptions were not the first to bring the cuneiform script to the notice of the learned world. A version of cuneiform was used by the Old Persian kings, and in 1778 the great Danish traveler Carsten Niebuhr had published excellent copies of the inscriptions he had seen at Persepolis and other sites in Persia. The Persian kings had used two scripts and three languages: Babylonian and Elamite versions of their inscriptions were written in the original cuneiform script derived from the first Sumerian pictographs, while the Old Persian texts were written in a specially invented alphabetic cuneiform which was no doubt inspired by the widespread Aramaic alphabets of the time. It was the Old Persian, with its much smaller repertoire of signs, which clearly offered the best opportunities for decipherment, and already by 1802 a German scholar called Grotefend had made considerable progress in this direction, only to have his discoveries quashed by petty academic rivalries at Göttingen. A new initiative was taken by an English army officer, H. C. Rawlinson, who had profited from his time in Kermanshah as a military adviser to the governor of Kurdistan to visit the neighboring rock of Behistun, which bears on its perpendicular face the longest known trilingual inscription. Between 1835 and 1837 he succeeded in completing a copy of the alphabetical Persian and the Elamite texts, but despite his use of ropes and other aids, the Babylonian remained inaccessible. Working along the same lines as Grotefend, although he could not have known it, Rawlinson first deciphered the kings' names in the Old Persian inscription, and by applying the letter values so obtained, he was able by 1837 to submit to the Royal Asiatic Society a translation of the opening of the inscription.

For Mesopotamia, however, the important step was the decipherment of the Babylonian version, and this was in itself an equally formidable task. In the first place there was the practical difficulty that in their concern to preserve the inscription from hostile hands, Darius' stonemasons had succeeded in making the Babylonian part of the text inaccessible even to Rawlinson. This was overcome eventually in 1847, by which time Rawlinson was back from India as the East India Company's Resident in Baghdad as successor to Colonel Taylor and Rich. He revisited the rock and, as he reports, "a wild Kurdish boy volunteered to make the attempt" and managed to "cross over the cleft by hanging on by his toes and fingers to the slight inequalities on the bare face of the precipice . . . passing over a distance of twenty feet of almost smooth perpendicular rock in a manner which to a looker-on appeared quite miraculous . . . Here with a short ladder he formed a swinging seat, like a painter's cradle, and, fixed upon this seat, he took under my direction the paper cast of the Babylonian translation of the records of Darius."

We cannot follow the process of decipherment step by step, partly because Rawlinson himself seems to have had no very clear idea of how it progressed, and partly because at the same time other scholars, notably Hincks, were working along the same lines. With the aid of the Old Persian text the meaning of the Babylonian version was approximately known; but the Babylonian was, unlike the Persian with its descendant Pehlevi, an entirely unknown language, and the system of cuneiform writing was far more complex than the simple alphabetic Old Persian character. Many signs had several quite distinct values (e.g. *ud*, *par*, *lih*), and although most were syllabic (e.g. *ma*, *gu* or *tum*), some signs could also stand for whole words or merely indicated the kind of word which followed (the "determinatives"). Nevertheless, once the bit was between his teeth, Rawlinson forged ahead, aided by a knowledge of the Semitic languages to which Babylonian is closest akin, and soon he was in a position to lay before the Royal Asiatic Society translations of inscriptions which his countryman Layard was in the course of digging up. So in 1853 Layard was able to introduce his second book called *Discoveries in the Ruins of Nineveh and Babylon* with the comment that "much progress has been made in deciphering the cuneiform character" for which "we are mainly indebted to the sagacity and learning of two English scholars, Col. Rawlinson and the Rev. Dr. Hincks" – although he characteristically does not fail to add that he is "aware that several distinguished French scholars . . . have contributed to the successful decipherment of the Assyrian inscriptions."

As with any new decipherment, skeptics persisted, and in 1857 the Royal Asiatic Society agreed to put the matter to the test: four scholars – Rawlinson, Hincks, the scientist Fox Talbot, and for France M. Oppert – sent in sealed translations of the historical annals of the reign of Tiglath-pileser I, which had been found at Assur (Qalat Sherqat) in 1853. The result was conclusive: although there were naturally many divergences in detail between the versions, it was clear that the Assyrian inscriptions had indeed yielded up their secrets, and from henceforth Rawlinson and his colleagues at home and abroad devoted themselves energetically to the solution of outstanding problems and the publication of new texts. The library of King Assur-ban-apli provided the most fertile source, and during the latter half of the 19th century it gradually emerged that its range of subjects and the types of document were even more varied than Layard had imagined, so that with the advance in knowledge a new vista of the whole of Mesopotamian civilization emerged, with its multifarious dialects and 3,000 years of literary creativity.

The later 19th century. Layard left the world of archaeology for politics after his second spell in Assyria, and there followed a rather ignominious episode in Mesopotamian exploration. Large-scale excavation at any one site was abandoned in favor of a series of unsatisfactory soundings at a great number of sites. The evidence of the Biblical and Classical sources, combined with the increasing comprehension of the cuneiform texts, showed that Babylonia must have been quite as important as Assyria, and it should therefore yield equally startling results. However, techniques of excavation were still inadequate, and the diggers only came upon late occupation or unspectacular mud-brick buildings from which they were incapable of extracting information to match

Rawlinson's difficulties in obtaining reliable copies of the Behistun inscription are easily understood. This picture was taken while a cast of the cuneiform was being made by Professor G. G. Cameron of the University of Michigan in the 1950s. In the center is a relief sculpture of Darius receiving the submission of 10 rebel kings; below and to each side are the three versions of the inscription.

Portrait of Rawlinson in 1850 with copies of Assyrian inscriptions in front of him. British Library.

that from the Assyrian capital cities. Rawlinson, who had taken over as the British Museum's agent after Layard's departure, superintended a variety of ventures: work by W. K. Loftus at Warka, by J. G. Taylor, the British vice-consul at Basrah, in Ur and Eridu, and under his own supervision at Borsippa. Work also continued in Kouyunjik, where the superb lion-hunt reliefs of Assur-ban-apli were found in a new palace, primarily under the direction of Layard's erstwhile assistant, Hormuzd Rassam. The French, also conscious of the potential of southern Iraq, sent a distinguished three-man expedition to Babylon in 1852, but the continuation of political unrest and the unpromising character of the site itself led them to no great results either, and fully bore out Layard's comment, based on his visit to Babylon in 1851, that "There will be nothing to be hoped for from the site of Babylon except with a parliamentary vote for £25,000, and if ever this sum should be voted, I would solicit the favour of not being charged with its application."

With Rawlinson's departure from Baghdad in 1855 organized archaeological activity in Mesopotamia came virtually to a standstill. As it chanced, the French consul at Mosul, Victor Place, who had taken over the work of Botta at Khorsabad with the greatest of energy and talent, also left Mesopotamian archaeology in this year after the numbing loss of the greatest part of his finds when his raft was wrecked and plundered near Qurnah. Rawlinson now threw his energies into the publication of the inscriptions in the British Museum, assisted by certain members of the staff to whom in due course he was happy to entrust the major part of the work. One of these was George Smith, an engraver's assistant who had been taken on by the Museum in view of his passionate interest in the cuneiform documents and his manifest talents as a decipherer of the Assyrian texts. He was in fact directly the cause of the next resumption of excavations in Assyria by the British Museum: for during his routine recording of the great mass of tablets from Kouyunjik, Smith discovered "half of a curious tablet which had evidently contained originally six columns . . . On looking down the third column, my eye caught the statement that the ship rested on the mountains of Nizir, followed by the account of the sending forth of the dove, and its finding no resting-place and returning. I saw at once that I had here discovered a portion at least of the Chaldaean account of the Deluge." This result was announced to the Society of Biblical Archaeology in 1872, and the sensation was such that the *Daily Telegraph* at once offered to provide £1,000 to send out an expedition to Kouyunjik to search for the missing part of the tablet. George Smith himself was to lead the expedition, and by May 1873 he was digging through the old trenches and spoil-heaps of Layard and Rassam. Considering the odds against success, one is almost forced to assume divine intervention, since on only the fifth day of work Smith identified among the newly rescued fragments a piece which filled the one major gap in the story – which we know now forms the 11th tablet of the great Epic of Gilgamesh.

This venture brought the Trustees of the British Museum to realize how much of the Kouyunjik library still lay neglected on the site, and Smith was sent out twice more to work there at the Museum's expense. Although he had considerable success, he was inexperienced of eastern ways and suffered many setbacks which Layard would have taken in his stride, and in the end he succumbed to an illness contracted while trying to cross from Mosul to Aleppo in the height of the Mesopotamian summer, when even Layard was wont to take refuge in the mountains. Although the Museum had thereby lost perhaps the most gifted cuneiform scholar of the day, it felt that the recovery of the tablets should continue, and understandably turned to Hormuzd Rassam whose familiarity with local conditions recommended him. As luck would have it, his selection coincided almost exactly with the arrival of Layard in Constantinople as ambassador to the sultan, and in 1878 as a result of his influence Rassam received a *firman* of unexampled generosity, allowing him to work anywhere in the Vilayets of Van, Aleppo, Baghdad and Mosul. Consequently, although Rassam's brief from the Museum was to "try to find as many fragments as possible from the libraries of Assur-bani-pal and Sennacherib," he was "more eager to discover some new ancient sites than to confine my whole energy on such a tame undertaking."

As a result, he left overseers with gangs of workmen at Kouyunjik and Nimrud, and after a small but profitable operation in which he salvaged the magnificent bronze plaques from the gates of Shalmaneser and Assur-nasir-apli at Balawat, he engaged in an archaeological steeple-chase through the south of the country, which took in Assur, Sippar, Tell ed-Der, Babylon, Borsippa, Cuthah and Tello, while on a second trip he also initiated work at the Urartian capital on the shores of Lake Van. In each place workmen were set digging under the supervision of a local foreman, without a shadow of the concern for accurate observation or recording which is already present in Layard's reports. One can only concur with the opinion of Hilprecht, that the methods employed by Rassam were "diametrically opposed to all sound principles of a strict scientific investigation." Although the British Museum's original aim had been to secure the remainder of the Kouyunjik library, it seems that Samuel Birch, the keeper, had condoned Rassam's treasure-hunting for tablets because he thought it would be the last chance to carry on excavations before Russian influence paralyzed all future work in Mesopotamia.

It is fortunate that after Rassam's activities the new director of the Imperial Museum at Constantinople introduced laws under which no person might explore more than one site at a time, and the Turkish authorities had the right to the antiquities found. There was, however, a backlash after Rassam's departure: huge archives of tablets began to find their way to the museums of Europe and America, and it became clear that the Baghdad antique dealers had struck up a very profitable arrangement with the "watchmen" Rassam had left to guard the British Museum's interest at the sites he had dug. Whether or not the British Museum had condoned Rassam's own methods, it was not happy to be buying on the markets tablets which had been excavated at sites it claimed a right to itself. To remedy the situation a member of the Museum staff, Ernest Wallis Budge, was sent out to Baghdad in 1888 with explicit instructions from Rawlinson himself, who had never ceased to uphold the paramount value of the inscriptions: "There is a leakage of tablets from our sites; either find the source of that leakage and stop it, or secure for the Museum what comes from the leakage . . . The vitally important thing is to secure the tablets; for, as compared with tablets, money has no value; money can be replaced, but tablets cannot, and once gone into the Museums of other countries, they are, so far as the British Museum is concerned, gone for ever." Budge succeeded in his mission and on two subsequent occasions, and after engaging in some rather questionable maneuvers to avoid the unwelcome attentions of the Turkish customs authorities, brought back to England a very considerable body of tablets, primarily from Sippar and Tell ed-Der. With this the end of this episode is reached, and from now on at least the motives, if not the methods, of Europeans working in Mesopotamia are essentially scientific rather than acquisitive.

The beginnings of Sumerian archaeology. Although back in the 1850s the Sumerian cities of Uruk, Ur and Eridu had been broached by Loftus and Taylor, this was a short-lived episode, and the results had not been sufficiently spectacular to distract public attention from the great Assyrian palaces. Nor had successors been encouraged by conditions in the area: the majority of big Sumerian sites were isolated from the main caravan routes by desert or marsh, and the population of these regions was especially wild and rarely acknowledged the Ottoman authorities. It was only after study of the cuneiform documents had demonstrated the greater antiquity of the civilization in the south of the country, and detected the existence of a strange early non-Semitic language (now known to be Sumerian), that the search after origins naturally attracted the attention of scholars to the desolate southern sites and induced them to brave the hazards of the terrain.

First in the field of Sumerian archaeology, as with Assyrian, were the French. Like many before and since, the French vice-consul at Basrah, Ernest de Sarzec, sought an agreeable occupation during the gaps in his duties by engaging in antiquarian research. His local informants soon guided him to the considerable mounds of Tello, where inscriptions and statues were known to have been found, and in 1877, having first secured the goodwill of Sheikh Nasir of the Muntafiq Arabs who at that time ruled the area virtually independently of Istanbul, de Sarzec began excavations on the tell. That he was breaking new ground was obvious from the start, and during the years 1877 to 1881 he recovered a fine collection of antiquities from the Sumerian period, including in particular at least nine superb dolerite statues of the *ensis* of Lagash, primarily Gudea. These he shipped back to Paris successfully, and the enthusiasm evoked by their exhibition was such that de Sarzec himself was voted a member of the Institute of France, and the collection was acquired for the Louvre, where a new Oriental Antiquities section was opened under the direction of Leon Heuzey. He and the excavator immediately began work on the book *Découvertes en Chaldée* which undertook the publication of the results in a worthy format – a rare enough event when museums often seemed content to bestow their acquisitions in dusty corners for future generations.

In 1888 de Sarzec, now promoted to consul at Baghdad, returned to Tello with an official *firman*, and was able to carry on the excavations until his death in 1901, when he was succeeded by de Cros and, in the 1930s, by de Genouillac and Parrot. De Sarzec was rewarded by the discovery of major antiquities belonging to the pre-Sargonid Lagash dynasty, which to this day remain the major source of our knowledge of the early civilization of Sumer, and in the subsequent seasons, although the main outline was now well established, valuable additions to the picture could be made in detail, especially because of the cooperation of the great French Sumerologist François Thureau-Dangin in whose hands the extremely difficult historical and economic documents from Tello were made to throw a bright light on this remote age of Mesopotamia.

The first American participation. With a strong tradition of Biblical teaching, the American colleges and universities naturally followed with lively interest the new discoveries in the lands of the Bible. The first outward sign of a desire to participate in the rediscovery of the Mesopotamian world was an expedition sent by the Archaeological Institute of America in 1884, which was privately financed and, clearly influenced by de Sarzec's recent successes at Tello, concentrated its attention on the major southern mounds. This venture bore fruit only indirectly in the shape of an ambitious plan for excavations in the city of Nippur which was launched by the University of Pennsylvania in 1888. Unfortunately the whole affair was vitiated from the start by bitter personal differences, primarily between H. V. Hilprecht, the German-born Professor of Assyriology, whose judgment – admittedly very often borne out by subsequent events – was never tempered with the consideration which might have made his opinions more palatable to his colleagues, and the field directors J. P. Peters, Professor of Hebrew, and J. H. Haynes.

Although careful plans were laid, the whole venture got off to a bad start, and went from bad to worse: funds were not adequate, it became increasingly difficult to find suitable staff, and the local situation around Nippur was distinctly unhealthy: they had to deal with tribes described by Layard as "the most wild and ignorant Arabs that can be found in this part of Asia," and indeed, the first campaign ended in chaos after a night thief from a neighboring tribe had been shot dead, and in retaliation the camp was burned to the ground and plundered. Nevertheless, in the course of this and subsequent seasons important discoveries were made, in particular the main body of Sumerian literature known today; but unlike Tello the site of Nippur is capped by a heavy overburden of the less significant later periods, and Hilprecht is unfortunately right to deplore the lack of trained assistants for Haynes, who spent three years almost entirely alone "near the insect-breeding and pestiferous 'Afej swamps, where the temperature in perfect shade rises to the enormous height of 120° Fahrenheit, and the stifling sandstorms from the desert often parch the human skin with the the heat of a furnace."

The work at Nippur and Tello breathes a new spirit of scientific research which stands in laudable contrast to the activities of the British Museum, but in other respects it must be admitted that these undertakings belong with the 19th century. The aspirations of the American expedition failed to match its achievements, while de Sarzec's work, admirable for the singleness of purpose with which he and his backers in Paris pursued the investigation of the one site, fell short of perfection in technical respects. His untrained workmen were not able to recognize the mud-brick walls for what they were, so that the priceless plans of several important Sumerian buildings were lost to posterity, although their presence can be posthumously detected from the disposition of foundation deposits and other unmistakable indications. Moreover the curious failure of de Sarzec to appoint effective guards on the site during his several absences had disastrous results, for during the span of his work there more cuneiform tablets from Tello appeared in the antiquities markets than were ever found during the excavations, even though the latter amounted to something over 30,000.

Opposite: statue of Gudea dedicated to the wife of his personal god, Ningizzida; he holds a vase from which flow streams of water with fishes. One of the finest pieces found at Tello by de Sarzec (c. 2130 BC). Louvre.

Woolley's Excavation of Ur

VISUAL STORY

The Pennsylvania and British Museums sent Woolley to Ur for the first time in 1922, and he finished work in 1934, having recovered the most complete picture of a Mesopotamian city and its history ever achieved. This might have been expected, but even Woolley cannot have foreseen the Royal Cemetery: during his first season graves with golden jewelry were encountered, but only four years later, when he deemed his workmen adequately trained, did he return to the area and reveal the first of the Royal Tombs. The gold and other splendid works of craftsmanship were sufficient to furnish prize exhibits in the museums of Baghdad, Philadelphia and London, but equally important was the discovery of funeral rites which involved the burial of human slaves as well as inanimate property, to accompany the rulers to the underworld. Abraham came from "Ur of the Chaldees," and Woolley was aware of the interest aroused by Biblical associations: hence the stratigraphic sounding, in which prehistoric ("Ubaid") pottery lay beneath a deep water-laid deposit, was called the "Flood Pit." Whether there can be a real connection with the Biblical Flood is still debated, but such considerations never interfered with the accuracy of his archaeological observation or the quality of his recording.

Above: the ziggurat at Ur with the staircases leading to the first stage, built by Ur-Nammu and restored 1,500 years later by Nabonidus. The ziggurrats of the major temples were so characteristic of Mesopotamia that they find an echo in Genesis as the "Tower of Babel." That of Ur is the best preserved of all (except one near Susa, at Choga Zembil), and Woolley's painstaking work enabled him to distinguish the two different periods of construction. He found evidence for three stages, perhaps all there were in Ur-Nammu's structure, but suggests five or seven stages for the later version.

Opposite: Woolley and his team before the expedition house in 1926: on Mrs Woolley's left is Father Eric Burrows, the epigraphist, on her right Woolley himself, Hamoudi the foreman Woolley brought from Carchemish, and M. E. L. Mallowan.

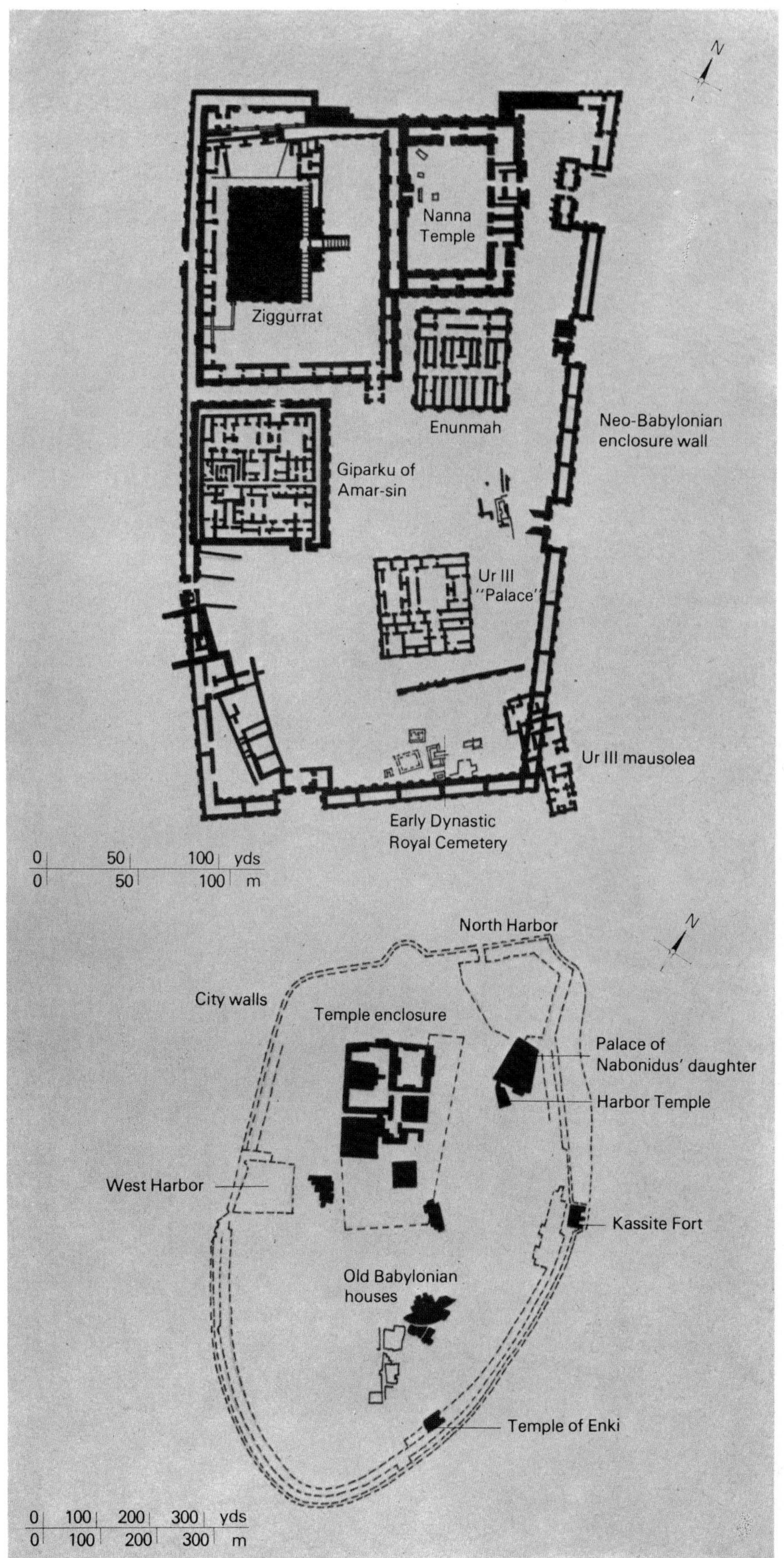

Right: although the great days of Ur were in the third millenium B C, it survived as an important city for many centuries. On the town plan (after Woolley) we see town housing of the Old Babylonian period where Woolley found a crowded merchants' quarter, a Kassite fort and several Neo-Babylonian buildings, mostly the work of Nabonidus who had a special reverence for the city god, Sin: he completely rebuilt the ziggurrat, rebuilt existing temples and outside his new temple-enclosure wall he made a residence for his daughter, high-priestess of Sin.

Above: at Ur important Early Dynastic buildings were buried under later layers, but the unique decorations on the Temple of Ninhursag at Ubaid compensated. Of this stone inlaid frieze Gertrude Bell, responsible for selecting the antiquities to go to the Iraq Museum, wrote, "I had to tell them that I must take the milking scene. It's unique and it depicts the life of the country at an immensely early date . . . it broke Mr. Woolley's heart" (ht 22 cm). Baghdad.

Left: this solid gold dagger with its lapis lazuli handle and golden "wickerwork" sheath is one of the most exquisite of all Woolley's finds (length 37 cm). Baghdad.

Below: despite the immense scale of his work, Woolley seems always to have had time to give to the detailed recording and delicate rescue of works of art. In the grave dubbed the "Great Death-Pit" (which contained 74 human skeletons) was this group of three musical instruments: large lyre with golden bull's head, lying over the sounding-box of a smaller silver lyre, with the boat-shaped base of another silver lyre in the center of the picture.

Opposite: the golden lyre as restored (ht. 1.20 m). Baghdad.

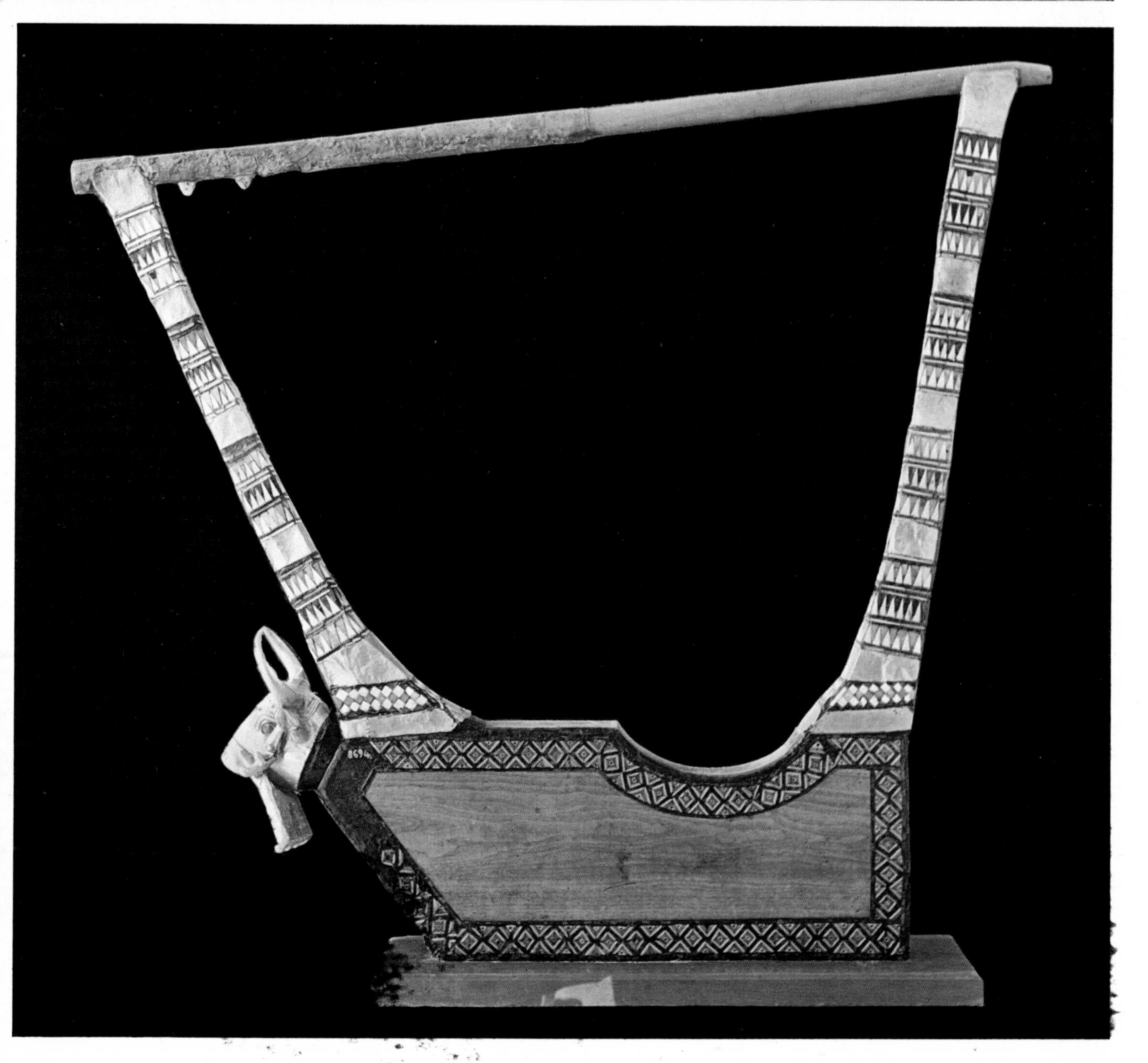

Two matching statuettes of a goat in a tree were found in the Great Death-Pit; they must have supported some object on the golden projection from their backs. This one is 50 cm high, and was of wood covered in gold leaf with lapis lazuli, the belly in silver leaf and the fleece in shell; originally both were hobbled to the branches of the tree by a silver wire around their forefeet. British Museum.

Above: in 1919 at Ubaid H. R. Hall had already discovered this unusually large relief: it measures 1.07 × 2.38 m, and was originally of wood with copper plating. Hall and Woolley suggest convincingly that it was set above the lintel of the entrance to the temple of Ninhursag. The lion-headed eagle is the symbol of Ningirsu, of Girsu, but he grasps lions, not deer. Ninhursag is the goddess of birth and fertility, and, unlike the milking scene, it is difficult to know what connection this relief has with her. British Museum.

Right: in a very richly furnished grave which Woolley considered not to be royal, belonging to a certain Meskalamdug, was this helmet. That it was intended to be worn may be doubted, but Eannatum on the Stele of Vultures wears a very similar helmet, and Woolley observed cloth padding on the interior, which was brought round to the outside to be secured with the holes around the edge. The elaborate hairstyle with plaited hair neatly bunched and held by a fillet at the back is also found on the bronze Akkadian head, and must be a sign of high rank. Baghdad.

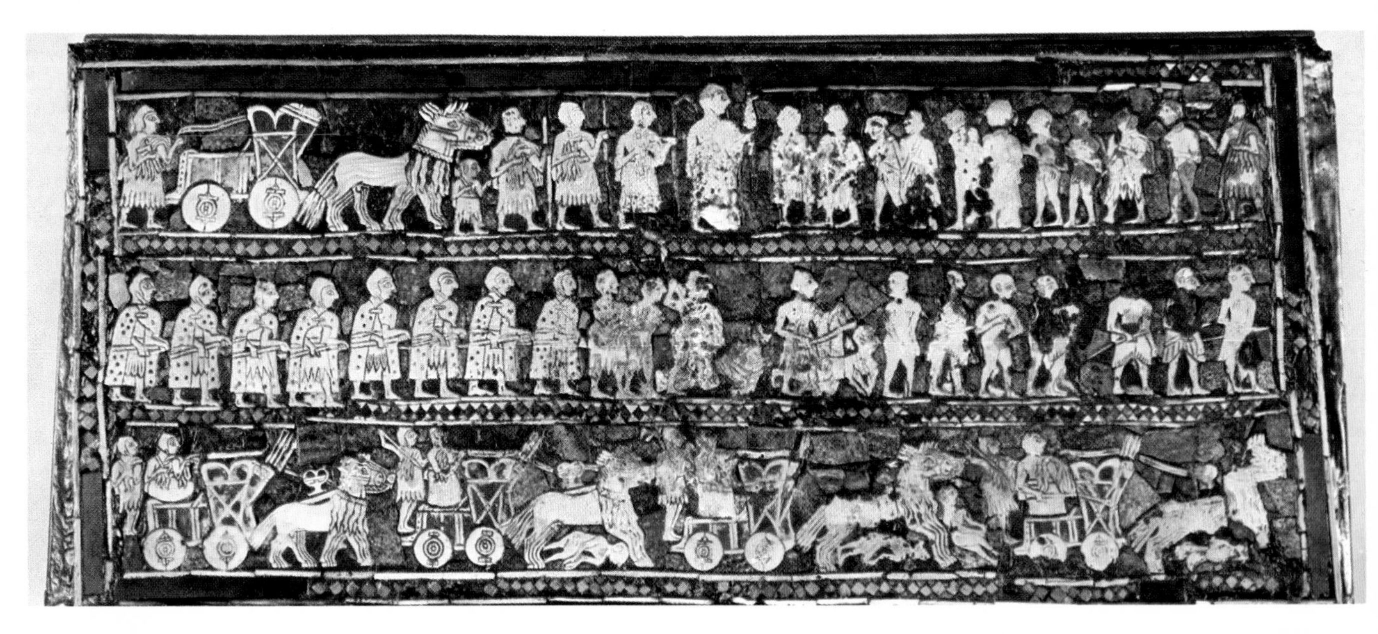

The typical Sumerian technique of inlay, already seen in the Ubaid milking scene, is here at its most elaborate. The object, whose purpose is unknown, is dubbed the "Standard of Ur" and comes from Grave 779. It must surely date from the time when Ur held the "kingship of Sumer." On one side (*top*) is a battle scene, leading up from the solid-wheeled chariots hauled by pairs of onager to the ranks of infantry urging the stripped and roped prisoners towards the king himself, who stands before his chariot to receive their submission. On the other side (*above*) are doubtless the victory celebrations: the king – in a fleeced skirt – sits with his drinking companions and musicians while a procession brings tribute or provisions for the feast. British Museum.

Left: the figure of an onager in electrum (alloy of gold and silver) stands on a double ring for the reins of a type illustrated by the Standard. It was found in the grave of Queen Puabi (Shub-Ad) with the bones of the two oxen (originally wrongly thought to be onagers). Some experts doubt the identification of our animal with the onager, a Mesopotamian wild ass which became extinct this century, but it still seems likelier than mule, which would presuppose the existence of the horse; the same animals haul the chariots on the Standard. British Museum.

3. Mesopotamian Archaeology in the 20th Century

The weathered Kassite ziggurrat at Aqar Quf (c. 1400 BC).

The 20th century begins, as far as Mesopotamian archaeology is concerned, on 26 March 1899 when Robert Koldewey on behalf of the German Oriental Society opened their excavations at Babylon. Like the American decision to work at Nippur, this undertaking had been preceded by a careful preliminary inspection of possible sites, led by Professor E. Sachau accompanied by Koldewey, who had already worked in 1887 for a brief spell at the Sumerian sites of Al-Hiba and Zurghul. Koldewey wrote of the trip "I have seen the ruins of Abu Habba, Babylon, Nippur, Warka, Senkereh, Tello and Seleucia ... Warka and Senkereh are without doubt excellent candidates for excavation, but after my recent more detailed inspection Babylon itself looks a very worthwhile and promising site . . ." Influenced by the bright glazed bricks visible on the surface of the palace mounds, Koldewey was clearly in favor of Babylon, but his opinion alone was not sufficient: on his return to Germany he heard rumors that Sachau's choice had fallen on Warka, then on Assur, but in due course the responsible committee accepted the recommendations in Koldewey's report and Babylon was selected.

From the start it was plain that Koldewey and his masters were determined to make a thorough job of it: the staff included not only a young architectural assistant, Walter Andrae, but a trained Assyriologist to read the texts, and before long two more assistants were sent out to help with the recording and supervision. Funds were adequate, no doubt partly because of Kaiser Wilhelm's personal interest in the work, and, to quote the excavator, "we have worked daily, both summer and winter, with from 200 to 250 workmen." Yet even Koldewey must have been taken aback by the scale of the operation he had started; again, he writes himself: "The city walls, for instance, which in other ancient towns measure 3 meters, or at the most 6 or 7 meters, in Babylon are fully 17 to 22 meters thick." It was as well that the leader of the expedition was an architect at heart, trained in the German traditions of Classical archaeology; one need only look at the chapter headings in his popular book on the excavations to see that for him the city was a collection of buildings enclosed by a wall, and unquestionably the main result of the years of devoted work was the meticulously recorded series of temple, palace, house and fortification plans of the late Babylonian period.

In other respects the work at Babylon must have been a little disappointing; works of art were few and far between, and even the haul of inscriptions was relatively meager. This was perhaps one reason why there was little love lost between Koldewey and his first "Assyriologist" Bruno Meissner, of whom he wrote on one occasion: "I have little of the Assyriologist here, and the influence of his scientific activity on the progress of the excavation is precisely nil, because weeks and months go by before he gives me his report on the inscriptions found . . . by which time the excavation has naturally long since moved on to another place." Be that as it may, and later Assyriologists happily cooperated more effectively, we may fairly say that it was at Babylon that for the first time adequate archaeological observation and recording were combined with the inscriptional evidence to extract the maximum possible information about the site.

Although Koldewey continued to receive support for the work at Babylon, the paucity of finds, and the fact that the water table did not permit him to penetrate below the later Babylonian levels, led to some disenchantment in Germany, and it was no doubt partly for this reason that the German Oriental Society decided to expand its activities in Mesopotamia. In 1902–03 Koldewey was asked to dig at Fara, an important Early Dynastic city recommended to the German Oriental Society by Hilprecht who had actually done some digging on the mound himself, but the work was not congenial to Koldewey and was soon stopped. Far more significant was the inauguration of the excavations at Assur in 1903. The direction of the work, which ran continuously until the Great War, was in the hands of Walter Andrae who had by now served his apprenticeship at Babylon and proved himself well worthy of the task. Assur did not have the immediate worldwide appeal of Nineveh or Babylon, but in the words of the excavator, "The choice . . . was a wise one . . . here the earlier and earliest history of Assyria yielded up a good part of its secrets, and the choice was also wise because of its relatively small size . . . Assur was overshadowed by the later Assyrian capitals only by their size, not in its historical importance."

If the work at Babylon was unique in the area uncovered, at Assur Andrae revealed a historical sequence of even greater value. The major part of the work consisted of disentangling the complex stratigraphy of the northern "public" side of the city with its temples and palaces, and this gave us not only a picture of the traditional Assyrian capital in the first millennium but the first Middle Assyrian remains, and below them still earlier levels. One of the most interesting results is described by Professor Seton Lloyd: "Selecting a major building, the Temple of Ishtar, . . . they carried down the excavation through the ruins of half a dozen earlier temples to an original archaic shrine dating from the days when Assyria was a tiny province on the borders of prosperous Sumer. It was a brilliant feat of excavating, and the prototype of all stratigraphic investigations in later times."

Above: view from the ziggurrat at Assur looking north up the River Tigris, showing the ruins of an Ottoman police post which hampered Andrae's excavation of the Assur Temple.

Opposite: Koldewey's most spectacular find at Babylon was the Ishtar Gate, with glazed brick reliefs of dragons, lions and bulls (reign of Nebuchadnezzar II, 604–562 BC). Baghdad.

Below: Miss Gertrude Bell: a rare picture, since she was usually far too busy writing or taking photographs herself to pose for another.

Archaeology in Iraq between the wars. All archaeological work came to a halt in 1914, and since after the Great War the land of Mesopotamia found itself under British military administration, it was some time before a German expedition returned to the country. After complex political negotiations, the state of Iraq emerged in 1921 and included not only the lands south of Baghdad but also the province of Mosul, therefore virtually all of the heartland of ancient Mesopotamian civilization. In the early days of the new country much of the administration inevitably rested in the hands of British officials, and one of the most distinguished of these, who had from the start played a crucial role in the creation of Iraq as a political unit, was Gertrude Bell. This was particularly fortunate for the archaeology of the country, because Miss Bell, who was made Honorary Director of Antiquities, had in addition to an intimate knowledge of the country and its people, an absorbing interest in its past and in particular in the Classical and Islamic architecture of the Near East. It was this which had led her to the discovery and publication of the Islamic fortress-palace of Ukhaidhir, and had taken her to Assur in 1909 when Andrae reports that "she wanted to know *everything* and crawled indefatigably with me into all the crannies and trenches of the excavation." Having been entrusted with the care of Iraq's antiquities she carried out her trust with her accustomed conscientiousness, finding the new king, Faisal, "perfectly sound about archaeology, having been trained by T. E. Lawrence" (who had been digging with Woolley and Hogarth in Syria before the war). A museum was started in Baghdad, and with a new antiquities law reserving all unique finds and half the remainder from any excavation for Iraq, it rapidly needed a new, larger building and Miss Bell had difficulty finding time to catalog the museum's acquisitions and have adequate showcases made for them. For before long Iraq was to become the host to more foreign expeditions than it had ever seen whilst still an Ottoman province, and happily with the new regulations the quality of work was also improving.

As the end of hostilities was in sight the scent of renewed stability in Mesopotamia under a British administration had occasioned an anticipatory quivering of the nostrils of the British Museum, and already in 1918 R. Campbell Thompson, an Assyriologist serving with the armed forces in Mesopotamia, had put some exploratory trenches into the mounds of Abu Shahrain (Eridu) on the Museum's behalf. He was followed in 1919 by H. R. Hall, who turned his attention to Ur, and in particular to the small mound called Tell Al Ubaid nearby, where he made some fascinating discoveries before he was recalled. By this time the appetite was fairly whetted, and on this occasion the world can be grateful that the British Museum was lucky on two counts: it found the University of Pennsylvania able and willing to assist with the funding of the proposed work, and it found as director of the excavations C. L. Woolley, who had been prepared for

Sir Leonard Woolley holding one of the harps from the Ur Royal Cemetery: its frame consists of plaster of paris which he had poured down the narrow holes left by the decay of the wood, an intuition of which he was justly proud.

the job by his experience at Carchemish and elsewhere, and subsequently showed himself the equal of a task whose magnitude no one could have guessed at the outset.

The results of the excavations at Ur are described elsewhere, and we must now briefly mention the other expeditions which followed in their wake. Clearly the attention of the scholarly world was now concentrated on the earliest historical phases of Mesopotamia, and so, for the same motives as Ur was chosen, we find expeditions at a variety of Sumerian sites: the French returned briefly to the scene of their former triumphs at Tello, the Germans were able to resume their prewar work at Warka in 1928, where their meticulous recovery of the unique complex of later fourth-millennium temples continues to the present day, an American expedition returned to Fara for a short while, and at the important northern city of Kish, first seat of kingship after the Flood according to the King List, a joint Oxford–Chicago expedition set to work. All these individual digs were, however, dwarfed by the arrival on the scene in 1927–28 of the Oriental Institute of the University of Chicago.

Financed primarily by Rockefeller resources, the Institute under its director, J. H. Breasted, had since the war been conducting a carefully planned assault on the centers of ancient civilization in the Near East, and in Iraq this realized itself in the reexcavation of the palace of Sargon at Khorsabad, and in new excavations on an almost unprecedented scale at four separate sites in the Diyala region east of Baghdad. The logistics of the operation matched the scale of its aspirations. As one of its members has written, "These excavating establishments . . . were to be research centres of Western character, established in these countries with the collaboration and protection of the local government. There seemed no reason to suppose that their efficiency would be impaired by provision of the equipment and amenities enjoyed by similar institutions in America . . . at Tell Asmar, forty miles east of Baghdad, a desert station with fully equipped photographic studios and laboratory provided a centre for the excavation of a whole group of most productive Sumerian sites."

While the initial impetus for choosing Khafajah and Tell Asmar was given by the appearance on the Baghdad antiquities market of remarkable Sumerian statuary from sites in the area, the choice of these two cities accorded perfectly with the expressed aims of the Oriental Institute and the archaeological approach of the Field Director, Henri Frankfort. Frankfort worked throughout in the closest cooperation with Thorkild Jacobsen, an unmatched Sumerian scholar, and as archaeologists Seton Lloyd and Pinhas Delougaz, and the result was the constant interrelation of archaeological, art historical, architectural and historical data, the outcome of which was immediately reapplied to currently accepted views and frequently upset them. In 1929 a congress of the archaeologists working in Iraq had met in Baghdad and determined among other things a nomenclature for the early historical and prehistoric phases of Iraq: yielding the sequence Al Ubaid, Uruk, Jamdat Nasr, and Early Dynastic. Throughout his work on the Diyala sites Frankfort's aim was to establish lines of development within these "static entities," and by 1935 he was able to write that "we can undertake this task with a greater degree of confidence and a higher measure of precision. For we now possess six parallel series of stratified remains connecting the Jamdat Nasr period with the age of Sargon of Akkad."

This Diyala project thus succeeded in its intention of establishing an archaeological sequence into which could be slotted all previous and indeed contemporary work on Sumerian sites: the corroboration of the stratification of the Khafajah Sin Temple by the Abu Temple sequence at Tell Asmar – to name but the two major instances – removed any risk of an error resulting from peculiar local conditions which can easily lead the unwary archaeologist astray, and in consequence the division of the Early Dynastic period into phases I, II and III, proposed on the basis of the Diyala sequence, provided a backbone through which the disjointed finds from Kish, Tello, Warka or Ur could be related to one another, and still today remains the only common yardstick to link the more recent discoveries at Nippur, Al-Hiba, Abu Salabikh, Isin etc.

Outside Iraq. Although the kernel of Mesopotamian culture always lay within modern Iraq, obviously it did not stop short at the present-day borders, and nor need Mesopotamian archaeologists. Sumerian and later Babylonian and Assyrian merchants filtered up the Euphrates and Tigris, into Iran, and down the Gulf towards the sea route to the Indus, and along these routes there sprang up outposts of Mesopotamian culture whose affinity to the central area naturally shades off as new spheres of influence make themselves felt. The closest of these cities is Susa, latterly the residence of the kings of Persia, but from before the earliest writing intimately bound up with the culture of the Sumerian south. Here at the turn of the century the French were granted an unusually generous concession by the Persian government, and over the years their excavations at Susa itself and in the surrounding country, which have produced such Mesopotamian monuments as the code of Hammurapi and the stele of Naram-Sin, have exposed the entire spread of Elamite civilization with its language, local culture and the dynasties whose members proved such a persistent thorn in the Mesopotamian side.

After the Great War French influence was also paramount in Syria, and it was no doubt partly a result of political conditions that their major Mesopotamian undertaking moved from Tello to the now famous site of Mari, Tell Hariri, just north of the Iraqi-Syrian border on the Euphrates. Here A. Parrot struck it rich as soon as his picks broke the surface of the mound, and over the 20 seasons of work the flood of discoveries illuminating the Old Babylonian and the pre-Sargonic periods has shown no signs of wavering. Further light was thrown on the presence of Mesopotamian culture in Syria by M. E. L. Mallowan's excavations further north on the tributaries of the Habur in the 1930s: at Tell Brak was a military palace built by the Akkadian king Naram-Sin, while at Chagar Bazar an archive from the "Mari period" showed that here there was one of the many little city-states so characteristic of the north of Mesopotamia at the time. Both Mari and the Habur basin lay on the routes from Assyria and Babylonia to the Mediterranean and the interior of Anatolia, modern Turkey, and both inscriptions and other finds attested the close relations between these areas in the early second millennium. A yet more eloquent testimony was provided by the Czech Orientalist, Bedrich Hrozny, who traced to their origin in the plain below the mound of Kültepe (near Kayseri in Cappadocia) the business documents of the Old Assyrian merchant colony, which had been appearing for many years in the antiquities market. The capital of the Hittite empire, Hattusas (modern Boğazköy) had begun to yield its secrets in 1906 when excavations started under the German Hugo Winckler, but the Kültepe archives with their vivid correspondence illuminated the economic conditions of the time in an entirely unexpected way, and offered a view of the interior of Anatolia with its multifarious kingdoms at a date when the heroic days of the Trojan War were still far in the future. Today the investigation of the site of Kültepe is in the hands of Professor Tahsin Özgüç of Ankara University, and he and other Turkish colleagues have also opened up the field of Urartian archaeology, which is beginning to provide a complementary source of history for the days of the Assyrian empire. At the other extreme of Mesopotamia's trade network lies the barren island of Bahrain, identified with the Sumerian Dilmun, which has served as an entrepôt for seafaring merchants down the Gulf since before the days of Abraham. Here in the 1950s and 1960s a Danish expedition recovered the major cultural phases of the island's past, and succeeded in tying them in to the Mesopotamian archaeological sequence and in demonstrating the close links with the Indus Valley civilization. Although the business archives of merchants – which must have existed – have so far eluded the archaeologists, enough has been found to allow us to recognize this as one of the outposts of Sumerian and Babylonian civilization.

Iraqi initiative. While the spread of Mesopotamian culture was being traced in distant parts, new ground was also being trodden within Iraq itself. Many blank patches

One of the finest statues found by Parrot at Mari: a boring allowed water to flow up and spill out of the vase held by the goddess (c. 1800 BC). Aleppo.

in both the geographical and chronological canvas still remain to be filled, and despite the number of foreign expeditions, there had been an understandable tendency for them to concentrate their attention on the periods which seemed significant in the context of world history – notably the age of the great Assyrian palaces and the early days of Sumerian literacy. However, the Directorate of Antiquities in Iraq was naturally concerned with all ages of Iraqi history and prehistory, and when World War II led to the departure of all foreign expeditions, excavations were initiated by the Iraqis – in particular Taha Baqir and Fuad Safar – with the realization that there was much new ground to break. Advised by Seton Lloyd, who had been a member of the Chicago Diyala expedition, they undertook relatively short excavations at carefully selected sites, by which much new light was thrown on a whole range of neglected periods. Famous though Hammurapi and his laws had been for many years, there was no archaeological work to balance, and the sites of Tell Harmal (on the fringes of Baghdad) and Tell ed-Der produced not only letters and documents of the Old Babylonian period, but a well-documented archaeological context for them, an urgently needed complement to the very detailed picture of social, economic and political conditions afforded by the hundreds of contemporary tablets of the time which have found their way without any archaeological provenance into the museums of the world. Equally neglected in Iraq had been the archaeology of the late second

Above: Kültepe in central Turkey. Jars and other household vessels stand as found in the merchants' quarter of the city of Kanesh during Prof. T. Özgüç's excavations.

Opposite: view of the great temple complex at Hatra, in the desert west of Assur.

Below: jars crushed by debris uncovered in the storerooms of the Temple of the Storm God at Boğazköy (Hattusas), during Prof. K. Bittel's excavations.

millennium BC – except for the Hurrian city of Nuzi excavated in the 1920s by an American team – and here again the Iraqis broke new ground at the Kassite capital of Dur-Kurigalzu, modern Aqar Quf, where both a temple and a palace were located with interesting results. Moving back in time, there were profitable excavations at Tell Uqair, illuminating the rather neglected Uruk period, and at Eridu where the sequence of prehistoric pottery was placed on a solid footing and fascinating light was thrown on the age of continuous settlement at the site. Finally, we should mention the beginning of a project which is still in progress today, the rediscovery of the desert city of Hatra with its stone-built temples, fortifications and houses.

The activities of the Iraqi Directorate of Antiquities, which continue through to the present day, introduced a new approach to excavation in Mesopotamia and a sense of problem which had in the past often been drowned in the desire to work at a major site regardless of its characteristics. Although soon after World War II two ventures were resumed with a conscious link to the pioneering days of the 19th century – British at Nimrud and American at Nippur – the number of less ambitious projects has multiplied during the last 30 years and so have the methods employed. Before mentioning some of the most recent archaeological work in Mesopotamia, it is time therefore to consider the framework within which it must operate, and some of the objectives underlying it.

Mesopotamian archaeology today. Writing at the time of his richest finds in the Royal Cemetery at Ur, Sir Leonard Woolley asserted that "The aim of the field archaeologist is to discover and illustrate the course of human history," and except in the very darkest days the Mesopotamian archaeologist has always sought for information rather than treasure. In the 19th century the original motive was the wonder of a long-dead world suddenly resurrected, with the startling revelation that the events of the Bible were described by contemporary documents and that we could trace back the history of Mesopotamia to a period hitherto only hinted at mistily in the Book of Genesis. The specific hunt for Biblical allusions was soon replaced by a more general interest in the origins of Near Eastern civilization, and in the 1920s this interest was rationalized by J. H. Breasted of the Oriental Institute at Chicago, when he described the Institute's purpose as "to contribute to the understanding of human life by furnishing a fuller knowledge of the processes and stages of the long development by which we have become what we are. This purpose involves us in the task of recovering a great group of lost civilizations in the Near East, which contributed the fundamentals of civilization to the Western World." Although not everyone would cast it in such terms, this must express the underlying self-justification of any historian or archaeologist working with the ancient Near East, and the special draw of Mesopotamia is confidently explained by Professor S. N. Kramer in the subtitle of one of his books on Sumer: "twenty-seven 'firsts' in man's recorded history." While our vocabulary may change with the changing fashions in archaeology, anthropology, economics and sociology, the appeal of ancient Mesopotamia is constant and resides in the two not unrelated priorities: the first literate civilization and the first truly urbanized society.

Means and motive. Perhaps more than elsewhere, in Mesopotamia every archaeologist is the prisoner of a triangle of interconnected variables: resources, methods and information. The end goal of all respectable archaeology is the recovery of information, and the constant (and usually inadequate) factor is the resources. This leaves the archaeologist's major field of decision in the sphere of method, and it must be admitted that even during the 20th century the methods of Mesopotamian archaeologists have come in for criticism. Sir Mortimer Wheeler could write in 1952: "In face of this achievement at home, what has gone wrong with Eastern or Near Eastern field-archaeology?", and although it was not a Mesopotamian site on which were employed something over 1,300 laborers with one supervisor, it must be admitted that there has at times been "wholesale mass-excavation, rewarded by extensive building-plans and ample finds which gratify the patron but are far beyond the capacity of anything approaching exact record."

Egged on against his better judgment very often by the pressure to produce good finds with which to attract more resources for future seasons – a position which starts already with Layard – the excavator has not always resisted the temptation of equating volume of earth moved with information recovered, and the resulting inadequacies of recording are indeed deplorable, since the deficiency can never be made good. Nevertheless the contention that Near Eastern excavations should follow slavishly the methods universally applied to Romano-British sites has been vigorously rebutted by at least one distinguished Mesopotamian archaeologist, and one must agree that methods have to be adapted to the site. It may be that "There is no method proper to the excavation of a British site which is not applicable – nay, must be applied – to a site in Africa or Asia" (R. E. M. Wheeler), but not even the most fanatical would insist that the sections through the one-period Assyrian palace at Khorsabad should have been drawn at a scale of 1:10 at intervals of 5 meters: the additional information this might have yielded could by no means have justified the enormous expenditure of time and money it would have required, and the same result would have been achievable in other ways. There are certain constant factors in historical Mesopotamian excavations which must be allowed to affect the digger's choice of method and to dictate deviations from the practice, if not the principle, of what has been termed the "procedural liturgy" of Romano-British archaeology.

To define the problems let us quote the words of one of the most experienced of practicing Near Eastern archaeologists, David Oates: "The Near Eastern excavator may be faced . . . with two fundamentally different situations. He may meet monumental buildings, filled with the barren debris of their own massive walls, and often with little or no stratified occupation because the original floor of a temple or palace was usually kept clean and might remain in use for centuries . . . Alternatively the excavator may find himself in areas or levels of essentially domestic occupation, where more flimsy structures were replaced at shorter intervals and a steady build-up of occupation debris was permitted." One common factor of these two different situations is the presence of mud-brick. The cheapness and permanent availability of the mud-brick are

The overlying mass of earth forced Layard to excavate at Kouyunjik by tunneling along the slab-lined walls, against his better judgment. British Library.

part of the reason why Mesopotamian public buildings could be planned on so vast a scale, and why the private dwellings could be altered, knocked down and rebuilt with such regularity. Moreover, it is mud-brick which has provided the Near Eastern archaeologists with one of their greatest headaches: mud-brick, especially old, decayed mud-brick, is hard for the untrained eye to distinguish from the surrounding soil, and in the early days mud-brick walls were generally not recognized as such. "There are still pictures which have become familiar in every text-book on excavation, like those of the Hittite palace at Sakjegeuzi, where mud brick walls six feet thick have been laboriously cut away and removed, leaving only the sculptured slabs standing, which had adorned their faces." It was the architectural instincts of Koldewey and Andrae at Assur and Babylon which first accorded to mud-brick walls and buildings the attention which is their due, and when the American excavators after the Great War first sought trained archaeological pickmen they found them at Sherqat among Andrae's old workers. Today the majority of foreign and Iraqi expeditions rely for their skilled wall-tracing on the descendants of the Assur crews, and rightly so, for after a lifetime's acquaintance with different types of soil and brick, the "Sherqati" who is worth his salt is far better able to detect the presence of a mud-brick wall than the enthusiastic volunteer hot with his trowel from Roman Britain.

The inscribed evidence. There is one respect in which the typical Mesopotamian historical site differs from almost any other, and that is in the presence of inscribed documents. Of course an Egyptian or a Greek temple or other public building will very often bear monumental inscriptions which allow its identification, naming the builder, restorer, the god to whom it is dedicated and a hundred and one other relevant facts which are dear to the archaeologists' hearts; and very often too the site where one is working in the Mediterranean or even as far afield as Roman Britain plays a known role in the history and geography of the area, which greatly assists the historians' assessment of the archaeological results, even if no inscriptions have been turned up on the site itself. All these advantages are also present on the Mesopotamian historical site, but the nature of the clay cuneiform tablet is such that we also are privileged to recover a type of written evidence which can supply the archaeologist with intimate detail about the building or room he is excavating in a way which should completely transform the significance of his work. We do not mean to imply that the presence of written information about a house or its owner should permit the excavator to pay less attention to some of the archaeologically recoverable detail: quite the reverse. It is true that if a list of copper vessels belonging to the master of the house were found, we should not need the discovery of a copper vessel in the concrete to tell us that he owned one; but the combination of the archaeological with the

Account tablet listing copper objects including "327 copper sickles weighing 1 talent 1 mina" (from Umma, c. 2050 BC). British Museum.

written evidence enhances the significance of both and therefore the presence of tablets actually imposes on the archaeologist a yet stronger obligation to keep his recording impeccable. It may be that most of the houses in a town dwelling quarter suffered minor alterations during their lifetime, and there is often little that the archaeologist unaided can say on the subject: when however he finds in the houses the deeds of sale or inheritance, there is a good chance that he may be able to disentangle the share of one brother from another, or point with confidence to the partition wall constructed when it proved necessary to sell off a part of the house after father's death.

What is true for a single house applies on a larger scale as well. We are only just beginning to realize the unique opportunities afforded by the fact that, whether intended or not, even the most ephemeral documents of Mesopotamian civilization have come down to us. The abundant details of the business transactions of the Assyrian merchant houses in Anatolia about 1800 BC, the contemporary sources for social conditions in the Babylonia of Hammurapi, or the daily records of the internal economy of the Ur III empire, churned out with amazing industry by Shulgi's bureaucracy – such sources give us an angle on Mesopotamian history which is of special significance for the archaeologist. Indeed in many ways work on a Mesopotamian city-site is most closely comparable with the problems of medieval urban archaeology in Europe. With this detailed knowledge of social and economic conditions, the excavator is no longer obliged to depend on his own results and extrapolate either intuitively or statistically more general conclusions. Rather he must welcome the opportunity to dispense with the speculation necessary in a non-literate archaeological context, and to replace it by a search for precise facts: to relate his building plans to social conditions, to distinguish private dwellings from public buildings and to establish their exact identity, and to tie his stratigraphic phases in to historical events. Thus, although the opinion is sometimes expressed that a moratorium should be imposed on all digging in Mesopotamia until the cuneiform tablets at present languishing unpublished in the museums of the world have been read and exploited, there is a benefit to be derived from the controlled excavation of inscribed evidence by both the archaeologist and the readers of tablets. The archive of nearly 2,000 legal documents found in 1975 at Tell ed-Der by a Belgian expedition will yield far more information than the much greater number of tablets excavated at the site in the 1880s, simply because their archaeological context was meticulously recorded and will be equally meticulously published.

Choice of a site. When the gentlemen of Pennsylvania were seeking a site at which to start their excavations in Mesopotamia, and inclined towards the impressive ruins of Nippur, Hilprecht, by his own account, urged strongly against this choice, and attempted to steer them to the less formidable challenge of Fara, where he later did persuade the German Oriental Society to work for a year. In retrospect, we must admit that Hilprecht's reasoning was, as always, sound, but it is also easy to sympathize with those who preferred the attractions of the larger site, and indeed even today the archaeologist in search of a site in Mesopotamia is faced with the same dilemma. For whereas it is obvious that for important results in a major urban civilization one must turn to the largest cities, it is also true that the larger the site the smaller the proportion one can hope to uncover, and that a great many of the major ancient cities now lie buried under later – Hellenistic, Parthian, Sassanian or Islamic – levels, which are of importance in themselves and cannot merely be bulldozed but must be adequately recorded before removal, thus consuming valuable time and labor. It was indeed the scale of the Mesopotamian cities which induced some of the worst crimes committed in the name of archaeology: large sites require large exposures for the work to show significant results, and large buildings require many workmen to clear them. The existence of this dilemma is indeed recognized by R. E. M. Wheeler – although the solution is not condoned – when he writes: "One of the most dramatic and revealing of all excavated cities is prehistoric Mohenjo-daro . . . Technically the methods adopted by a succession of excavators there became almost an international scandal . . . but the primary marvel of the great Indus city is not that it did (or did not) develop in such-and-such a fashion . . . but that it existed at all in the remarkable form that extensive, if disproportionately summary, excavation has revealed to us . . . There can be no question that Mohenjo-daro takes its place as the representative of one of the great civilizations of the world in some measure by virtue of the crimes of its explorers."

Nowadays, with the shift in acceptable archaeological practices, such wholesale ventures can no longer be undertaken so lightly, and one way in which an adequate harvest of information is sought without "disproportionately summary" excavation is by the careful selection of the site to meet a limited objective or answer a specific problem. The Iraqi work already mentioned provides some instances of this, and another illustration is afforded by the British expedition to Tell Al-Rimah (1964–71). David Oates, the excavator, noting the sparseness of information on the history of Assyria during the second millennium BC, wrote at the outset of the work: "The reason for this lack of information from Assyria itself is a practical one. The geographical and climatic advantages which made the plain around Nineveh a sufficient nucleus for the conquest of an empire have ensured intensive and continuous occupation of most of the obvious village or town sites. Old and Middle Assyrian settlements, not to mention the towns and villages of the third millennium BC, lie beneath the massive remains of Late Assyrian buildings and are all but inaccessible to the excavator. Material and documents of the earlier periods must be sought in less favoured areas, where individual settlements had a shorter life."

In the event the site of Tell Al-Rimah justified the care and experience with which it was singled out. A major

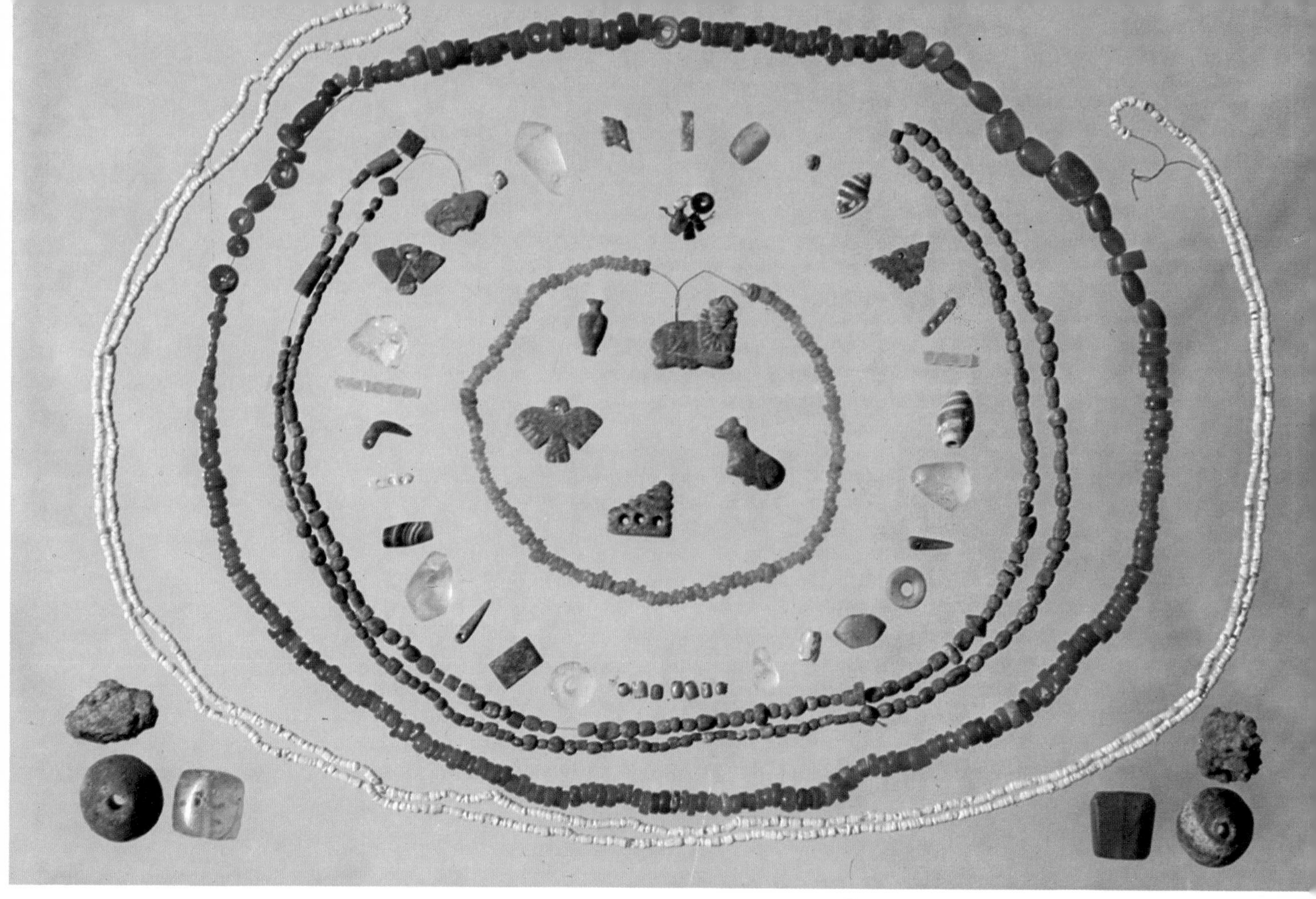

temple with unique architectural features, a palace, and in each building an archive of Old Babylonian letters and administrative tablets reveal the city's position in the complex politics of the early second millennium; there follows an invaluable archaeological sequence which leads unbroken to the period of the Middle Assyrian expansion, from which time we have an archive of business and administrative documents which disclose the city's status and the activities of some of its chief citizens; and after a significant break in the stratification, reflecting the years of Assyrian weakness, the new inhabitants left us a shrine in which stood a fine Neo-Assyrian stele with invaluable evidence about the policies of resettlement in the area. Although this excavation was highly profitable in terms of information recovered weighed against the resources, the earlier levels are buried fairly deep, and the same considerations which led to the choice of the site indicated at least a temporary suspension of the digging. That on every site there is a point where further work will be less productive of information, if not finds, was keenly recognized by Woolley, who wrote that although "only a minute fraction of the city's area was thoroughly explored, none the less we did secure a reasonably detailed picture of Ur throughout its four thousand years of existence and had made discoveries far surpassing anything we had dared to expect; now there was the danger that more digging would yield results more or less repetitive, and the preparing of our material for public-

Excavations conducted by the author at Abu Salabikh in 1975 aim at reconstructing a picture of a Sumerian city during the Early Dynastic period: here we see a crushed jar *in situ* with a hoard of beads (*opposite*) and the same beads after excavation (*above*).

Below: the excavations at Tell Al-Rimah uncovered a magnificent temple of the Old Babylonian period (c. 1800 BC), decorated all round its exterior with engaged mud-brick half-columns imitating date-palm trunks or with a "barley-sugar" twist (as here).

ation, an imperative duty, could not be undertaken while field work was still in progress."

This latter point is all too often ignored. However much information is recovered, and however scientifically the excavation is conducted, it is useless until the excavator has interpreted his results and made them available to the public. Although many Mesopotamian excavations have a good record of publication – such as Assur, Babylon and Ur – there are also exceptions, among which we would number the expedition which has been at Warka (Uruk) off and on since before World War I. In view of their handsome monographs on certain categories of finds, and an annual report containing many detailed architectural plans and descriptions, this may well seem an unfair example; and yet the format of an annual report is so ill suited to the orderly presentation of archaeological results, and the buildings at Warka are so complex, that the scholarly world is hardly better informed that the general public about the great series of fourth-millennium temples which are of extreme importance in the history of architecture. The fault lies not in the scientific quality of the excavations or of the reports, but in the lack of any single publication in which the results of different seasons are recast by those who were present into a coherent description of the buildings themselves rather than of the process of their excavation.

Of the historical excavations currently under way in Mesopotamia Warka is now the doyen; the old tradition of selecting a major, multi-period, city and devoting to it an almost indefinite number of seasons is also shared by the expeditions at Nippur, Isin and Larsa. At Lagash (Al-Hiba) an American expedition has selected a major city, but since it was largely abandoned after the Early Dynastic period, the most interesting Sumerian levels are easily accessible on the surface, and the same considerations applied to the resumption of excavation at the Early Dynastic site of Abu Salabikh, near Nippur, where a small city lies unencumbered by later occupation directly below the surface of the mounds. Another foreign expedition with more limited objectives is the Belgian investigation at Tell ed-Der: here the Old Babylonian layers are immediately accessible and by careful observation of the stratigraphy of a housing quarter it has been possible to tie the architectural sequence in with dated tablets of different reigns at three different levels.

Hitherto we have mentioned almost exclusively town or city sites, and indeed it is hard to find anything else in Mesopotamia. Small tells are usually only villages and have consequently received little attention from those in search of historical data, and there is nothing comparable to the tumuli and Roman villas of western Europe, which have provided such invaluable small self-contained units for the archaeologist. There are of course a few exceptions. An Assyrian stone-built aqueduct was uncovered at Jerwan by the Chicago expedition in 1933, and another equally well-tailored operation was the investigation of a Roman frontier post at Ain Sinu near Jebel Sinjar in north Iraq. In each case the essential historical and architectural details were provided by a single season's work, and if one measures the information recovered against the expenditure of resources, these must be counted among the most successful of all historical excavations in Mesopotamia.

Sennacherib's aqueduct at Jerwan (reconstructed *below*, after Lloyd) carried water from Nineveh across a small wadi; built of fine rusticated masonry, with a bitumen-plastered bed for the water, it was supported by pointed arches (*opposite*) through which the waters of the wadi flowed in the winter and spring floods.

The site in context. Both the investigations just mentioned were undertaken within the framework of larger projects: at Jerwan the recording of the aqueduct was accompanied by a survey of the course of the canal it served and by a study of the rock reliefs and hydraulic arrangements at the canal head at Bavian. The work at Ain Sinu by David Oates was complementary to his soundings in the Roman fortifications at Sinjar itself and at a 6th-century church nearby, and formed part of a general study of the historical geography of this area, with special reference to the Roman frontier. A similar concern for the archaeology of a whole region, rather than any one site, was imposed on archaeologists in the 1950s when the construction of two dams in northern Iraq flooded the Rania and Shehrizor plains and with them a great number of ancient sites. The Iraqi Department of Antiquities surveyed both areas and a number of the mounds were at least partially excavated, producing results both historical and prehistoric from areas which would otherwise have had to wait a long time before attracting the attention of the archaeologists. A similar regional approach has grown out of dam construction in Turkey and Syria on the Euphrates in recent years, and here also the combination of sites has given the areas in question a depth of archaeological identity quite unlike anything that could have been achieved by the excavation of a single capital city.

We would not like to give the impression that excavation is the only method for the archaeologist concerned with the history of a whole landscape. We are fortunate in Mesopotamia that most large and many small ancient sites are immediately detectable as large or small mounds; and the potsherds which litter their surfaces give the expert evidence for the period or periods of the site's occupation, so that in theory, by recording all visible sites in an area and noting the periods of their use, the distribution of settlements at any date could be mapped, giving an invaluable indication of social, economic or even political conditions. The principle that the surface remains could betray the period of a site was not of course lost on the early explorers, and a keen appreciation of the geographical circumstances was forced on them by the mere realities of existence in those days; the works of Layard and Place abound with references to ancient sites sought out by them and inspected for their archaeological potentialities. Nor were the surface sherds the only clues: even at a totally unexcavated site the configuration of the mounds may enable the trained eye to distinguish with confidence the city walls, gates, ziggurrat and other public buildings. Indeed at Tell Taya near Tell Al-Rimah the streets and houses of the third-millennium city can be planned without excavation, as the stone foundations appear on the surface, and in future it seems certain that air photography will disclose fascinating detail, both about the ancient landscape as a whole and on the surface of individual mounds.

The northern plains of Mesopotamia, where Layard saw "as far as the eye could reach" the "grass-covered heaps marking the site of ancient habitations" and was able to count them to as many as 200, are especially suitable for this kind of survey work. In the south the task is more complicated but the potential results are correspondingly more significant. The first conscious efforts at area survey were made in the Diyala region by the Chicago expedition, and subsequently it has been American scholars – Jacobsen, Goetze, Crawford and Adams – who have refined the process and gradually filled out the map. From the start it was evident that the distribution of sites in the south was significant only if they could be located in relation to the irrigation system of the time. To determine the position of the two great rivers and their derivative canals at different periods is not an easy task: textual evidence is scarce and often ambiguous, and the earlier procedure of reconstructing an ancient watercourse wherever an alignment of contemporary mounds showed up, although undoubtedly correct in many instances, is methodologically suspect since it makes presuppositions about the character of the ancient irrigation systems which are what we should be trying to prove. Fortunately more impartial witnesses can be found: geomorphological methods are already in use by the Tell ed-Der expedition in an effort to trace by borings the courses of the Euphrates and its major canals near Sippar, and can obviously be applied elsewhere. In the modern desert between Tigris and Euphrates Adams, now very much the protagonist of area survey, has recently detected on aerial photographs ancient meander patterns which can only have been created by one of the two great rivers, and point to much more drastic changes of course than had been previously suspected. Finally, the visible banks of the more recent canals give a secure basis for the reconstruction of Islamic and Sassanian irrigation systems.

Even if the entire network of watercourses could be mapped out for a given period, the interpretation of survey data remains subject to a variety of factors. Silt is deposited unevenly, more thickly near the canal banks than elsewhere, and this may be deceptive: an apparently small tell in a heavily alluviated area may simply be the tip of a much larger mound now buried, and in fact much more important than a contemporary and seemingly bigger site in an area which is not silted up. With regard to his recent surveys Adams has written that "close scrutiny of geomorphic processes makes it clear that the land surface surveyed by the archaeologist is a complex product of variable, interacting agencies rather than the outcome of uniform, general alluviation as has generally been assumed. Both wind erosion and wind deposition have played a very significant part, with the latter in particular probably serving far more than alluviation to obliterate surface traces of smaller settlements."

Despite the obstacles, it is not likely that any major or second-rank sites will long escape detection, but to the human geographer even the smallest settlements are significant: it is here that statistical sampling methods must inevitably be invoked, not because the evidence is absent, but because it would take too long to collect. To map out the "scattered traces of rural settlement" which supplemented the built-up centers Adams holds that "only an extremely intensive gridding of small areas on foot will suffice." Yet another problem is that in the quantitative assessment of individual sites a sherd collection from the surface may be a very inadequate reflection of what lies beneath: the lower layers will obviously be less represented among the surface sherds, and the natural irregularities of archaeological sites mean that even sophisticated statistical processing of the results would yield only a hazy image of the earlier phases of the settlement.

Nevertheless, there is little cause for pessimism. The size of the available sample must compensate substantially for the multitude of possible hitches in detail, and the technique of archaeological survey has taken its place alongside excavation and the use of written sources as a third avenue by which we may approach the ancient Mesopotamian world. It can throw light on subjects beyond the reach of the other techniques, and its potential value is evident to anyone concerned with a subject such as the agricultural structure which underpinned the military expansion of the Assyrian empire, or the exact nature of the urban revolution in early Sumer. In each of the three approaches both the quantity and the quality of the evidence are of almost unmanageable richness, and the task of archaeologists in future will be to combine all three and profit from the combination. As yet this process is in its infancy, but it is clear that closer liaison between the diggers and surveyors of sites and the readers of tablets will create for ancient Mesopotamia the opportunity of resurrecting in intimate detail the mechanics of the society which fostered one of the great early civilizations. The only limiting factor appears to be the shortage of workers both at home and in the field, and the problem is not so much to refine new scientific or statistical techniques through which the maximum of evidence can be extracted from the available material – although such techniques will of course be applied – but rather to decide the strategy by which the most significant results will be obtained from the embarrassing wealth of epigraphical, geographical and archaeological sources.

4. Sumer and Akkad

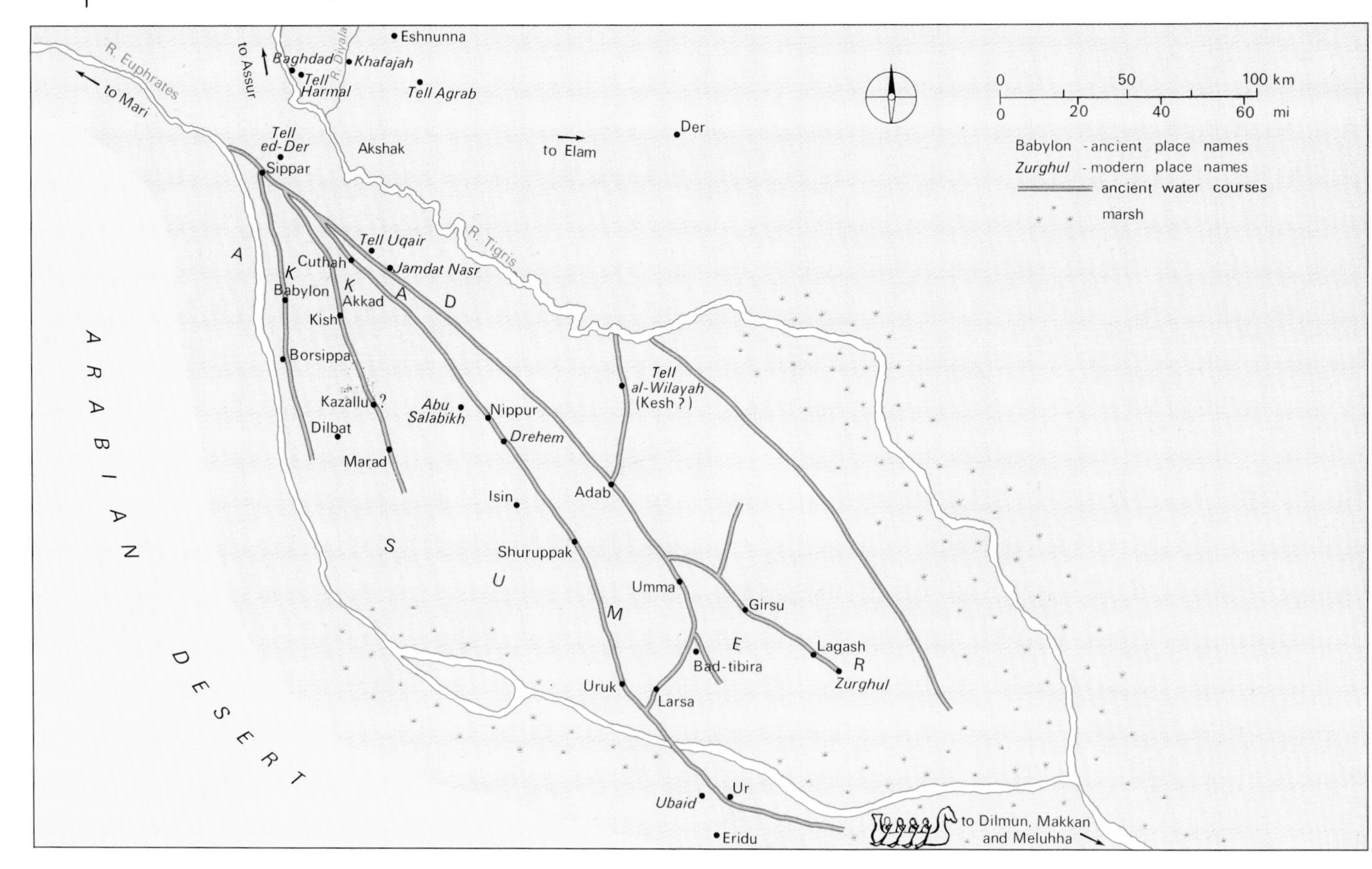

Cities of Sumer and Akkad.

The beginnings of literacy. Within the last decade a team of German archaeologists has discovered a city dating to before 3000 BC, which lies for more than a mile along the west bank of the Euphrates in Syria. The site, Habuba Kabira, is fortified by a unique double wall with complex gateways and towers at precise intervals, and within this huge enclosure are well-constructed stone houses, in one of which was found a collection of the clay lumps used for the sealing of merchandise, with the impressions of cylinder seals indistinguishable from similar finds made in Proto-literate Uruk (Warka) and Susa. They have also found clay tablets with numerical signs, sealed with typical Mesopotamian seals, and the excavators can hardly be wrong to describe this as a trading city, forerunner of many encountered in later years in this situation on the Euphrates bend, where they can control traffic coming up the river from the south, or across the plains from the east, as well as strike out westwards towards the region of Aleppo and the sea.

In 1973 an expedition from the Royal Ontario Museum uncovered at the site of Godin Tepe, between modern Kermanshah and Hamadan in Iran, a complex of buildings in which was pottery characteristic of Susa and Mesopotamia in the Proto-literate period, and 43 tablets or fragments bearing numerical signs and seal impressions, which might just as well have come from Susa itself or even Habuba Kabira. As the excavators suggest, these discoveries point unmistakably to the presence at Godin Tepe of merchants from Susa eager to control the lucrative trade with Mesopotamia.

Previous page: statuette from Uruk (c. 3000 BC). Baghdad.

More than 600 miles southeast of Susa, in the arid hills of southern Iran, the mound of Tepe Yahya has been under investigation by an expedition from Harvard University. This has disclosed the existence during the fourth and third millennia BC of a flourishing city which was evidently in close contact with Susa not only because of the discovery of the well-known Uruk and Jamdat Nasr pottery, but because here too were found tablets with typical Mesopotamian seal impressions and not merely numerical signs but even pictographs identical with those in use at contemporary Susa.

Although each of these far-flung sites has its own local setting, and there is no reason why such large and prosperous urban societies should not have emerged independently, they are in fact linked in a loose network with its center in Mesopotamia and neighboring Susiana – the alluvial lands of southeastern Iran which for centuries were ruled from the city of Susa. Naturally, the diffusion of earlier pottery styles, such as Halaf or Ubaid, and of raw materials like copper or obsidian, is sufficient to show that even before the Proto-literate period these regions must have been in close contact, but at this stage there seems to come a change in the relationships. For it is during the Proto-literate age that a truly urban society can first be recognized in Mesopotamia, and this is reflected by the contemporary expansion of sites such as Tepe Yahya and

Habuba Kabira, far from the central area. Both in the way of international trade, and in every other way, there seems to be a real divide at the beginning of this period, which marks off the civilization of Mesopotamia from all surrounding cultures, and makes it not only the kernel of a new literate urban society, but also the source of the cultural traditions of the whole Near East for the duration of cuneiform writing.

The archaeological record. It is therefore all the more aggravating for the historian that archaeological work on the Proto-literate period within Mesopotamia proper has hardly extended beyond the single site of Uruk (modern Warka). It is true that important finds have been made at Susa and neighboring sites on later Elamite ground, but apart from the good but restricted work in deep levels at Khafajah and Nippur, serious investigation of Proto-literate levels in Sumer is virtually confined to the shrines of Tell Uqair (near Kish) and Eridu, to the unreliable work at Jamdat Nasr, and of course to Uruk itself. All the same, even from this unsatisfactory sample, the virtuosity of the age is plain enough. At Uruk we are confronted by a succession of precincts in which the German architects have lovingly distinguished brick by brick the sophisticated plans of temples often of enormous size, some in plain mud-brick but others making use of limestone blocks or with their exteriors decorated by complex patterns achieved by mosaics of colored cones of clay or stone inserted into the mud plaster of the walls. Nothing has yet been found, except perhaps at Tell Brak in the far north, to rival these structures in size, conception or complexity, but at Tell Uqair an interesting small shrine of this date was erected on an irregularly shaped platform and decorated with wall-paintings of leopards and worshipers bearing offerings, and it is certain that the building techniques of Uruk were in use throughout Sumer, since the tell-tale cones may be picked up on the surface of many a site as yet untouched by the archaeologist's pick.

The sophistication of the architecture is matched in the other arts. From the temple precincts at Warka and elsewhere there come some of the finest pieces of sculpture known from the entire span of Mesopotamian art, and the cylinder seals which make their first appearance now, are as well conceived and technically as expert as any that follow, even if they do not reach the exquisitely minute perfection of the finest Akkadian work. Other finds attest to the skill of the metal-worker in silver or copper, but unquestionably the most significant achievement is the invention of writing. No one can yet say with certainty when or where the long development of the cuneiform script started; the earliest phases are still known almost exclusively from Uruk, but in view of the lack of contemporary excavated sites this need not be significant. By the later Proto-literate period the scribes of Jamdat Nasr (near Kish in the north of the country) are using precisely the same repertoire of signs as their colleagues at Uruk, and there is even evidence of a common tradition of sign lists. Evidently, though, the cumbersome corpus of over 2,000 often complex signs was a hindrance to the easy transmission of the system outside Sumer itself, and apart from the simple numerical notations which we have already encountered at the outer fringes of the Mesopotamian sphere of influence, it was only the idea of writing, and not the signs themselves, that spread further, to Susa, where a similar but independent set of "Proto-Elamite" signs was introduced, perhaps to Egypt and the Indus valley, and maybe even as far afield as Romania where a similar script has recently and most unexpectedly cropped up.

Since the writing on the earliest tablets is entirely pictographic – that is, each symbol stands for a whole word, not for a sound or sounds – we cannot easily determine whether they are written in Sumerian, but the consensus of scholarly opinion now holds that this is almost certainly the case. This need not of course imply that Sumerian was the only or even the dominant language, and it would be naive to suppose that the population was much purer ethnically then than in later times. Nevertheless, whether entirely Sumerian-speaking, or, as one may rather suspect, with a strong admixture of Akkadian or even pre-Akkadian Semitic people, the culture of urban Proto-literate Mesopotamia was as uniform as ever it was before or after. It was at this time that in the arms of the two rivers there first crystallized the Sumerian civilization whose technological achievements and intellectual creativity made it the fountainhead of all Mesopotamian culture.

The beginnings of history. Although the invention of writing is the precondition for history to supersede prehistory, in Sumer at least we cannot claim to be able to use the earliest writing as a historical source. The accounts of the temples of Uruk were certainly not designed to convey historical information, nor indeed do they. It is only after the lapse of some centuries that the first "historical" text can be identified, and that, as we shall see, is no more than the name of a king scratched on the side of a stone bowl. It is therefore only in the course of the Early Dynastic period (c. 3000 to 2400 BC) that the anonymity of prehistory is supplanted by the rich detail of historical times, and it is perhaps for this reason that this period has attracted more archaeological activity than any other – except perhaps the imperial palaces of Assyria – in sharp contrast to the neglected Proto-literate levels. Major excavations began with the French work at Girsu (Tello), and this was followed by expeditions at Ur, Uruk and Eridu in the south, Shuruppak (Fara) and Nippur in central Sumer, and in the north by work at Kish. The stratigraphy of the period was put on a firm basis, and the terminology Early Dynastic I, II and III was initiated, by the Diyala expedition's work at Khafajah, Eshnunna (Tell Asmar) and Tell Agrab, and the geographical limits were

extended up the two rivers by the excavation of Assur and Mari. Nor is that all, since recent years have witnessed new excavations at Lagash (El Hiba) and Isin (Ishan al-Bahriyat), and the still unidentified city at Abu Salabikh near Nippur has yielded an important collection of Early Dynastic literary tablets. As a result of this relatively intense activity, we can now trace with some confidence the transition from the classical phase of Proto-literate art through a degeneration into the ferment of the Early Dynastic period when style followed hard upon style in an artistic tradition which was always interesting, if not endowed with the classical beauty of the best Proto-literate pieces.

Naturally the excavators also discovered inscriptions, and these should enable us to add a further dimension to the picture. And yet they do not offer us the precision we might have hoped for. At those sites – chiefly Ur, Girsu, Kish and Shuruppak – where large numbers of early tablets have been found, there is rarely a reliable sequence of stratified material, whether through no fault of the excavator or as a result of outdated or simply indefensible methods, and it is impossible to tie any of the major finds of tablets into the established archaeological framework of pottery or other artifacts. It was left to the Diyala expedition to seek out sites where a well-recorded sequence of Early Dynastic levels could be dug, but as luck would have it the inscribed material here, to the northeast of Sumer proper, was so scarce that it did little to remedy the situation. We are left with the curious result that there are three concurrent classifications for these centuries: the purely archaeological, for which the work in the Diyala suggested the divisions Proto-literate and Early Dynastic

Above: limestone macehead found at Tello, but bearing the name of Mesalim, king of Kish. Lions attack each other and a spread-winged eagle occupies the top of the mace. Louvre.

Opposite above: well in the Early Dynastic Shara Temple at Tell Agrab, built with the typical "plano-convex" bricks, flat on the bottom and lightly humped on top.

Opposite below: silver vase from Lagash. Incised on the body is the lion-headed eagle grasping two lions; the inscription around the rim dedicates the vase to Ningirsu. Louvre.

I, II and III, the epigraphical, which can order in sequence the different groups of tablets on the basis of the stage of development reached by their script, and the purely historical, which makes use of the scanty written sources for the time before Sargon of Akkad, and may even attempt to extract from them an absolute chronology into which the archaeological and epigraphical schemes could eventually be fitted. Ultimately these three channels can only be united by further well-controlled excavation, not unmixed with good fortune.

In the meantime we have a classic instance of the intersection of different avenues of approach. While the archaeological record persists, unchanged, from prehistoric times, there gradually accumulate wisps of written evidence which come in time to overwhelm the archaeological sources with the wealth of detail and depth of insight they can offer. Whereas sometimes the one line of approach merely confirms and enlarges what was already known from the other, it is amazing how often the texts may reveal whole facets of Sumerian civilization which could have appeared in the archaeological record but have not, or else excavation has demonstrated the existence of something which the philologist may have sought expectantly but in vain in his documents. To take but one instance, of all the sites within the boundaries of ancient Sumer none has been as rich or as informative as Ur. Woolley's excavation of the Royal Cemetery, with its enormous wealth of objects and macabre mass burials, revealed at once a luxury and sophistication in the early phases of Mesopotamian civilization which were previously unsuspected, and a side of religious belief and practice which could never have been divined on the basis of the texts alone. This same cemetery also illustrates the frustrations of trying to coordinate the written and the excavated evidence: although ruling dynasties are mentioned in the historical texts at both Ur and Kish – where similar though slightly earlier royal tombs were discovered – we are still in no position to state with any confidence whether the tombs belonged to any of those dynasties, or to other rulers who came before or after.

Later written traditions. Although by the accession of Sargon writing had come to serve a variety of purposes, including the description of historical events by kings who wished their deeds recorded for posterity, it is not these contemporary inscriptions that constitute the backbone of our conception of the political history of these early days, but a document which dates in the form known to us from a good 500 years later. This is the "Sumerian King List" which records the names and lengths of reign of the kings believed to have ruled Sumer not only "after the Flood" but even before it. Since not only the ancients but also modern scholars have been inescapably influenced by the contents of this document, we must turn aside to examine it in greater detail.

The list begins by saying that "when kingship came down from heaven" it was in Eridu, and names two kings who ruled from there. The kingship is then said to have moved in succession to dynasties ruling from Bad-Tibira, Larak, Sippar and Shuruppak. At this point, it is announced, the Flood swept over the land, but after the Flood the kingship came down once more from heaven, to the city of Kish. Twenty-three kings are recorded as having ruled Sumer in the 1st Dynasty of Kish, finishing up with a certain En-mebaragesi and his son Aka. There follow much shorter dynasties (or even single reigns) in the order: Uruk, Ur, Awan (in Elam), Kish, Hamazi (Kerkuk area), Uruk, Ur, Adab, Mari, Kish, Akshak, Kish, Uruk (for the third time), and finally Akkad and its successors.

In the early days of cuneiform studies it was assumed by scholars that each dynasty came after the one before it in the list exactly as it appears in the text, and there was the presumption that even though – as in the Book of Genesis – the early lengths of reign (e.g. the 625 years assigned to Aka of Kish) were plainly miraculous, for the later part of the list it would only be necessary to add together the total number of years attributed to each dynasty to recover a secure absolute chronology for the period. However, when it was realized that some of the kings named in apparently successive dynasties were in fact contemporaries, it became clear that we should envisage each dynasty as overlapping with those before or after it. Once this is done, we lose any direct assistance the Sumerian King List might have given towards the establishment of an absolute time-scale, but the list's overall credibility can still be cautiously affirmed: at least for the kings after the Flood, there is no reason to doubt that the political hegemony of Sumer did indeed pursue the rather erratic course described by the King List.

This is fortunate, since other written sources for these rather shadowy events at the outset of recorded history

Above: trade within Sumer is demonstrated by clay sealings, like this one from Jamdat Nasr, with which bales were secured. Ashmolean.

Left: the best-preserved copy of the Sumerian King List (from Larsa); this side lists the kings before the Flood. Ashmolean.

draw much of their significance from their associations with the King List. One of the most encouraging of recent discoveries was the identification of the inscription on a stone bowl from the excavations at Khafajah as being of "En-mebaragesi, king of Kish." This was especially satisfying since En-mebaragesi is given as the penultimate king of the 1st Dynasty of Kish, and is said by the King List to have defeated Elam, which would accord with the discovery of this bowl east of the Tigris. Apart from this shortest and earliest of royal inscriptions, other kings named in the King List have left us records of their presence at sites such as Adab, Kish, Nippur, Ur and Uruk in numbers sufficient to show that the list is based on genuine historical traditions and need not be dismissed as a mythical composition.

There were indeed reasons for doubting the historicity of the early stages of the list: after the 1st Dynasty of Kish we find rulers of Uruk whose names feature largely in the heroic tales recorded hundreds of years later, and include the figure of Gilgamesh himself, whose achievements in later tradition may confidently be dismissed as mythical inventions. And yet one of these literary compositions described in vivid detail a conflict between Gilgamesh and Aka, the son of the very En-mebaragesi whose historicity is no longer in question. This tale, in terms irresistibly reminiscent of the Homeric epics, tells how Aka of Kish descended on Uruk to do battle with his unruly vassal Gilgamesh, and how it was only the timely apparition of Gilgamesh himself on the walls of Uruk which caused the men of Kish to fall back like the Trojans before the face of Achilles. For us this epic is doubly precious: it must reflect a real event, however distant, and it shows that the heroic figures of Sumerian literature – Lugalbanda, Enmerkar and Gilgamesh – belong to a time that can already be called historical. The discovery of that vase is as if Greek archaeologists had unearthed a sword bearing the name of Atreus.

Nonetheless, these scraps of information are no more than drops in an ocean of ignorance, and if we have dwelt on the sources for the period it is more to emphasize than to obscure how tenuous any reconstruction of its "history" must be. Various converging lines of evidence have led scholars to postulate a long period at the start of the Early Dynastic times during which the city of Kish was the seat of kings who claimed the hegemony or "kingship" of Sumer. This is not only indicated by the King List, but also by the curious fact that later "kings of Sumer" adopted the title of "king of Kish" in preference to any other, wherever their own particular dynasty was at home. Moreover, the excavations at Kish uncovered two strongly fortified secular buildings of the Early Dynastic II to III periods, and it is quite as revealing that on one occasion the cities of Umma and Lagash called in Mesalim "the king of Kish" to settle one of their innumerable border disputes.

A different picture is presented by some curious sealings from the early levels at Ur, in which the names of cities such as Kesh, Adab, Uruk, Ur and Nippur are written together in a way which argues a degree of cooperation which is hard to explain except in terms of a political confederation of some kind between these widely separated states, even though the immediate application of these sealings must have been to articles of trade. It has even been suggested that at the date of these sealings – approximately Early Dynastic I – Sumer had created a league of city-states centered on Nippur, which although the residence of Enlil, chief god of the Sumerian pantheon, never in historical times appears as the seat of any temporal power. How such a confederation stood in relation to the 1st Dynasty of Kish, or to the even earlier dynasties implied by the King List, is a problem to which we can hardly hope ever to be granted the solution.

Sumer in the Early Dynastic III period. The last king of the 1st Dynasty of Kish, Aka, may have reigned about 2600 BC. Thereafter Sumer entered a "warring states" era, so that between the reign of Aka and the accession of Sargon, scarcely more than two centuries, the King List records 13 changes of dynasty, and, as can be seen from the map, no one part of the country held a monopoly. While both before and after this time the "kingship" was a reality, during the Early Dynastic III period it seems doubtful that any dynasty succeeded in exercising more than a transitory overlordship. Sumer was composed of vigorous and independently minded city-states, each with its own ruler and its own city-god, and naturally unwilling to be controlled from any other city. On the other hand this should not obscure the essential unity of the country. The general acceptance of Nippur as the home of the chief deity of the pantheon was balanced by the recognition of all major gods by the whole of Sumer, even though each deity was specially at home in one or another city – the moon-god Nanna at Ur, An the sky-god in Uruk, or Ninhursag the goddess of birth at Kesh. Nor was this sensation of unity affected by differences in language: certainly Sumerian was most at home in the south, and probably the majority of the population in the area of Kish was already Akkadian speaking, since even the first kings to rule there after the Flood are given Akkadian names by the King List, but this did not necessarily mean that the rule of Kish was felt to be a foreign occupation. In tablets of the Early Dynastic III period from Salabikh near Nippur the majority of the scribes who wrote these purely Sumerian texts bore Akkadian names, and there seems to have been a real symbiosis of language in pre-Sargonic Sumer.

Although by this time we begin to encounter historical inscriptions, it would be fruitless at present to attempt to reconstruct the course of political events. That the "kingship" recorded so carefully by the King List is only a very superficial clue is apparent from the instance of the city-state of Lagash. Largely as a result of the French work at Girsu (Tello), we know more about the rulers of Lagash than about any other Sumerian city-state. We have the list of their names for the last 150 years before the Akkad dynasty, and some of them were clearly important figures in the internal politics of Sumer. In military terms the most successful of them was undoubtedly Eannatum, who can claim to have defeated not only the ruler of Umma – the immediate neighbor and constant enemy of Lagash – but also three cities which figure in the King List: Mari, Akshak and Kish. Later his nephew Entemena, according to a recently published inscription, exercised some kind of control over Ur, Uruk, Larsa and Bad-Tibira, and yet the state of Lagash itself is not once mentioned in the King

Detail from Eannatum I's "Stele of the Vultures" celebrating his defeat of Umma. Louvre.

Evidence of trade connections with Iran is provided especially by stone bowls, such as this one from the Inanna Temple at Nippur showing combat between a lion and a snake. Baghdad.

List. This is not an omission to be held against the compilers of the list, but serves to remind us that to know which city held the precarious supremacy at one time by no means opens to us the true complexity of relations between the city-states of this heroic age of Sumer.

External relations. Although – or perhaps because – the cities of Sumer devoted much energy to fighting among themselves, they seem not to have carried their arms much beyond the borders of their land. It is true that there are references to the occasional brush with Elam, but relations between the two neighbors were always particularly close, and the existence of an Awan Dynasty in the Sumerian King List shows that the Elamites very likely gave as good as they got. More impressive may have been the achievement of Lugal-zagesi, the last king before Sargon of Akkad, since he claims to have "made the roads secure from the Lower Sea to the Upper Sea" (i.e. the Arabian Gulf to the Mediterranean). However, Sumer's contacts with the outside world are not to be judged by its military prowess. It is of course a commonplace that life was not possible in the land of Sumer without trade: even the indispensable grindstone had to be brought from the hills.

But trade to the Sumerians was not so much a grim necessity as one of the major ingredients of their civilization. It greatly transcended the exchange of goods between the hills and the plains, which could of itself have offered a tolerable economic basis for life in Sumer, and in search of copper and other metals, woods and stones, and other less bulky luxuries, the people of Sumer traveled far and wide to all points of the compass.

In the south the cities of the seaboard, chiefly Lagash (and Girsu) and Ur, sailed down the Gulf to the island of Dilmun (modern Bahrain), whence they brought copper and, as Ur-Nanshe, the first king of the Lagash Dynasty, proudly relates, wood for the building of new temples in his cities. In later years the *ensi*s of Lagash sent forth merchants to Dilmun with local products like pig's fat and perfumes, or barley and emmer, to exchange with the copper available in Dilmun, which was brought to this island staging-post from countries beyond, later to be known as Makan and Meluhha. Perhaps even more important was the overland trade with the east, and despite periods of hostility, the archaeological record bears witness to the close connection persisting between the cities of metropolitan Sumer, and Susa and the similar major cities of the plains of Elam. Once more the dry accountant's records from Lagash attest this trade: merchants plying between Girsu (Tello) and Der (near Iraq's modern border with Iran) or dealing direct with Elam itself, while a less direct route may have led through Adab, poised strategically on a major Euphrates channel on the northeast shoulder of Sumer proper. For the wife of the *ensi* (city ruler) of Lagash is found exchanging gifts with the wife of the *ensi* of Adab, and in return for boats going upstream laden with copper and bronze which no doubt originated in Dilmun, the northern city sends back ivory statues, pack animals and boat-loads of woods including young vines and apple saplings.

Echoes of foreign trading ventures even persist in the literature of the Sumerians many hundreds of years later. Although contact with the Iranian highlands must generally have been through the mediation of the cities of Elam, one epic tale suggests that the Sumerians did sometimes deal directly with their suppliers. In a poem known to modern scholars as "Enmerkar and the Lord of Aratta" we hear how Enmerkar, who is listed as a ruler of Uruk before Lugalbanda and Gilgamesh, desires precious stones for the temple of the goddess Inanna which he is building. He sends a messenger to the city of Aratta which lies to the east over seven mountain ranges, and after many exchanges resulting (in this Sumerian version!) from the intransigent behavior of the Lord of Aratta, the coveted stone is sent. The economic reality behind this story is clear from the demand of the Lord of Aratta for grain: early in the poem a caravan of donkeys is laden with sacks of grain from the storehouses of Uruk, and sent winding through the mountain passes to Aratta "like a trail of ants."

We are unlikely ever to be able to identify Aratta with

any one site, but archaeologists working in eastern Iran have recently recovered fascinating evidence of the trade in lapis lazuli, with carnelian the object of Enmerkar's quest. Early texts almost coeval with Enmerkar himself mention this rare deep blue stone in the same breath as gold and silver, and throughout antiquity it was sought after by kings. The lapis lazuli mines were in remotest Afghanistan, and the new excavations at Shahr-i Sokhta produced massive quantities of the stone, together with the workshops and flint tools used in the process of rendering it into convenient lumps for transport or even finished products. From this distant clearing-center the caravans must have wound towards Sumer, either to the north of the great salt desert, where the site of Tepe Hissar was also involved in the trade, or southwards through the dry hills of southern Iran where we have already encountered Tepe Yahya with its early use of Elamite pictographs and close connections with Susa and Mesopotamia.

In the north and west as well there is ample evidence for the activity of the merchants of Sumer. Up the Tigris a settlement had grown up on the site later to become the city of Assur: here the German excavators uncovered a simple shrine of the Akkadian and Early Dynastic periods, richly equipped with the characteristic furnishings of a Sumerian temple, including the unmistakable round-eyed statues of worshipers with their shaggy skirts. Despite the traces of Sumerian influence already detected here and in sites in the Habur valley like Tell Brak and Chagar Bazar, it still came as something of a shock when

Top right: a splendid example of Early Dynastic III sculpture is this official from the Ishtar Temple at Mari; his name is given on his back as "Ebih-il, the captain." Louvre.

Center right: reconstructed view of the Ishtar Temple at Assur (level G, c. 2400 BC), showing the statues, temple models and other furnishings where they were found. After Andrae.

Below: lapis lazuli beads and slate smoothers from Shahr-i Sokhta in Seistan (Iran), c. 2400 BC (beads from grave G.12 and tools from workshop in area EWK).

these same Early Dynastic worshiper figures turned up at Tell Chuera in the desert lands between the Habur and Balih rivers in northern Syria, where the German expedition stumbled on a stone-built shrine of the third millennium.

Trade northwestwards followed the course of the Euphrates, and here in a position comparable to Assur's lay the city of Mari whose control of this major trade route had already rendered it an active participant in the affairs of Sumer during the Early Dynastic period. Digging deep below the more famous palace of Zimrilim, the French excavators of Mari have recovered parts of an equally impressive pre-Sargonic building, and in the contemporary temples of the city they have come upon statues of rulers inscribed with their names, which are often Akkadian. A particularly vivid illustration of the closeness of relations with Sumer proper came in the shape of a hoard of precious objects buried in a pottery jar: besides beads and human figurines of precious metals and stones, there was a magnificent gold and lapis lazuli lion-headed eagle, and a long lapis lazuli bead bearing an inscription of Mesanepada, one of the kings of the 1st Dynasty of Ur in the Sumerian King List. No doubt this was a gift from the king of Ur to his peer at Mari, designed to secure his goodwill for the trade with the regions beyond to the northwest. North of Mari, as in Uruk times, there must have been major trading centers on the great bend in the river, and from there routes will have led west towards the Mediterranean ports and the mountains of the Amanus and Lebanon, which throughout history served as a magnet to the rulers of Mesopotamia in search of cedar and other timber for the roofing of their latest architectural scheme, whether palace or temple. Unfortunately written documentation of this trade is still lacking, unless the new finds at Ebla (Tell Mardikh) near Aleppo will provide it, and so it is hard for us to tell whether the trading colonies at Assur or Tell Chuera, with their manifest Sumerian artistic conventions, were actually occupied by Sumerian speakers from the south, or merely reflect the strength of Sumerian influence on the neighboring peoples.

The structure of society. Although trade in luxuries may have been predominantly achieved by an exchange of gifts between rulers, Sumer's need for all raw materials forced upon it a trade of a more extensive kind. Since the only assets Sumer had to offer her trading partners were agricultural produce and the skills of her craftsmen, we are entitled to assume that in addition to the efficient organization of her trade relations, Sumer's success was due to a mastery in agriculture and industrial technology which enabled her to export significant surpluses and by the excellence of her products to hold the markets where she traded. All this must imply a sophisticated and well-organized society. If we seek the domestic details which lie behind the artistic and intellectual achievements of Early

Administrative tablet from the reign of Urukagina (2351–2342 BC) recording a delivery of fruit by the gardener. Louvre.

Gathering the date harvest in Mesopotamia today, traditional methods and equipment are still in use.

Dynastic Sumer, we must inevitably turn to the unique archives from Tello (Girsu), represented by some 1,600 economic tablets from the temple of Bau which were clandestinely unearthed during the French excavations at the site, and are now divided among the major museums of the world. These reveal in minute detail the work of the temple accountants as they record the temple's dealings with a great variety of people and the passage of goods in and out of the storerooms. They list receipts or issues of grain (wheat, barley, emmer), of garden vegetables and fruit, especially dates, and also huge quantities of fish; stock-breeding covered sheep and goats, oxen, pigs and donkeys. Many of the temple's personnel were free men, but slaves are also encountered. Craftsmen of various kinds are mentioned, and it is obvious that the temple's accumulation of capital was used to finance merchants in trading ventures. There are frequent lists of fields and of the crops sown or harvested in them, and in general the picture is of a predominantly agricultural institution, for which Professor A. L. Oppenheim has recently coined the apt phrase "landed sanctuary."

Although these archives present us with a vivid picture of daily life, it is hard to be sure which details are normal, and which are unique to this one temple. At Girsu the Bau Temple was not the only nor even the biggest of such "landed sanctuaries": the main temple of the city belonged to Ningirsu, and according to the theological theory of the time, this was administered by the ruler (*ensi*) who was the god's representative on earth. Logically enough, Ningirsu's wife Bau had her temple administered by the *ensi*'s wife, and the tablets attest to the fact that she did indeed take an active interest in the running of the sanctuary. Since the *ensi* was also the secular ruler of the city-state (even when he acknowledged the overlordship of the "king of Sumer" of the day) scholars in earlier years saw Girsu and the rest of the city-state of Lagash as a virtual theocracy, in which the whole state belonged to and was administered by the temples, and the same was held to be valid for the other city-states of Sumer. This view is now discredited. Plenty of evidence exists, even at Girsu itself, to contradict it, and in any case to formulate a general rule from conditions at Girsu alone was a faulty procedure: there is every reason to suppose that the city-states of Sumer were as diverse as those of ancient Greece or Renaissance Italy. Many documents, especially from Shuruppak (Fara), attest to the existence of a flourishing and equally well-organized secular administration, and sale documents for houses or for agricultural land prove that the ownership of property was in the hands of individuals, even though they may strictly have been controlled by a "clan" or similar organization.

And yet it is undeniable that the temple was a central feature of the Sumerian city, and perhaps more important in the long run than any purely secular institution. For the temple served as a focus around which the city's own identity revolved. No matter which family or city ruled the secular lives of the population, their city god remained the same, and his temple remained the expression of their city's identity. In these circumstances, it is not surprising that in some cases the administrators of the chief temple became also the secular rulers of the city: the rulers of Umma and Isin, for instance, were priests in the Early Dynastic period, and the disentanglement of the "religious" and the "secular" in the titulary of the different rulers of Sumer is a delicate operation which varies from city to city depending on the constitutional history of each.

The importance of the temple in Sumerian city life is one point on which the archaeological and the written records are in full agreement. While large secular buildings (i.e. "palaces") have been excavated, at Mari, Kish and Eridu, they are encountered far less often than temples. At virtually every Early Dynastic site it is the temples that occupy the key position in the city, and it is evident that the artistic and architectural genius of the community was directed to the benefit of the houses of the gods. Although the prime source of income for most temples must have been the possession of agricultural land, the community they served provided offerings as well, whether of free will or in some measure obligatory. In this way the temple might build up valuable reserves of gold, silver and precious stones, enabling it to function as a repository for the surplus wealth of the community, and as a source of capital – such as for the financing of trade ventures, as we have seen. As the city's fortunes rose or fell, so the temple was renovated or allowed to decay, as the prime recipient of, and so an index to, its prosperity. It is no mere piety which provokes the bitter tones of a poet of Lagash when he laments the ravaging of his city's temples by the hated men of Umma: when they "stole the temple's silver and lapis lazuli" they struck a heavy blow at the material economy of Lagash, as well as to its pride.

The Dynasty of Akkad. The classical age of Sumer came to an abrupt end with the advent of King Sargon (Sharrum-ken) of Akkad (also written Agade). If at the time this may have seemed no more than another of the many switches of dynasty recorded by the King List, this impression must soon have faded. Whereas in previous years the "king of Sumer" seems to have been content to allow each local ruler to continue as before, while accepting his submission, Sargon's attitude to the kingship was rather different, and his horizons were not bounded by precedent.

The seat of the new dynasty appears to have been a new foundation, and although the precise site of Akkad remains the most alluring enigma of Mesopotamian archaeology, it is certain that it lay in the north of Sumer, perhaps in the neighborhood of the ancient capital city of Kish and of later Babylon. No doubt one reason for the choice of a new capital was that Sargon himself was a "new man." The King List, supported by later legendary

Bronze life-size head found at Nineveh, but surely of the Old Akkadian period and often ascribed to Sargon. Baghdad.

compositions about him, makes Sargon's mother a priestess, and his adoptive father a gardener, and he is said in his early days to have served as cupbearer to Ur-Zababa, the king of Kish, whose overthrow he later witnessed. But perhaps the most significant fact about Sargon himself is that he was Akkadian – that is to say, he spoke the Semitic language subsequently to be called Akkadian after the city he founded. For many years before, as we have seen, the north of the country had been inhabited by speakers of this language, but until the accession of Sargon it is impossible to detect any differences between Akkadian and Sumerian parts of the population. This situation was without doubt deliberately changed by Sargon. His inscriptions and later texts inform us that he relied for his military elite on Akkadian troops, and from the time of his accession the Akkadian language is introduced for royal inscriptions, letters and administrative documents, a startling innovation which, even if not entirely without precedent, is sufficiently abrupt to be shown up as the result of a deliberate policy.

Sadly, Sargon's own inscriptions are poorly preserved, but what does survive points another contrast: whereas Lugal-zagesi's triumphal inscription lays its emphasis on the age of peace and prosperity he had brought to the land, Sargon's suddenly boast of the king's military prowess, of the battles won, cities taken and rulers defeated. For us there is the bonus that his inscriptions do at least provide us with historical detail: after conquering Lugal-zagesi himself and taking control of all the cities of Sumer, Sargon turned his ambitions to the outside world. He or his successors have left us their inscriptions at Susa, and up the Tigris at Assur and Nineveh, while a large number of Old Akkadian business documents found at the city of Gasur (later Nuzi) show that the new regime had taken over there.

Towards the northwest the kings of Akkad reached even further. At Mari, the halfway stage to Syria on the Euphrates, we know that Akkadian speakers had held sway even before Sargon's accession, and at one time had even been powerful enough to be accorded the "kingship." But without more written evidence it is impossible to say how far north and west Sargon's troops may have encountered populations speaking their own language. It may well be that he and his dynasty had kept close ties with their non-urban background and were able to establish a loose but effective network of allegiance and alliance over northern Mesopotamia without installing large garrisons or undertaking extensive administrative organization. For although it is scattered, there is evidence that they ruled the whole tract between the Tigris and the Euphrates: monuments of Naram-Sin have been found in the foothills of the Turkish mountains both east of the Tigris and in the far north near modern Diyarbakir, while a strongly fortified palace of his was excavated at Tell Brak and both there and at Chagar Bazar, also in the Habur basin, administrative tablets in the Old Akkadian dialect turned up.

Their rule was certainly also felt west of the Euphrates: Sargon proclaims his conquest of the city of Ebla, among others, now known to be Tell Mardikh south of Aleppo, and both he and his grandson Naram-Sin marched as far as the Mediterranean, there in the Amanus to fell the coveted cedars. Indeed later tradition takes both kings across the mountains into Anatolia in search of the silver mines and other sources of precious metal, or even, in one legend, in support of a colony of Akkadian merchants, and these traditions gain in credibility as the evidence accumulates.

Finally the kings of Akkad followed the merchants of Sumer southwards as well. Whereas the *ensis* of Lagash and kings of Ur had traded for their copper with the island of Dilmun, Sargon boasts that, not content to be served by middlemen, he brought "the ships of Meluhha, Makan and Dilmun to moor at the quays of Akkad," and his son Rimush even claims to have marched to the land of Makan and defeated it, bringing back booty. The exact location of Makan and Meluhha has been one of the most thoroughly debated problems of ancient history, and is still unsolved, but with the evidence for trade with the Indus valley especially strong in the island of Bahrain, the ancient Dilmun, it is now agreed by the majority of scholars that wherever these two lands may have been, they were closely associated in trade with the great civilization of the Indus valley.

Part of an Akkadian victory stele: the prisoners-of-war with strange hairdos and elbows tied back are held in a ladder or "neck-stock." A vivid illustration of Akkadian imperialism. Baghdad.

The stele of Naram-Sin, one of the masterpieces of Mesopotamian art. It shows Naram-Sin, with horns on his helmet symbolizing divinity, receiving the submission of his opponents in their mountain terrain; note the two battle standards (on left). Louvre.

The new spirit which enters the world of politics with Sargon also breathes in the art of the time. While the germs of a new and more naturalistic style can be detected towards the end of the Early Dynastic period, and the artists of the Akkadian period retained many of the forms and conventions of their predecessors and only gradually adapted them to their own preferences, anyone who sets the acknowledged masterpieces of Akkadian art against the finest products of Early Dynastic III cannot fail to be amazed at the transformation which is apparent. The detailed naturalism with which the human and animal forms are portrayed is balanced by a feeling for composition – most apparent in the stele of Naram-Sin – which greatly surpasses anything produced in Mesopotamia until the culmination of the Neo-Assyrian sculptor's tradition under Assur-ban-apli.

Sumerian revival. The concluding reigns of the Akkad dynasty are veiled from us by a lack of straightforward sources, but they represent a period of transition of a kind encountered more than once in Mesopotamian history and neatly termed by German scholars a "Zwischenzeit" or "between-time." A later Sumerian literary composition ascribed the fall of the dynasty to the end of the reign of Naram-Sin himself, and saw in it divine nemesis: Ishtar, goddess of Akkad, had deserted her own city in anger at the sins committed by Naram-Sin against Enlil (i.e. perhaps against his sanctuary at Nippur). However, less emotional sources make it clear that even if most of Naram-Sin's empire was lost, his son Shar-kali-sharri continued for some decades to rule over at least the north of the country – the area subsequently known for 2,000 years simply as "Akkad." When the house of Akkad finally succumbed, it was to the Guti, a tribe ruled by kings with outlandish names, and probably having descended from the Zagros Mountains where they are to be encountered in later years. No sources record any details of their incursions, nor have these barbarian kings left any significant inscriptions of their own, but there are indications that their rule was acknowledged as far south as Umma. How long this state of affairs lasted it is impossible to gauge with any accuracy, but it was in any case less than a century.

In the meantime it seems that some of the old-established southern cities were profiting from the fall of Akkad to reinstate local dynasties, and it is perhaps at this point that the city-state of Lagash enjoyed the first stage of a new prosperity. The major figure of this dynasty was Gudea, and he consciously or unconsciously epitomizes an ideal view of Sumer devoted to the gods and the peaceful arts. Although to have achieved what he did, and to have engaged in the wide-ranging trade which brought him the precious materials for his building schemes, he must have won considerable political prestige, his own inscriptions, like those of Lugal-zagesi before him, make virtually no mention of wars and triumphs. His major undertaking was the rebuilding of the E-ninnu, the chief temple of Ningirsu at his city of Girsu (Tello). To celebrate this achievement a long hymn was composed which was written on two or more giant clay cylinders now in the Louvre. This composition, which serves to Sumerian scholars as the first and in many ways the most important of all Sumerian literary creations, relates how Gudea received in a dream a divine command to rebuild the temple, symbolized by certain visions such as a mythical winged figure flanked by lions, a goddess writing on a lapis lazuli tablet, and an "ass which pawed the ground" – this last being a symbol for Gudea himself, in his impatience to carry out the work. After traveling to Sirara (Zurghul) he consulted the goddess Nanshe, who explained the import of the dream, which was that his lord Ningirsu was instructing him, Gudea, to build his temple. The remainder of the text explains how the building proceeded, with the cooperation of the people of the state of Lagash, and describes in detail the different parts of the new temple and their divine occupants.

If this unusually vivid poem was not sufficient to endear Gudea to us, he has ensured his remembrance by the many statues of himself which were placed in the temples of the different deities of his city and country. Two of these commemorate his activities as an architect visually as well as in their inscriptions, showing him seated with an architect's rule in his lap and in one case with a temple plan as well. Others show the ruler standing with his hands clasped in an attitude of veneration, or seated. These statues, which are mostly in a hard black stone, show clearly the influence of the naturalistic school of Akkadian sculpture, but they also have the static quality of the older pre-Sargonic statuary, and the proportions of head to body, for instance, are far from naturalistic. It is clear that to the Sumerian mind a statue such as these, which stood in the temples in order to represent Gudea permanently before each god, was more of a symbol than a likeness.

The Ur III Dynasty. If Gudea may stand for the revival of a true Sumerian culture, the credit for ridding Sumer and Akkad of the physical presence of the barbarian must go to the cities of Umma and Ur. The details of this process are unclear, but if we may believe their own accounts, the initiative was taken by a certain Utu-hegal of Umma, who routed the Guti forces, only in due course to be defeated himself by Ur-Nammu of Ur, who proceeded to extend his rule over the whole of the land, although his own inscriptions, as far as they have been recovered, make little mention of his warlike activities and concentrate on his peaceful deeds. He records the restoration of temples, and is clearly proud of having restored commerce by sea with Makan. To us he is best known as the promulgator of the first "code of laws" we now know, and the only military event he refers to is the defeat and killing in battle of the *ensi* of Lagash, Nammahani, which may in fact have been the major hurdle he had to surmount.

According to the Sumerian King List, Ur-Nammu was the first king of the 3rd Dynasty of Ur, and hence the ensuing century or so during which his descendants ruled Sumer and Akkad is usually known as the Ur III period. Originating in the ancient city of the moon god, it is perhaps no surprise that, proud of their independence from the supremacy of the Akkadians and subsequently the Guti, this dynasty self-consciously stressed its Sumerian roots. But although the Guti incursions were not destined to leave any permanent marks on the civilization of Mesopotamia, the effort to shake off the effects of the years of Akkadian domination was largely vain. Even though Sumerian was reinstated as the sole official language throughout the whole of the new Ur III empire, the occasional lapse of a scribe into Akkadian bears witness that Sumerian was on the wane, and even more telling are the names of the kings of this dynasty themselves: Ur-Nammu and his son Shulgi have good Sumerian names, as does Shulgi's son Amar-Sin; but the last two rulers, Shu-Sin and Ibbi-Sin, have Akkadian names testifying to the dominance of the Akkadian language, if not of the Akkadian population.

Another respect in which the Ur III kings lived in the shadow of Sargon and his dynasty was in their style of government. Gone was the old tradition of autonomous city-states loosely acknowledging their allegiance to one among their number. Although the old title *ensi* was still used, and indeed in some cases it may even have been the *ensi* himself who stayed on, the new dynasty was not content to leave each city to run itself. Instead the *ensi*, now to be understood as a "provincial governor," was accountable to his overlord for all that went on within his territory, and from him down to the meanest scribe a draconian bureaucratic system of accounting ruled the lives of the administration. It is this administrative policy which has left us the most conspicuous relics of the Ur III period: late in the last century illicit excavations in the sites of southern Iraq unearthed tens of thousands of the tablets written by

Black stone weight in shape of a duck; the inscription states that Shulgi "for Nanna established [its weight as] 5 minas"; crescent of Nanna just visible on other side. Baghdad.

Copper statuettes of King Shulgi carrying a builder's basket, from the foundations of the Ziggurrat of Enlil at Nippur. Baghdad.

the clerks of the Ur III administration. The main archives, which are only painfully slowly being reconstructed from the tablets scattered throughout the major and minor collections of the world, come from the cities of Girsu (Tello), Umma (Tell Jokha) and a site close to Nippur called Drehem, through which passed all the livestock destined for the central shrines of Sumer at Nippur. Other archives of equal size obviously have yet to be uncovered, and smaller groups have been excavated by the archaeological expeditions to Ur and Nippur.

The amazing feature of these archives is not merely the weight of numbers – well over 30,000 tablets being already published – but the loving detail and passion for exactitude which must qualify the Ur III empire for the title of the world's first bureaucracy. Work quotas on canal digging or agricultural labor were calculated not to the nearest man, but to fractions of a man, and each commodity – whether gold, wool, foodstuffs, reeds and so on – was recorded as it entered or left the department to which the scribe belonged, and the responsibility for each such transaction carefully noted. Although one may sometimes be moved to incomprehension when faced with a tablet whose entire purpose is to record the fact that "one sheep has died" and the date, the ultimate effectiveness of the system becomes apparent when we see the monthly or yearly balance sheets. Thus tablets from Ur itself record as much as 6,000 tons of wool passing through one government organization in one year of the reign of Ibbi-Sin, and a text from Drehem informs us that during three years of the reign of Shulgi they handled "28,601 cattle, 404 deer, 236 wild sheep, 38 horses, 360 onagers, 2,931 donkeys, 347,394 sheep, 3,880 gazelles, 457 bears, 13 monkeys and 1 unidentified animal."

It is hard to define with any confidence the reasons for this unprecedented passion for accounting. To some extent it must reflect the wish of the kings to control the economy of their empire as tightly as an old-style *ensi* had been able to supervise his city: to prevent the misappropriation of "state property" and with the resulting statistics to plan the economy. Probably, though, it is less of an innovation than it seems, since Akkadian tablets of equal competence are known, and even before the accession of Sargon the accounts of the Bau Temple at Girsu are remarkably detailed. However, the scale of the operation is certainly unparalleled, and it is interesting that very few documents from the reign of Ur-Nammu or the early part of Shulgi's reign have so far been discovered. This suggests that Shulgi was himself the initiator of the system. Ur-Nammu proudly proclaims in his law code for the reunited cities of Sumer and Akkad that he standardized the weights and measures in use, but it was probably Shulgi who put these measures into effect, and took other steps to ease the administration of the new empire, such as the unification of the different local calendars.

Although the Ur III kings did indeed write royal inscriptions, ironically these are very rarely informative about the history of their dynasty, and instead we can cull much useful information from the economic tablets, with their date formulae (each year is named after a major event), with mention of provincial governors from different parts or of foreign messengers and dignitaries visiting Sumer. The extent of the Ur III empire at its zenith must have coincided fairly closely with that of the Akkadian kings, stretching up the two rivers as far as the Anatolian highlands and encompassing Susa and other Elamite areas to the east. Maintenance of these conquests was not a peaceful task, and it is obvious that especially in the northeast continuous campaigns were needed to contain the belligerent tribes. Another menace, which subsequently proved critical, was the persistent pressure from Amorite nomads in the west, who caused so much trouble that as early as Shulgi's reign a wall called "Excluder of the Amorites" was built along the northwestern shoulder of the settled area, near Babylon and Sippar. This wall is mentioned later in correspondence between Ibbi-Sin, the last ill-fated king, and his governors in the north, who were fighting a losing battle against the fresh waves of nomadic intruders. From the absence of documents dated to his later years it has proved possible to show how Ibbi-Sin's authority was gradually eroded from the north, until his rule extended little beyond the city of Ur itself; and even the documents from Ur tell the same tale of impending disaster, for the prices of grain have risen so high that famine must have been abroad.

The Indus Civilization

VISUAL STORY

Cuneiform records show that the Sumerians pursued an active trade in carnelian, precious woods, etc. down the Arabian Gulf with lands called Dilmun, Makan and Meluhha. Already in 1880 Rawlinson identified Dilmun with Bahrain, but only in the 1920s, with the discovery of Harappa and Mohenjo-Daro, was it apparent that Meluhha could be the Indus civilization and Makan somewhere en route. Even today their exact identity is disputed, partly because "Indus" sites have been located across a region far greater than Mesopotamia. Their uniformity of material culture proves that close relations were maintained between the different lowland districts, and the cities themselves, with their well-planned housing – complete with built-in sanitation and municipal drainage – are proof of an effectively organized society. Although the Indus script has defied decipherment, the frequency of seals and sealings betokens flourishing trade, and the granaries and workmen's barracks imply centralized economic institutions. Unquestionably the Indus cities enjoyed a culture equal to that of Egypt or Mesopotamia, but in the second millennium they declined, and the Gulf trade with them. Makan and Meluhha were remembered only in tradition, and Dilmun mainly for its esteemed date crop.

Opposite: a modern *dhow* on the Gulf: the ancient trade routes still persist, and are reflected in the presence of a large Indian and Pakistani mercantile community in places like Bahrain and Kuwait, which were trading ports before the advent of oil.

Besides the "classical" sites in the Indus Valley continuing research has disclosed "Indus" sites along the south coast of Pakistan at least to the Iranian border, and in India in the Gulf of Cambay and even as far as the River Jumna near Delhi. *Below:* view of the Mohenjo-Daro citadel from the north, with the south end of the Great Bath just discernible. The universal baked-brick masonry, which required immense outlay of labor and valuable fuel, is one of the most impressive testimonies to the organization of the Indus cities, whatever its motive.

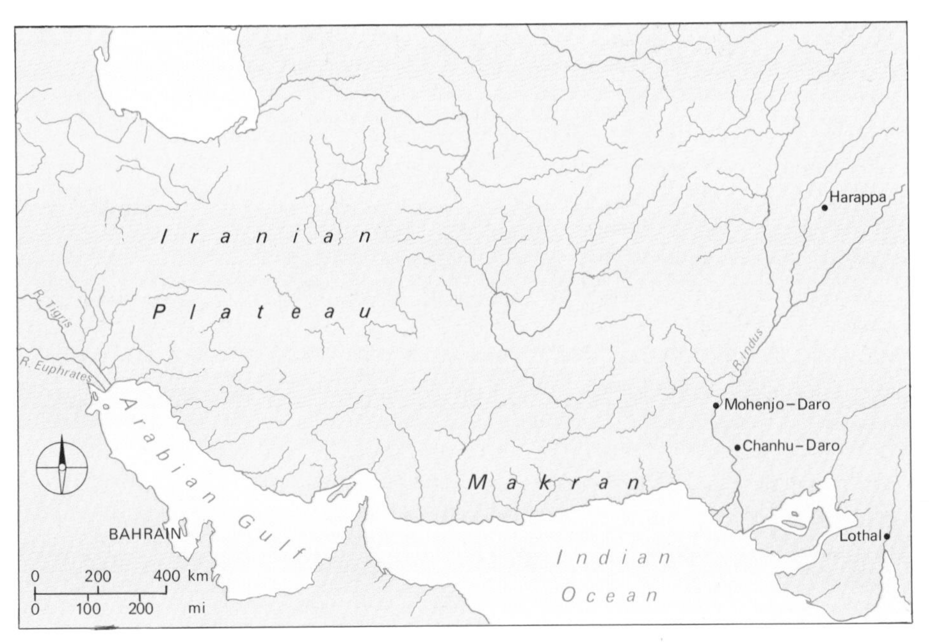

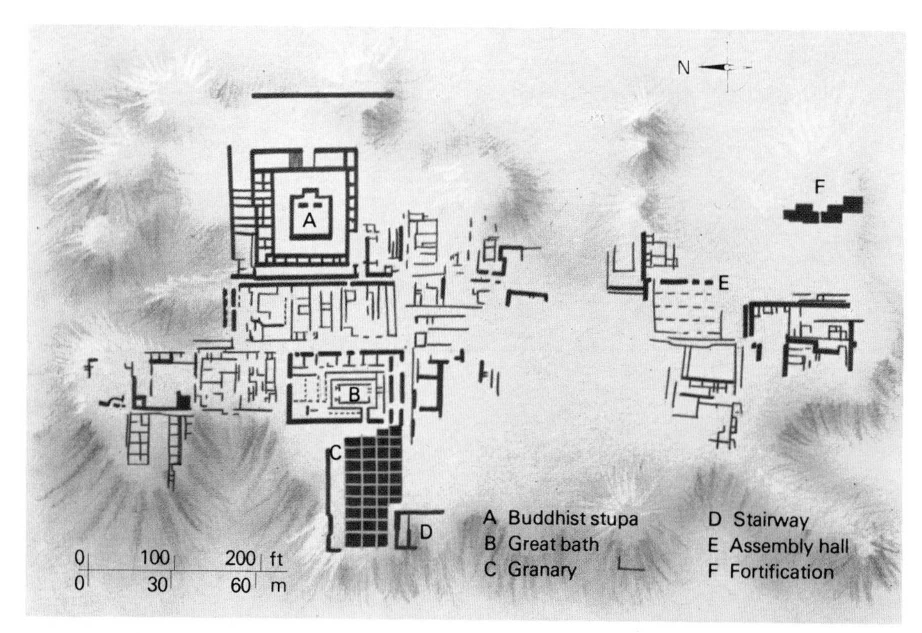

Left: the citadel at Mohenjo-Daro was chiefly excavated by Sir John Marshall, whose methods left something to be desired, and the only unmistakable building identified by him was the Great Bath. Structures to the west, which he thought were a "hot-air bath" were shown in 1950 to have been the base of a granary by Sir Mortimer Wheeler, who also re-excavated the nearby stairway and the fortifications at the southeast corner. After Wheeler.

Below: Mortimer Wheeler's workmen haul a sack of grain up from the loading bay at the foot of the granary to demonstrate its purpose.

Above and right: with its confident marriage of naturalism and stylization, this bearded figure is the equal of the best Mesopotamian statuary. It is of glazed steatite, and the trefoils on the cloak were filled with red paste, the slit eyes inlaid with shell (about 18 cm high, from Mohenjo-Daro, the lower town, area DK). Karachi.

Below: although sculpture is as yet rare on Indus sites, this delicate dancing girl (11·5 cm high) with bangles on her arms and legs was found in the lower town at Mohenjo-Daro and shows what we may look forward to. Karachi.

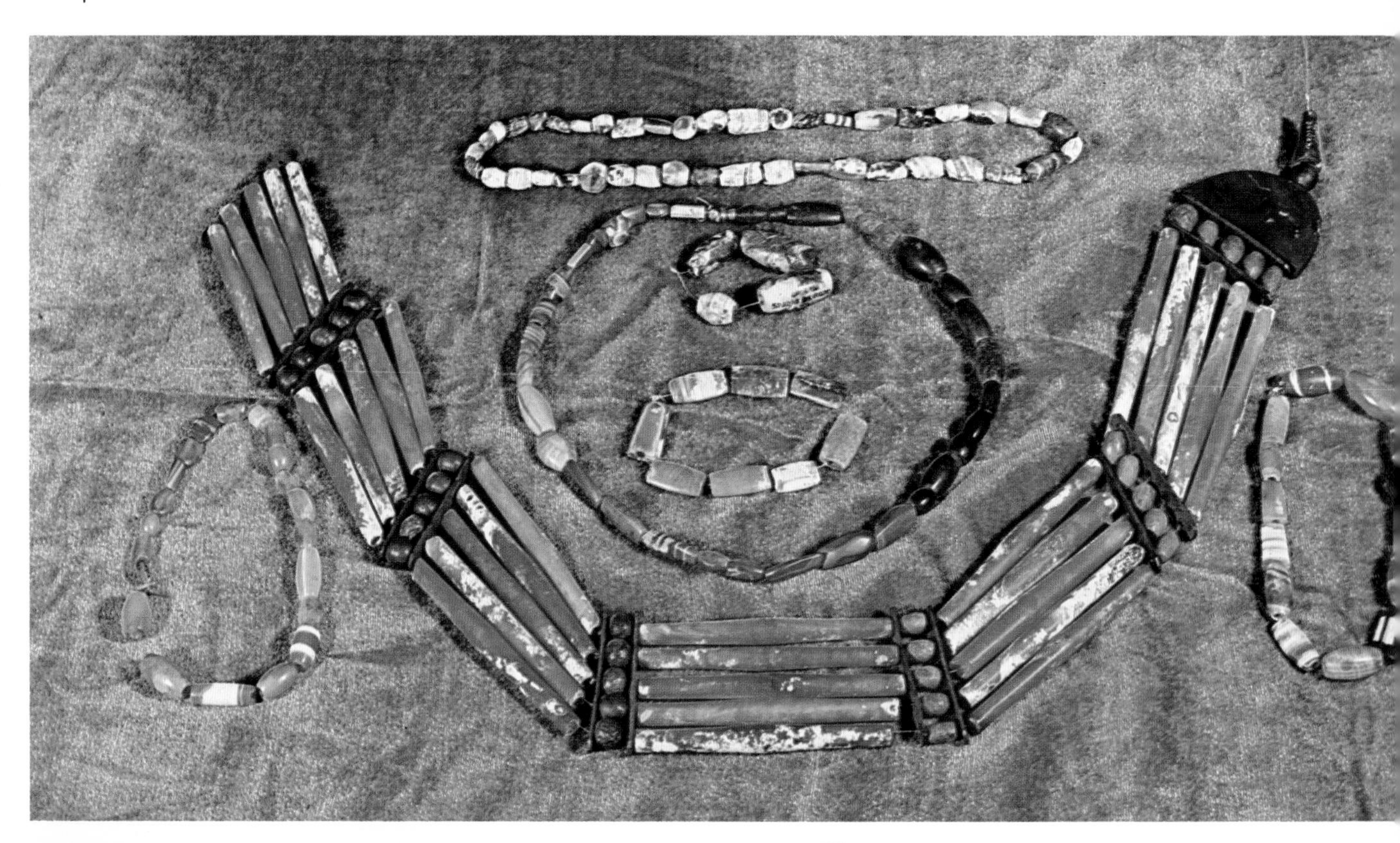

Left: bull stands before an unidentified object (perhaps a "manger"). Indus seals are usually of steatite and square (with sides 2 to 3 cm). Karachi.

The Indus civilization resembles that of Mesopotamia in its use of writing and seals, and although they are quite different in detail, they no doubt were an integral part of the mercantile and administrative structure as in Sumer.

Above: jewelry of differing periods from Mohenjo-Daro: most typical are the long carnelian beads, which were made in the Indus cities as we know from a bead-maker's workshop at Chanhu-Daro. Karachi.

Below: seals with characteristically Indian fauna (the rhinoceros survived in India till the 16th century AD). Karachi.

Above: the economy of the Indus civilization must have relied greatly on land transport, and it is clear that then, as now, the ox-drawn cart was the most prevalent means of transport. This cart, with its pair of solid wheels, not unlike those still in use in Sind, is a terracotta model, possibly only a toy. Karachi.

Only the "official" areas of Harappa have received much attention from archaeologists. The citadel itself (*right*), was raised on a platform and shown to have had a mud-brick wall 40 feet thick. The granaries (reconstructed *below*) lay conveniently close to the river, and are in two rows of six units (each 20 × 50 feet). After Wheeler.

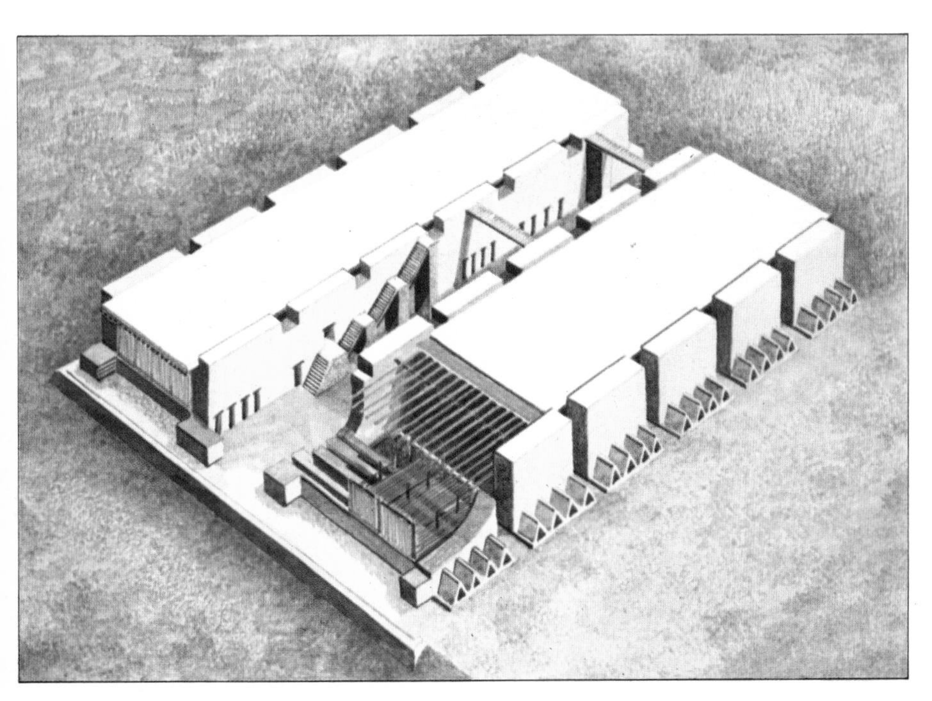

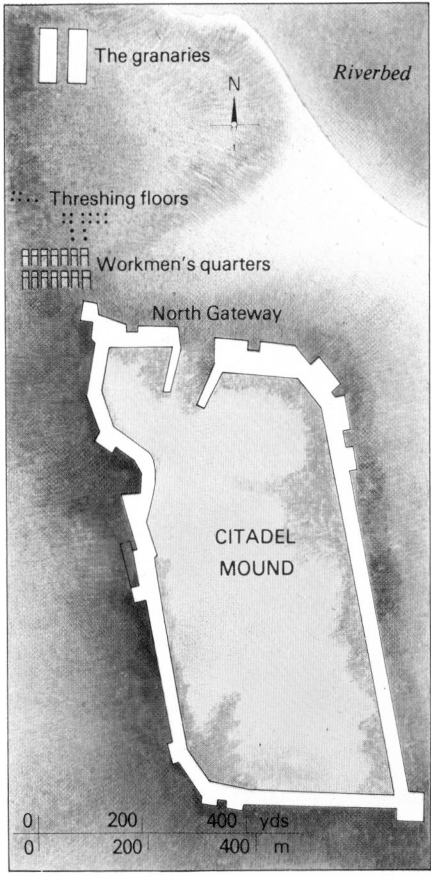

Above: these circular baked-brick features, some 9 feet across, must have served as places for pounding (rather than threshing) grain; 18 of them were found between the granary and citadel, just north of the "workmen's quarters."

Above: in Saudi Arabia and other lands on the western shore of the Gulf, one of the commonest ancient sites is the burial mound, entirely alien to Mesopotamia. Here on Bahrain huge areas of the interior of the island are occupied by mound-fields, but they are mostly robbed. Pottery found in association favors a date c. 2300–1800, when the Dilmun trade was at its peak.

Opposite: whether or not one accepts the identification of the island of Bahrain (off the Saudi Arabian coast) with Dilmun of the Sumerians, there is no doubt that it was a trading entrepot between Mesopotamia and the Indus cities. Here, beside the Portuguese fort, a Danish expedition in the 1950s and 1960s located a handsome building of roughly "Neo-Assyrian" date, seen in this photograph superimposed on even more impressive stone walls of the "Kassite" period.

Right: flat-roofed modern housing nestles in among the extra-high "royal" burial mounds at A'ali in the center of the island; although these too were robbed, the scanty evidence available suggests a similar date, perhaps a little later.

Above: five seals found on Failaka, a small island in the Gulf, off the coast of Kuwait; it was obviously in close touch with Bahrain, since dedications in cuneiform to Inzak, god of Dilmun, have been found in both places, and these seals are of a type identical with some found on Bahrain (and datable to the Old Babylonian period). Moesgärd.

Above left: buried under the floor of the "Neo-Assyrian" building at the Bahrain fort, there were more than 10 shallow bowls holding the bones of a snake, and sometimes a single bead. No close parallel is known, but to this day the snake is a symbol of eternal life, and there must be some ritual significance in these deposits. Moesgärd.

Left: though Makan and Meluhha vanish from the scene after the Old Babylonian period, Mesopotamian connections with Dilmun persisted: this silver hoard buried under a floor in the "Neo-Assyrian" building includes a 7th-century Phoenician signet ring, and Sargon, Esarhaddon and Assur-ban-apli all mention Dilmun and refer to its king or "governor." Moesgärd.

5. The Second Millennium

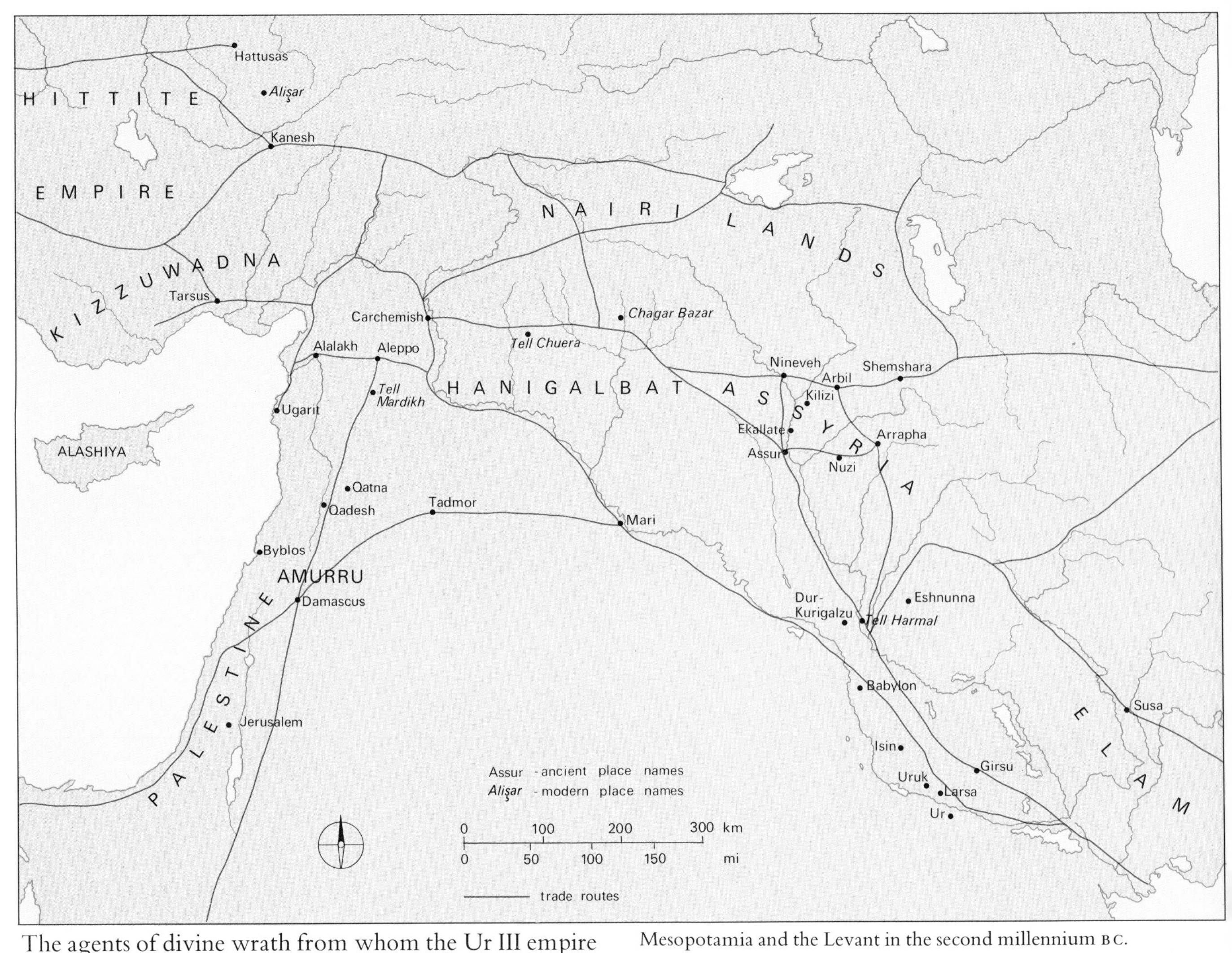

Mesopotamia and the Levant in the second millennium BC.

The agents of divine wrath from whom the Ur III empire received its deathblow were the armies of Elam from outside the borders of Sumer, but there followed no period of foreign domination such as the Guti had imposed after the disintegration of the Akkadian empire. If in language Sumerian now finally succumbed to the speakers of Akkadian, it was not they who fell heirs to the hegemony of the cities of Sumer and Akkad, but another Semitic race, the Amorites. Amorites are already encountered in the days of Shar-kali-sharri, who fought with them in the desert lands south of the Euphrates in later Syria, and although they appear during the Ur III empire as barbarous opponents to be kept out of the settled lands of Mesopotamia, there is also ample evidence that they penetrated the urban areas as peaceful infiltrators, herding the sheep of the town dwellers or serving the settled population in other ways. It is clear that within the rigid bureaucracy of the empire Amorites had built up loyalties and connections and attained to positions of trust, which enabled them to contend vigorously for the control of the dismembered cities of the empire.

Although in the "Zwischenzeit" following the collapse of the Ur III Dynasty the course of events is too complex for us to hope to reconstruct in full, one figure of these years may stand out as typical. To judge from his name, Ishbi-erra, he may in fact have been Akkadian rather than Amorite, and he is referred to, perhaps disparagingly, as "the man from Mari" by King Ibbi-Sin whom he served in the latest years of his reign as a high official. When Ibbi-Sin's fate was clearly sealed, he profited from his position of authority, and established himself as an independent ruler in the city of Isin, south of Nippur – one of the areas where Amorite penetration seems to have been strongest. Other vigorous dynasties, with kings with Amorite names, were founded at Larsa, Kish and Babylon, but this was by no means the full extent of the Amorite "takeover." Within two centuries we have met Amorite dynasties in the Diyala region, up the Tigris at Assur, and, besides minor states in Sumer and Akkad proper, throughout the northern Mesopotamian plains and up the Euphrates, notably at Mari. Towards the west our sources peter out slightly, but we also know of strong Amorite kingdoms across the Euphrates at Yamhad (Aleppo) and further south at Qatna. Whether this Amorite occupation

Previous page: alabaster statuette from Ishchali, near Khafajah; c. 1900 BC. Baghdad.

in the north and west was the direct consequence of the collapse of the Ur III administration in these areas, or the infiltration had already begun during and even before the empire, it is hard to say without fresh documentary evidence. What is certain is that the new Amorite kingdoms introduced a shift in the political center of gravity, since the bond of common origins and a common language meant that close contact was maintained between the furthest extremes of the area, from Larsa to Qatna.

The Old Babylonian empire. One factor which contributed to the intense diplomatic activity of these years was the introduction of the Old Babylonian dialect of Akkadian as the normal means of communication throughout the whole area. It is indeed possible that Akkadian had remained in use in the north and west since the days of the Akkadian kings, but in the south the cuneiform syllabary was readapted to the new dialect and the resulting freedom from the Sumerian scribal traditions brings with it a flood of revealing and instantly vivid correspondence, which underlines how dry and uninformative were the sources for earlier times. One of the most revealing documents of this time comes, like so many, from the archives of the palace at Mari. It is a letter to the king of Mari, Zimri-Lim, from one of his governors who has evidently been given the task of winning the allegiance of certain petty princelings in the north. He explains that he convened these "kings" at the unknown town of Sharmaneh, and addressed them thus: "There is no king who is strong by himself. Hammurapi of Babylon has a following of 15 kings, Rim-Sin of Larsa the same, Ibal-pi-el of Eshnunna the same, Amut-pi-el of Qatna the same, and Yarim-Lim of Yamhad [Aleppo] has a following of 20 kings . . ." This sums up the politics of the day, although, significantly perhaps, no mention is made of the arch-enemies of Zimri-Lim, Samsi-Addu and his sons.

Zimri-Lim, a contemporary and sometime ally of Hammurapi of Babylon, was the son of Yahdun-Lim who ruled Mari before him, but he did not succeed him directly on the throne of Mari. For despite Yahdun-Lim's successes, which included marching to the Mediterranean in emulation of greater conquerors before him, his reign ended in disaster when his realm was conquered by another Amorite king called Samsi-Addu (in Akkadian, Shamshi-Adad). This figure, who has been brought to life for us by the Mari correspondence, succeeded in founding a kingdom which stretched from Assur on the Tigris and Mari on the Euphrates northwards to the Turkish mountains. He made his own capital somewhere in the Habur basin, perhaps at Chagar Bazar, in a city he named "Residence of Enlil" (Shubat-Enlil), but installed his two sons Yasmah-Addu and Ishme-Dagan as vice-regents at Mari and a city called Ekallate on the east bank of the Tigris north of Assur, from where the turbulent lands across the river could be watched. The incredible profusion of petty states whose submission or alliance he had to win, with Amorite or Hurrian kinglets, is illustrated not only by the letter to Zimri-Lim we have just quoted, but by Samsi-Addu's own letters to his rather feeble son Yasmah-Addu at Mari. From these documents it is clear hat Samsi-Addu was an energetic and forthright ruler, equally at home in politics and war. The range of his diplomatic activities can be judged from a small collection of letters excavated by a Danish expedition at the mound of Shemshara high in the Kurdish mountains, which show that his son Ishme-Dagan at Ekallate kept up – at times – an amicable alliance with the local chieftain of the area, while the distant inhabitants of Dilmun thought it worth their while to send envoys to Samsi-Addu himself, and we have his peremptory instructions to Yasmah-Adad at Mari to speed them on their way with provisions, water bags and even new sandals.

The reason for diplomatic visits of this kind was certainly the promotion of trade, and in this age we are lucky to have a glimpse of the mechanics of commerce which is not equaled until the Classical age. At one level, the trade in luxuries, there was the exchange of goods in the guise of gifts between friendly rulers, best attested in the subsequent Amarna Age. A more significant phenomenon was the large-scale trade in staple commodities such as metals like copper or tin. Business documents from Ur have revealed an interesting shift in the financial management of this sort of trade. During the Ur III empire merchants employed by the temple of Nanna at Ur undertook the sea journey to Dilmun (Bahrain), where

Terracotta plaques are common in the Old Babylonian period; this one (from Khafajah) shows a god dispatching a solar being. Baghdad.

they exchanged the products of Sumer (especially textiles) for copper and various precious items available there. This was a venture financed by the temple, which did not involve its employees personally in the financial risks, and as such we may see it as a continuation of the long-standing Dilmun trade which is first mentioned by Ur-Nanshe of Lagash. By the time of Rim-Sin of Larsa, who also ruled Ur, a different system had evolved.

Now the merchants, individually or as a group, organized the trading fleets themselves, sometimes borrowing capital from the temples, but bearing the risks and taking the profits in person. We have legal deeds recording the establishment of partnerships for the specific purpose of raising capital for a single Dilmun trading mission, and it is clear that these innovations are symptomatic of a change in the whole style of government. In place of the Ur III system, when virtually everyone was a state employee, held liable by the rigid accounting system for every item which passed through his hands, the state was now in the habit of "farming out" transactions, including not only activities like foreign trade and stock breeding, but even the collection of agricultural taxes, with an arrangement whereby the contractor paid a prescribed amount to the state and creamed off whatever he could make in excess of that. This tradition of private enterprise dominates the administration of Babylonia from this time forward to the disappearance of cuneiform records, but it is now time to turn back to the north, where at the city of Assur we meet an even more impressive illustration of the growth of private business.

The Anatolian connection. As it happens, the activities of the merchants of Assur are known to us not from any documents discovered in their own city, but from thousands of letters and business records excavated – legally and illegally – at the site of Kültepe in central Anatolia, some 1,000 miles distant from Assur. Once scholars had demonstrated that these tablets were written in a dialect of Akkadian, Old Assyrian to be precise (and not, as had been surmised quite understandably, in some unknown ancient Anatolian language), it soon became apparent that they constitute the business archives of some three generations of merchants from the city of Assur, who maintained resident Assyrian agents in the city of Kanesh, which proved to be the ancient name of Kültepe. The essential part of the trade was the transport of tin for the making of bronze to the towns of Anatolia, from Assur where it had been brought from sources further east. Annually caravans of donkeys left Assur after the winter rains, and made the long journey across the plains of northern Mesopotamia, where they might indulge in some subsidiary dealings en route, and then through the passes of the Taurus to unload at Kanesh or even further afield, at a healthy profit. Textiles were usually also included in the consignments, either from Assur itself or from further south – the best textiles, from Babylonia, are the "Akkadian" – and, in exchange, the profits were brought back in the shape of silver or gold.

The Kültepe texts display a sophistication of business methods and organization which is somehow the more impressive in the remote setting of the Anatolian plateau. Although the merchant quarter at Kanesh seems to have functioned as the main Assyrian center, other such trading colonies were established elsewhere, and similar Old Assyrian documents have already been discovered at the sites of Boğazköy (later the Hittite capital, Hattusas) and Alişar nearby. There is even a hint that similar trade relations had existed as much as 500 years before, in the legends that Sargon and Naram-Sin crossed into Anatolia to come to the rescue of Akkadian merchants in Purushhanda, a city which had a colony at the time we are considering, and was the seat of one of the most powerful local rulers. The colony at Kanesh was governed by a council which had authority over Assyrian merchants both there and in the other outlying colonies. This was necessary not only to arbitrate in transactions between the Assyrians themselves, but also to represent the entire body in dealings with the native princes; and to enforce the decisions of the council, disciplinary officials were appointed from among the respected members of the community and taxes were exacted. Predictably, perhaps, it was the exaction of taxes, usually customs dues, by the local rulers that was the most frequent cause of strained relations between the merchants and their host country.

Obviously the Anatolian princes stood in need of the Assyrians to bring them their tin and other goods, and indeed they profited from the trade by the taxes they could impose; but in the last resort they held the upper hand, and they were not afraid on occasion to punish by imprisonment any merchants detected smuggling, which was a regular and accepted practice, if we may judge from the Assyrians' own correspondence. In one typical letter the writer warns his correspondent that an agent had "sent his contraband goods to Pushu-ken [the merchant] and they were confiscated, and the palace has arrested Pushu-ken and thrown him into prison with a strong guard. The queen has written round to the towns of Luhusatia, Hurama, Shalahshua and the rest of her land about the

Valley of the Tohma Su in central Anatolia: one of the routes available to the Assyrian donkey caravans making for Kanesh.

smuggling, and they are on the lookout. So please don't smuggle anything . . . and leave the iron [at this date a great rarity] which you were going to bring through in a house you can trust in Timilkia."

Although this trade was organized and financed by great private merchant houses or "firms" at Assur, it was of course as susceptible to political upheavals as any state-run venture. It flourished in the years after the collapse of the Ur III empire and before the appearance of Samsi-Addu. It was perhaps the disruption associated with his seizure of power which led to a brief interruption of the trade, since Assur too was incorporated into his realm, but he certainly permitted a resumption of the trade once he had restored peaceful conditions. However, shortly after his death, Zimri-Lim, assisted by the king of Yamhad where he had lived in exile, succeeded in taking Mari back from Yasmah-Addu, and although Samsi-Addu's other son still ruled over Assur and that district for some time, many of the northern cities of Mesopotamia which lay on the direct route to Anatolia fell into the area controlled from Mari, and the Kanesh trade soon lapsed.

Servant releases lion from its cage for King Assur-ban-apli to hunt; the tradition of the lion as "royal beast" goes back at least to the Mari letters. British Museum.

The Mari archives. The great majority of the tablets from Mari belong to the reign of Zimri-Lim, and his correspondence in particular illustrates the most intimate details of his government. His exchange of letters with the provincial governors embraces not merely affairs of war and politics, but also the mundane trivia of day-to-day administration. These hard-working officials were responsible for the control of the Euphrates, or the Habur or branch canals, and for the equitable distribution of their waters, and might at one moment be charged with the exaction of customs dues on boats passing up or down the river, and at another with the provision of delicatessen for the royal table, such as truffles or special kinds of fish; more than once we read of the efforts of a governor to dispatch to the king a particularly fine piece of stone, or a caged lion, for the lion was already a royal beast, and had to be conveyed alive to the king whenever possible.

Equally instructive with the tablets of Mari is the building in which they were found. Zimri-Lim's palace contained more than 300 rooms, and is estimated by its excavator as measuring 200 × 120 meters. Although no other major palace of this date has been so completely excavated, it is obvious that it was considered exceptional even by its contemporaries, and confirmation of this comes from a letter from the king of Yamhad, who tells Zimri-Lim that he is sending on to him the servant of the king of Ugarit on the seacoast, who has expressed the wish to see "the house of Zimri-Lim." Part of the need for such a vast complex of rooms is explained by occasional offhand remarks in the tablets: the king inquires of an official why only 100 of the 400 palace retainers are issued with clothing, or an administrative list records rations given to some 400 women all employed by – if not in – the palace.

A letter from Assur to the firm's agents in Kanesh: the tablet (*right*) was enclosed in the envelope which carries the writer's seal-impression. British Museum.

However, the fame of the palace of Mari and its king was in fact short-lived. Despite their earlier alliance, Zimri-Lim and Hammurapi of Babylon crossed each other's paths, and in Hammurapi's 33rd year he marched up the Euphrates and took Mari, destroying the famous palace and thus preserving in its ruins the tablets for which we are now so grateful. This is the more ironic because, as luck would have it, no comparable archives are known from Babylonia itself. It is true that some of Hammurapi's own letters do survive, but these and other documents which throw light on his government were excavated illicitly and therefore the buildings from which they come are sadly unknown. Nevertheless, drawing on all available sources, we are able to reconstruct Hammurapi's reign in its broad outline, and it is possible to see that it did constitute a turning-point in the history of the area, terminating the era of small warring city-states, and converting the lands of Sumer and Akkad into one country for the first time since the reign of Ibbi-Sin of Ur.

Henceforth the southern part of modern Iraq can be reasonably called "Babylonia" since from the time of Hammurapi until the foundation of Seleucia on the Tigris Babylon was the capital city of the country both in political and more especially in cultural affairs.

Hammurapi and his dynasty. The dynasty of which Hammurapi was the sixth king had been founded by the Amorite Sumu-abum at the city of Babylon, which had already existed in Ur III times but now for the first time became the capital of a small state. Although it soon swallowed up some small dynasties established in neighboring towns like Kish, Kazallu or Marad, by Hammurapi's accession the territory of Babylon had not expanded far beyond its original frontiers. Nevertheless, by the sheer fact of its independence it had become one of the major contenders for power in Sumer and Akkad: in the south Rim-Sin of Larsa, who already controlled the territories of Uruk, Ur and the state of Lagash, had finally succeeded in annexing the state of Isin, for long his major rival, and the only other strong kingdom of the time had emerged at Eshnunna (Tell Asmar) in the Diyala region, as we can tell from the Mari letter already quoted. In the north Samsi-Addu was probably at the height of his power.

Most of Hammurapi's long reign must have been devoted to internal affairs, but in his 31st year he finally defeated Rim-Sin of Larsa and so made himself master of ancient Sumer and Akkad. Two years later he took Mari from his old ally, Zimri-Lim, and his defeat of Eshnunna and the extension of his rule as far north as Nineveh did not follow until his 38th year. In the prologue to his code of laws, for which he is rightly best remembered, he begins by proclaiming that the chief gods of Sumer, Anum and Enlil, had exalted Marduk, god of Babylon, and entrusted to him the supremacy, and had summoned Hammurapi himself "to create justice in the land, to abolish the criminal and the dishonest, and to prevent the strong from oppressing the weak." He then enumerates the cities which he had brought under his beneficent sway: Nippur, Eridu, Babylon, Ur, Sippar, Larsa, Uruk, Isin, Kish, Cuthah, Borsippa, Dilbat, Lagash and Girsu and Kesh and Adab – all the great traditional cities of Sumer and Akkad – as well as the towns along the middle Euphrates including Mari, and Eshnunna, and finally Nineveh. It is true that this list significantly does not

Above: statue of Ishtup-ilum, ruler of Mari c. 1900 B.C. Aleppo.

Opposite: aerial view of the great palace of Zimri-Lim at Mari; the throne room and audience chamber lie to the right of the square, smaller courtyard (Room 106).

Right: Mari: wall painting in the smaller court of the palace; detail showing a supplicant goddess, winged beasts and trees. Louvre.

include Elam or Assur, and to the end of his reign Hammurapi seems to have had troubles on his north-eastern borders – like many before and after him – but he was nevertheless the first king to unite the central sector of the Ur III empire under one rule once more, and however transitory his territorial conquests may have been, Babylon under his successors remained the sole traditional seat of kingship and the chief repository of scribal culture.

The prologue to his code vividly illustrates Hammurapi's desire, which was shared by his predecessors and contemporaries, to appear as a wise and just king under whom the ancient lands of Sumer and Akkad were once more united, to live together in peace and prosperity. The practice of the age was to name each year for an important event, and from these year-names we can see that not only Hammurapi but all the rulers of the day, small and great, were ceaselessly engaged in securing the prosperity of their kingdoms by digging new canals and maintaining old ones, and in the emphasis laid on these activities, and in the absence of historical inscriptions with boastful accounts of successes on the battlefield, Hammurapi and his age show themselves to be guardians of the ethos of ancient Sumer rather than imitators of Sargon and his Akkadian dynasty.

The same applies, as we shall see, in the sphere of law, and it is to the enthusiasm of the Akkadian or even Amorite scribes of this time that we owe our knowledge of the great bulk of Sumerian literature.

Primarily from the scribal schools of Nippur – the spiritual center of Sumer – but also from Ur, Kish, Sippar and Isin, we have recovered a great variety of Sumerian texts which were lovingly preserved and even composed after the death of Sumerian as a spoken language by the scholars and pupils in temples and secular schools, during the years between the exile of Ibbi-Sin in Elam and the final demise of the 1st Dynasty of Babylon. While the efforts devoted to the copying of Sumerian literature were certainly in part the outcome of a genuine concern for the past on which the civilization of Sumer and Akkad was founded, scribes who learned their Sumerian would find it of practical use as well. No one any longer wrote letters in Sumerian, but for religious inscriptions such as a king might wish prepared for a new temple, for the long-winded year-names by which any legal document would be dated, and for the traditional formulae in which such a document would be drawn up, Sumerian remained the accepted medium, much as in the medieval world Latin was not only the language of Vergil and Seneca, but the vehicle for any official, legal or religious communication.

As for the history of Sumerian literature itself, it remains an enigma. Some poems, like those which praise rulers such as Lipit-Ishtar of Isin or Rim-Sin of Larsa, are manifestly composed after the Ur III period, and the same can be said of some religious texts which even to us are blatant translations from the Akkadian. No one can yet say exactly when Sumerian ceased to be spoken, and that major literary works could be written even after the Ur III empire is proved by the "Lamentation over the Destruction of Ur," a poem of over 400 lines bewailing the desertion of Ur by its goddess Ningal and the resultant destruction of the city: the streets are grown over with weeds, water plants choke its canals, and the festivals are not kept. A similar composition on the fall of the house of Akkad, which is blamed on the sins of Naram-Sin, probably dates from Ur III times, but what are we to make of works like "Gilgamesh and Aka" or "Enmerkar and the Lord of Aratta" which hark back to the dawn of history? Literary texts from the time of the Ur III kings or earlier are still extremely rare, and although no one has sought to deny the survival of traditions reaching back some 600 years or more, the problem, as with the poems of Homer, is when these compositions were first written down, and – if they had existed before that time as oral poetry – how accurately they were handed down from one generation to the next.

Statuette in bronze with gold covering, showing Lu-nanna praying to Amurru for the life of Hammurapi (c. 1760 BC). Louvre.

Till recently scholarly opinion had suspected that the literary works copied by the scribes of Babylonia were composed in their present form no earlier than the Ur III Dynasty. This was not to deny the possibility that earlier literary compositions may have existed, but if so they had not, as far as could be told, survived into the standard repertoire of the scribal schools. The discovery of literary tablets of the Early Dynastic III period at Abu Salabikh has compelled a revision of this position: we can now point to at least one major work, "The Instructions of Shuruppak to his Son," which is attested c. 2500 BC at Abu Salabikh, then some hundred years later at Adab (Bismaya), and reappears, recognizably the same composition, in the literary canon of the Old Babylonian scribes after the downfall of the 3rd Dynasty of Ur. Since it is improbable that the poem was preserved orally during the 500-year gap in our sources, it is obvious that we cannot hope as yet to reconstruct the history of Sumerian literature until new discoveries have been made which throw some light on the intervening centuries.

The care with which the age of Hammurapi preserved the literature of a bygone era did not hinder the growth of Akkadian as a literary language in its own right. Disparate Sumerian myths about Gilgamesh were combined at this time into a single epic, with a length and structure unrivaled in its forerunners, and other myths were welded together into an Akkadian poem describing the creation of man and the great Flood, also drawing on old Sumerian tales but lending a new vigor with the freshness of the Akkadian language. Royal inscriptions were also composed bilingually in Sumerian and Akkadian, and another innovation, for which the Akkadian language only was used, was the recording of omens and their meaning, derived at this period chiefly from the inspection of sheep's entrails – the liver or lungs – or from the shapes formed by drops of oil on the surface of water. At the same time the old lists of signs and words with which the apprentice scribes had learned to write cuneiform were greatly expanded and given a column of Akkadian translations. It is however in his code of laws that Hammurapi has left us a document which at once constitutes the classical text of the Old Babylonian dialect of Akkadian – used for the teaching of the language and cuneiform script even today – and bears witness to the successful amalgamation of different linguistic and cultural elements into a single "Babylonian" society.

Above: Old Babylonian geometrical exercise tablet (c. 1800 B C), calculating the area of subdivisions of a square. British Museum.

Left: the stele of Hammurapi: above, he stands before Shamash, god of justice; below are 16 columns of inscription. Louvre.

The law code. The laws of Hammurapi are preserved principally on a black stone stele, 2·25 meters in height, and carrying on the top a relief of Hammurapi himself standing respectfully before the sun god Shamash who was the god of justice. The remainder of the stone is taken up with the 49 columns of cuneiform writing, which records in clear, vigorous Akkadian the laws of Hammurapi, promulgated "so that the strong may not oppress the weak, and to protect the rights of the orphan and widow," as he states in the epilogue. Although this is no longer, as it was for many years, the "oldest code of laws in the world," it remains the most important single written document from the whole spread of Mesopotamian civilization. The laws cover many branches of life – agricultural disputes over irrigation or the terms of field or date-grove leases, business transactions between merchants, family law and the problems of inheritance, terms of employment for different craftsmen, and penalties for crimes like adultery, unintentional homicide or the leveling of false accusations. Each law is formulated in two parts: an "if" clause stating the crime or other circumstances envisaged, and the clause giving judgment. To quote but one example: "If a man has rented a field to a gardener to be planted as a date plantation, the gardener shall raise the trees for four years, and in the fifth year the owner of the plantation and the gardener shall divide the plantation equally; but if the gardener has not planted the land completely but has left some of it waste, they shall include the waste part in his share."

Despite the length of the code, it is of course obvious that it cannot have covered even a fraction of the cases which confronted the judges in real life, and this raises the question of its exact nature, which has been hotly debated ever since its first publication in 1902. It is significant that similar codes of law are known as far back as Ur-Nammu, founder of the Ur III empire, and another written in Sumerian was promulgated by Lipit-Ishtar of Isin while a code in Akkadian comes from the kingdom of Eshnunna, having been discovered at Tell Harmal on the eastern outskirts of modern Baghdad. Although none of these remotely approaches the size or complexity of Hammurapi's code, they all treat much the same subjects, and it is clear that although some of Hammurapi's provisions are entirely new, other laws are in fact traditional, and can be traced back almost without a change in the wording to the code of Ur-Nammu. Compare with the law just quoted above the following extract from the code of Lipit-Ishtar: "If a man gave uncultivated ground to someone to plant as a plantation, but he did not complete the planting of the plantation, the owner shall assign to the man who planted the plantation the ground still uncultivated as part of his share."

Where Hammurapi does seem to have introduced new provisions, there is generally an explanation. After his conquest of the kingdom of Larsa he instituted an extensive program of agricultural reform, reallocating land and bringing in new settlers, and fostering agriculture by overhauling the decadent canal system. This all emerges from his own letters to the governors appointed by him at Larsa, and in view of the frequent disputes over land tenure mentioned in these letters, it is no surprise to find sections of the code devoted to the sort of problem which might crop up as a result of the resettlement policies. Equally the inclusion in the code of provisions governing the rights of priestesses in relation to their husbands' families can confidently be associated with the contemporary phenomenon of "cloisters," or communities of woman associated with a temple, of which the *naditum* priestesses of Sippar are the best known. In comparison with the earlier law codes, there is also an innovation which we would consider a step backwards: Ur-Nammu prescribed that a man who severed another man's limb should pay 10 shekels of silver, or if he cut off his nose, 40 shekels, and a similar monetary compensation for the different parts of the body which might suffer injury is fixed in the Eshnunna laws. It is all the more disconcerting then to find Hammurapi reverting to the *lex talionis*, "an eye for an eye, and a tooth for a tooth": "If a man has put out the eye of another man, they shall put out his eye; if he breaks the bone of another man, they shall break his bone." Without doubt this barbarous departure from Sumerian tradition reflects the harsh law of the desert, from where Hammurapi's dynasty came, and it appears that however devoted Hammurapi may have been to the preservation of the ancient mores of Sumer

Stone tablet of an early Hurrian king of Urkish, held by a bronze lion; probably temple foundation deposit; Akkadian period. Louvre.

and Akkad, he was Amorite enough to impose his tribal customs throughout his dominions.

We have already suggested that the reign of Hammurapi marks a turning-point in Mesopotamian history. The nature of the change is vividly illustrated by the remainder of his dynasty. For although specifically historical sources for these years are scanty, the economic documents show that life pursued an even tenor in most of Babylonia itself, and that even if the extent of their realm was gradually eroded by internal revolt or attrition from without, the authority of Hammurapi's successors in the 1st Dynasty of Babylon was not seriously challenged from within Sumer and Akkad. Indeed with the disappearance of Mari and Eshnunna, and the absence of any vigorous rulers in the north, there was no effective rival to the kings of Babylon, and although in later years parts of the south split away under the kings of the "Sealand" dynasty, it must have come as a bolt from the blue when in the reign of Samsu-ditana a man called Mursilis marched down the Euphrates, plundered Babylon and took its gods captive.

It is with this event, or more precisely with the last year of Samsu-ditana, who was the last king of the dynasty, that a new dark age obscures the course of events in Mesopotamia. For some reason the periods of unrest coincide with the complete disappearance of written sources – as far as they have survived for the modern historian – and although the scribal traditions must have been kept alive, the scene after the 1st Dynasty of Babylon is particularly dark because not even any of the revealing letters or economic documents are known from these years. Consequently, as far as Babylonia is concerned, all we can say is that Hammurapi's dynasty came to an abrupt end with Samsu-ditana, and that when the curtain rises again the northern part of the country is under the thumb of the new Kassite kings, and the "Sealand" dynasty had strengthened its hold on the south. The length of time during which this transformation took place is a subject of dispute. Despite the application of philological, historical and archaeological arguments of every kind, there is no agreement as to how many years should be allowed; most writers accept that the final answer is yet to be determined, and settle for the "Middle Chronology" by which the end of Samsu-ditana's reign is placed in 1595 BC, and well over a century elapses from this date until the first well-attested Kassite king.

Kassites and Hurrians. Although during this time the Kassites succeeded in imposing their rule on Babylonia, and on the country to its northeast which linked them geographically with the mountain lands from which they almost certainly originated, they cannot be considered conquerors in the old pattern, and despite their foreign origins they were anxious to adopt and promote the traditions of Babylonia. A new capital was also built at Dur-Kurigalzu, near modern Baghdad, but they considered Babylon as the seat of kingship and recognized its claim to be the chief city of the land. During the four centuries of their reign, they succeeded in winning back for Babylon the southern districts of the "Sealand," but the major political events seem to have been indecisive confrontations with the armies of Elam and Assyria, and their borders seldom extended beyond the alluvial lands of southern Iraq. In fact the initiative has shifted during this time to the north of Mesopotamia, and in particular to the Hurrians.

Hurrian kings have been encountered in the north as far back as the Akkadian empire, and plentiful references in Ur III administrative documents demonstrate that Hurrians were present then in some numbers, even in the south. During the age of Hammurapi and the Mari archives, many of the local princelings in the "Upper Land" between the two rivers bore distinctly Hurrian names, and texts written in the Hurrian language have even been excavated at Mari. When the conquests of Hammurapi and the subsequent inertia of his successors had left a power vacuum in the north, it was the Hurrians who stepped in. A state called Hanigalbat existed already before the end of the Old Babylonian Dynasty, and was even powerful enough to have attacked the great Hittite king Hattusilis while he was absent on campaign in the west. Elsewhere, from the Zagros to the Mediterranean, there sprang up a chain of small Hurrian kingdoms, but by about 1500 BC these all appear to have been welded together under the one paramount ruler, Saushtatar of Mitanni, whose capital Washukanni, although still unidentified, must have lain somewhere close to the present

Symbols of the gods invoked on a boundary stone of a type introduced by the Kassites (c. 1120 BC). British Museum.

Very few genuine Hurrian artifacts have been discovered: this ram comes from the time of Mitannian domination at Alalakh. Antioch.

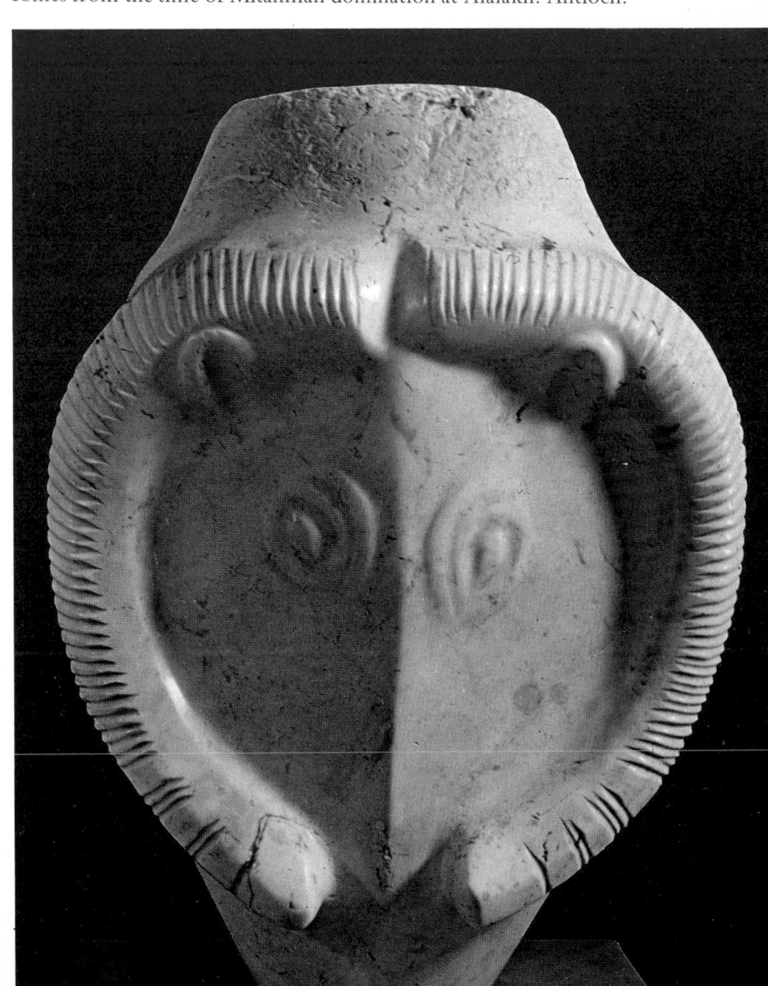

Syrian-Turkish border where it runs from the Tigris to the Euphrates. We are especially fortunate in that this very king happens to be mentioned in two archives discovered at the opposite ends of his empire: at Alalakh (Tell Açana) on the Orontes close to the Mediterranean seaboard, where legal documents have been excavated bearing the impression of his seal, and in the east beyond the Tigris at Nuzi (Yorghan Tepe) which has yielded a letter from Saushtatar himself to the local king of Arrapha (Kerkuk), and also bearing his seal impression.

Although all these documents were written in the Akkadian language, which had already established itself as the vehicle of international diplomacy, at neither site is there any shortage of evidence for the presence of the Hurrians. Especially at Nuzi a great proportion of the personal names are Hurrian, and Hurrian words, word formations (on an Akkadian base) and even sentence structures have permeated the local scribal dialect until it is sometimes scarcely recognizable. Similar, though less extreme, influences can be observed at Alalakh and Ugarit (Ras Shamra), and in each case the documents attest the existence of a sharply defined social structure which can also be attributed to the Hurrians. The archives at Nuzi were found both on the summit of the tell, where the administrative center or "palace" must have stood, and in the ruins of spacious mansions outside the town proper, in which members of the ruling class resided. The palace archives reflect the expected preoccupations. The palace is the administrator of justice, as it appears from the records of legal proceedings, and as well as running its own internal household, which included craftsmen and women as well as agricultural workmen, it was responsible to its superiors for the organization of the army. This is apparent from the lists of military equipment, including chariots and horses, and from the records of persons involved in military service. Although all the details are not yet clear, it seems that in the Hurrian states each petty king was responsible to the central regime for the supply of fighting men, and that in turn the heads of noble houses were responsible to their king. At Alalakh and other places in the west we meet a class called *mariannu*, who belonged to the highest rank of society and were distinguished by having to provide the charioteers of the army, reflecting the fact that the new masters of the region, like the Kassites in Babylonia, owed much of their military superiority to the new skills of horse training and the resultant changes in methods of warfare.

The almost feudal character of the state is vividly illustrated by the family archives from the rich men's houses at Nuzi. These did include loans, and contracts of personal service, but the most typical documents are the "adoption texts" which are in fact sales of property. For land was apparently held by a man, and his sons after him, from the king *in perpetuo*, and since it was the possession of this land that placed upon him and his family the obligation to serve under the king in battle when summoned, the law did not permit the land to be sold. The result, at least at Nuzi, was that in order to "sell" his land, the owner had to adopt the intending purchaser as a "son" so that he became entitled to receive it under the laws of inheritance, and it did not pass out of the "family." Since some of the ruling class at Nuzi had purchased large plots of land from different owners, this had the curious result that they were the adopted sons of several different "fathers," and a final circumvention of the system was necessary, whereby the obligation to military service was severed from the actual possession of the land and explicitly assigned to the now landless original owner.

The Amarna Age. It is ironical that the great age of the Hurrians should be known almost exclusively from petty states at the uttermost ends of their empire. When some fortunate archaeologist eventually succeeds in locating one of the major cities of the central core of the Hurrian empire, he will certainly find documents written not in the bastard Akkadian of Nuzi, but in the Hurrian language itself. At present, however, the main sources for the little-

Wall paintings with bulls' heads, female faces and floral motifs; found in the 15th-century palace at Nuzi.

Relief of Tudkhalias III or IV as the sanctuary of Yazilikaya in a natural rock formation near Boğazköy. He stands on twin mountain peaks holding the cartouche of his name.

Boğazköy (Hattusas) looking down towards the citadel from the city wall. Unlike Mesopotamian buildings, Hittite temples and palaces are generally of rough-hewn, massive stone masonry.

in the north and east were pushed back again to a safe distance from the capital.

When this son, called Suppiluliumas, took the throne in about 1380 BC, he faced in Syria the Mitannian Tushratta, who was allied by marriage to the Pharaoh Amenophis III. His first moves against this archenemy were diplomatic. He succeeded in making treaties not only with the ruler of Kizzuwadna, who remained independent, but also with the king of the "Hurri lands" which were a northern division of the Mitannian empire now ruled by a King Artatama who claimed the overall kingship from Tushratta as well. He was naturally willing to ally himself with any possible opponent of Tushratta, and in the far southeast Suppiluliumas found another state pleased to join hands against Mitanni, and cemented that alliance by taking the hand of the daughter of the Babylonian king in marriage.

With these preparatory moves, Suppiluliumas seems to have had no difficulty when the time came in sweeping up all the Mitannian dependencies west of the Euphrates, although he was careful not to tread on Egyptian toes. His first attack came not through Syria but by a march through eastern Anatolia which brought him out on Tushratta's northwestern frontier. He found the capital Washukanni abandoned, and marched unopposed back westwards across the Euphrates to take complete control of Syria as far south as Damascus, appointing his own nominees as local rulers. Subsequently he also took the important city of Carchemish, and perhaps his most significant innovation was to appoint sons of his to be the kings of Aleppo and Carchemish, much as in the past the king's close relatives had been given local kingships within

Anatolia. They were able to act in all except the greatest issues as entirely independent rulers, which gave them the freedom of initiative badly needed so far from the center of the empire. The success of the arrangement is shown by its prolongation by his successors and sons Arnuwandas (who died after a short reign) and Mursilis II, who proved a worthy heir. After some revolts in north Syria and the death of his brother, the king of Carchemish, he appointed new Hittite kings both there and in Aleppo.

The century after the accession of Suppiluliumas can be seen as the golden age of the Hittite empire. His successors, Mursilis II, Muwatallis and Hattusilis III, were able to maintain the extent of his conquests and stabilize Hittite government of these areas. In the southeast the defeat of Tushratta had removed any serious threat from Mitanni, whose rulers now became vassals of the Hittites or of the Assyrians, and although the growth of Assyria posed a new threat, Carchemish remained the bastion of the Hittite empire on its southeast flank, and even Adad-nirari I and his son and grandson did not seek to advance beyond the Euphrates. Furthermore, the link with Babylon initiated by Suppiluliumas proved equally effective against the upstart Assyria, and was perpetuated by Hattusilis III. In a lengthy missive addressed to the young Kadashman-Enlil he congratulates the king on his reported interest in hunting, and takes the opportunity to suggest that despite the caution of the new king's stick-in-the-mud elderly adviser, he should "go out and make a raid against the enemy," implying an attack on Assyria, which would, conveniently for Hattusilis, deflect the Assyrians' attention away from the west.

As far as we know, the Assyrians never went so far as to risk a serious confrontation with the Hittites, although Tukulti-Ninurta did plunder across the river, but in the south a resurgent Egypt under Sethos I and Ramesses II was unable to ignore their occupation of lands which had once been unquestionably in the Egyptian sphere of influence. Since the conquests of Suppiluliumas the Hittites had controlled the kingdoms of Amurru and Qadesh, traditionally Egyptian-aligned states. In one major effort to restore the *status quo*, Ramesses II planned a major offensive, and in 1300 BC he marched up the Orontes into Hittite territory. The two armies met at Qadesh, and despite the glowing accounts of the battle – in both words and pictures – from the Egyptian sources, it was evidently fairly evenly matched, and the Egyptians achieved nothing. Recognition of this came some 16 years later (1284 BC), when a treaty was concluded between the two great powers.

Something is known of the Hittite style of empire from sources in Syria as well as Boğazköy. They favored the system of vassal states already known from the Mitannian empire. Each vassal king was personally tied by treaty to the Hittite emperor, and the text of some of these treaties has survived, usually written out in Akkadian on cuneiform tablets, and sealed with the seals of the contracting

Incised Hittite rock sculpture at Kizil Dağ near Konya, with a "hieroglyphic" inscription of Hartapus, a little-known Neo-Hittite king.

parties. The king of Ugarit (Ras Shamra) was one such vassal, and although his allegiance was to the Hittite king in person, the day-to-day administration was carried out by the king of Carchemish. We have a letter from the king of Carchemish referring to this chief obligation of the vassal, the supply of troops for battle; he writes: "Talmi-Teshup, the chariot-driver of the 'Sun' [i.e. the Hittite king] is coming to you. He will inspect your foot soldiers and your chariots to see how many there are. Alert all the soldiers and the chariots assigned to you by the palace, the 'Sun' will make a count." The adoption of this Mitannian style of government may in fact partly reflect the advent of a Hurrian element in the Hittite royal house: starting with Tudkhalias II, the kings of this dynasty seem to have Hurrian names in the first instance, which were changed for linguistically Hittite names only on their accession. Indeed the brother of Suppiluliumas when appointed king of Carchemish discarded his Hittite name for the Hurrian Sharri-kusukh, and this may have been a deliberate attempt to lay stress on the local affiliations of the dynasty and belie the appearance of a foreign domination.

The Hittites and the west. In any assessment of the character of the Hittite empire we are at the mercy of our sources. These are almost entirely in cuneiform, whether their language is Hittite, Hurrian or Akkadian, and therefore must have a built-in bias towards the east. It is true that the Hittites developed their own script, known as "Hieroglyphic Hittite," but as yet it has been discovered from the time of the Hittite empire only on sealstones (and their impressions) and in monumental stone inscriptions. It seems probable that it was also in everyday use, but if so it was written on wood or other perishable materials, since no archaeological traces have survived. The script itself was an imitation of Egyptian hieroglyphs, simplified into a syllabary, and must have been conceived around the middle of the second millennium; its first known user was Isputahsus of Kizzuwadna, the contemporary of Telepinus, whose seal impression was found in excavations at Tarsus. Used sporadically thereafter for royal inscriptions, the script's golden age seems to have fallen in the era of the Neo-Hittite states, when it was used for writing the Luwian language closely akin to Hittite, and it seems clear that texts in Hieroglyphic Hittite, if only they had survived, would have shed more light on the indigenous Anatolian facets of Hittite civilization.

Although we have dwelt on the part played by the Hittite empire in the political millstream of the Near East, the empire was primarily an Anatolian phenomenon, and its main interest must be the light it sheds on this region before the Classical age. This makes the absence of a counterweight to the predominance of the cuneiform sources all the more aggravating. It is true that the royal inscriptions are written with a lucid detachment which may be an indigenous "Hittite" characteristic; in treaties or historical annals the Hittite kings display an objective attitude to history which comes as a welcome relief after some of their Near Eastern contemporaries, and both in their public inscriptions and private letters the kings seem concerned to show a sweet reasonableness, such that the reader is invited to judge for himself the expediency or morality of his actions. Perhaps this is an inheritance from the early days of the Hittite monarchy, when under Hattusilis and Mursilis I the king seems to have been much less the hereditary autocrat than he later became.

In the realm of literature the Hittite debt to Mesopotamia is especially strong. There are pieces of the Epic of Gilgamesh from Boğazköy in both Akkadian and Hurrian, as well as a special abridged Hittite version, and the archives of Hattusas included Hittite and Akkadian legends of Sargon and Naram-Sin of Akkad, no doubt specially popular because of their Anatolian campaigns. Hurrian influence is considerable in the later Hittite empire, but until more is known of Hurrian culture itself, it will remain very difficult to separate out any indigenous "Hittite" elements of the cultural amalgam. This is especially regrettable since in the literature at least connections with the Aegean world are becoming evident: the successive generations of the first gods are described in poems with a clear Hurrian origin in a way reminiscent not only of Mesopotamian motifs, but also of Hesiod's *Theogony*, and this is not the only possible connection, since it seems quite possible that the practice of divination by inspection of the entrails of animals reached the west, and particularly the Etruscans, through the mediation of the Hittites. However, considering that the Hittite kingdom must have been the major political force in Anatolia for most of the second millennium BC, it is surprising how few connections with the west can be detected. It is true, of course, that Near Eastern civilization was always diffused more easily through the Levant ports and the Mediterranean, to Cyprus, Crete and the Aegean, than across the inhospitable Anatolian plateaus, but it remains a little disconcerting that the excavations at Troy have revealed effectively no points of contact with the Hittites that can be detected in the material record, and that later Greek traditions show no awareness of the existence of this major world power inland from the cities on the west coast of Anatolia.

This is the more surprising because the Hittite sources record frequent contact with the lands to their west. The main rival to their hegemony was the land of Arzawa in the southwest, whose king had been important enough to correspond directly with the pharaoh, and which retained its identity, even though a vassal of the Hittites, until late in the 13th century BC. However, when Tudkhalias IV, who succeeded Hattusilis III, was obliged to fight to reassert Hittite authority over Arzawa, it was the result of the increasing power of a land called Ahhiyawa, whose location has been for many years one of the most hotly debated questions of ancient geography. For in the name Ahhiyawa some scholars have seen the Achaeans of Homeric tradition, and their land has been identified with parts of mainland Anatolia, Rhodes or even Greece itself. The problem is still far from settled, and indeed one author has recently written that "The Hittites had no cause to remember the Achaeans; they had never even heard of them." Whatever the truth, there can be little doubt in view of the Hittite records that it was the hostility of these westerners that did much to undermine the Hittite empire.

No serious threat was offered to the kings after Tudkhalias IV by the old enemies in the east, Assur and Egypt, but much effort was devoted to breaking up alliances formed between Arzawa, Ahhiyawa and other western Anatolian states. The end of the empire is shrouded in the usual darkness, but was occasioned by a great movement of peoples which affected the whole of the Near East: an Egyptian inscription describes the incursion of the "Peoples of the Sea" and says that "Not one stood before their hands from Hatti [=the Hittite empire] on; Qode [=Aleppo], Carchemish, Arzawa, and Alashiya [=Cyprus] were crushed." The destruction wrought by these invaders can be followed in the archaeological record, but their ultimate origin and their racial affinities remain a puzzle. When written sources return to Anatolia centuries later, the empire is nothing but a vague memory, and any Hittite traditions that remain are concentrated in a scatter of petty states each side of the Taurus mountains.

"The Palaces of Nimroud Restored" (from a sketch by James Fergusson). Although perhaps a little over enthusiastic, this recreation of ancient Kalhu, based on Layard's excavations, has an authentic imperial aura about it. While the colonnades are alien to Assyrian architecture, the massed frontage of public buildings as viewed from across the Tigris is convincing. British Museum.

Nimrud: an Assyrian capital

Assyria had four capitals: Assur, the oldest, Nineveh, the last and greatest, Khorsabad, and Nimrud (ancient Kalhu) which is overall the best known and most instructive. The acropolis mound, extensively investigated by Layard, attracted the attention of M. E. L. Mallowan, for many years Woolley's right-hand man at Ur, and in 1949 excavations for the British School of Archaeology in Iraq began, continuing until 1963. Results exceeded expectations. The city was refounded by Assur-nasir-apli II (883–859 BC), who built the Northwest Palace and brought a canal from the River Zab; Shalmaneser built the military palace dubbed "Fort Shalmaneser"; and Nimrud was the royal residence until Sargon moved to Khorsabad (c. 707 BC). It was understandable, therefore, though still gratifying, that palace rooms were strewn with tribute collected over the years, bronzes and especially ivories. There were also the royal correspondence of Sargon and Tiglath-pileser, and equally revealing, business documents of temples and private citizens, records from the administration of the palaces and the armies, and a new Assyrian library in the Nabu Temple, all rounding off the picture of this first experiment in empire.

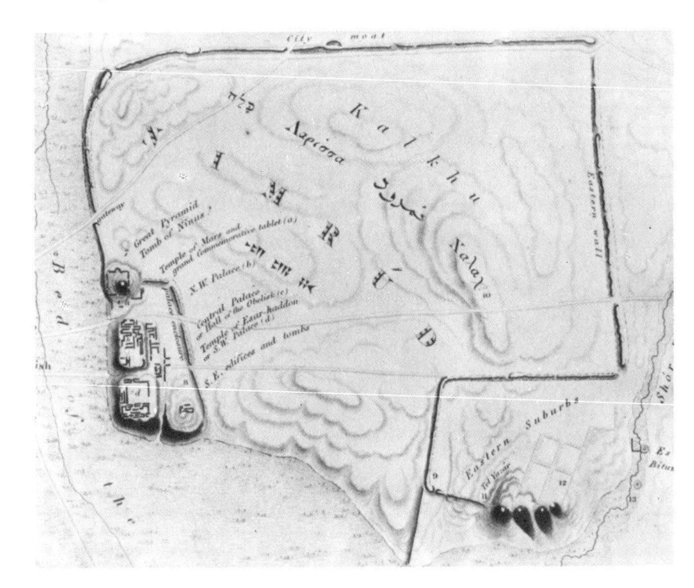

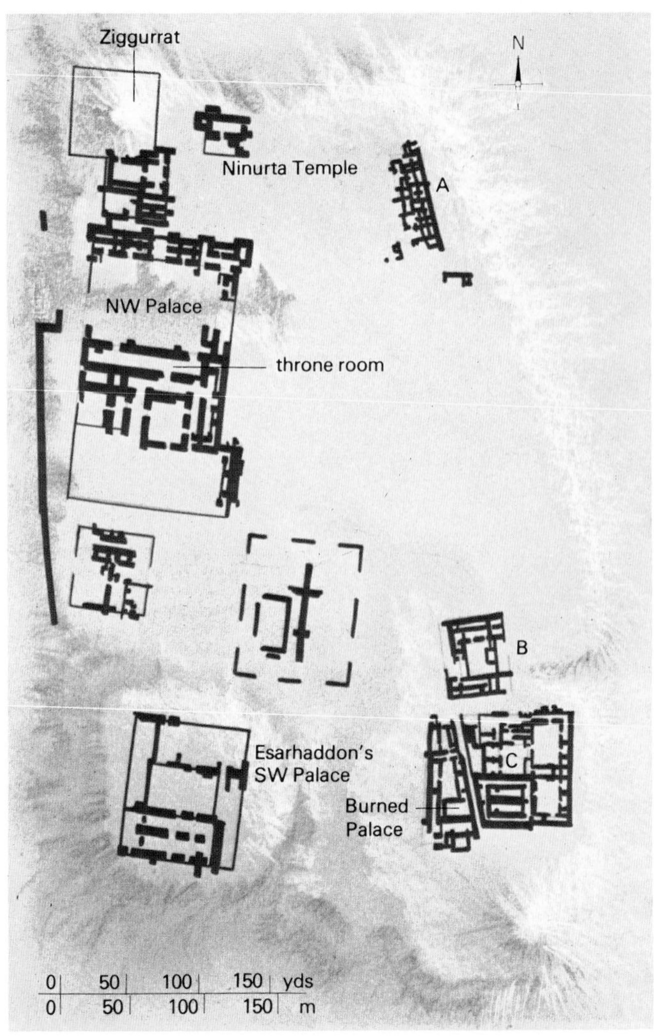

Above: a part of the superb survey of Assyria prepared for the British Museum in 1852 by Capt. Felix Jones, R.N. The city wall and main mounds of Nimrud (an area of 357 hectares) are accurately shown, with the old Tigris bed passing the west side of the city to join a natural wadi and Assur-nasir-apli's canal coming from the east past "T. Yazár", where Jones's "Eastern Suburbs" are in fact the single Fort Shalmaneser complex. Oriental Institute, Cambridge.

Right: although some of the identifications have been updated, today's plan of the acropolis differs little overall from Layard's. Chief new features are: wealthy houses by the town wall (A), the 8th-century Governor's Palace (B), and especially the Nabu Temple (C), which was unusually well preserved and yielded documents from its internal administration in addition to a large Assyrian library. After Mallowan.

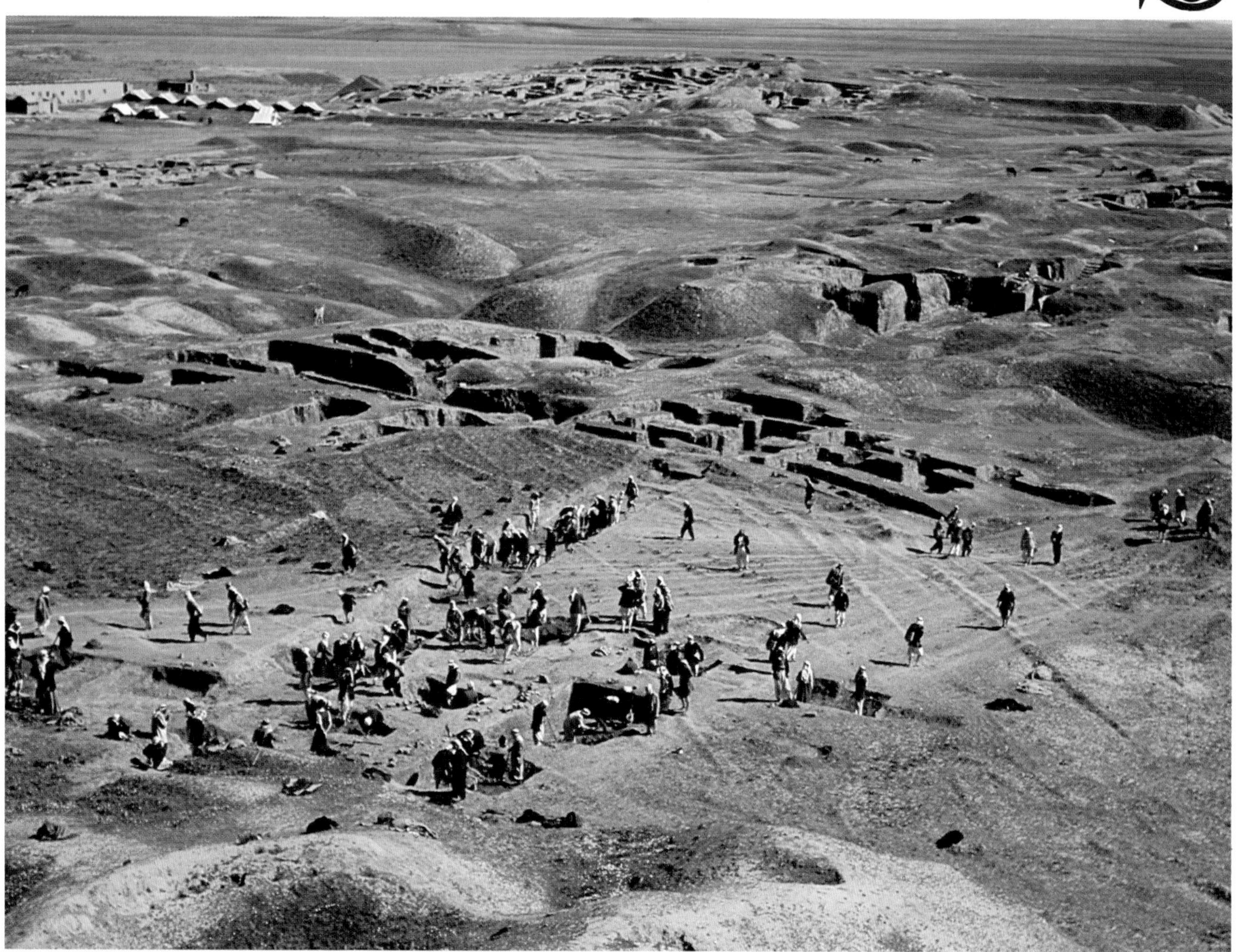

Above: standing on the Assyrian ziggurrat one can see almost all the acropolis mound, during the excavations of 1956. In the foreground is the Ninurta Temple, and beyond the Arab workmen the rooms of the Northwest Palace. In the middle distance the tents and house of the expedition, and beyond them at the south end of the mound, the Nabu Temple.

Shalmaneser III's great new military palace measured some 350 × 250 meters, and included three huge courtyards for the marshaling of the troops. In the southeast court was a throne base (*opposite*) from which the king could review them, and the south side of this court was formed by a massive throne-room suite, with walls 4·5 m thick and probably originally 12 m high. The throne room itself (42 × 9 m) housed against its east wall this unique stone dais for the king's throne and footstool. Around its sides are carved scenes of the king greeting his Babylonian counterpart and receiving tribute: here (*left*) Chaldaean tribesmen bring a model city signifying their submission, and a tray of precious ornaments and part of their tribute.

Above: Assur-nasir-apli's Northwest Palace was the first Assyrian building to be decorated with stone bas-reliefs and giant guardian figures at the gateways. This head of a winged bull is lying as it was left by Layard on the courtyard pavement, but today it is restored to its place at the eastern entrance of the great throne room.

Left: Sherqati workmen uncovering the remnants of bronze-plated furniture which was lying in the bathroom of the king's special throne-room suite in the Nabu Temple. The whole building had been destroyed by fire, and in the throne room itself fragments of the king's throne and ivory lay in a thick bed of ash, together with smashed tablets on which were written the treaties by which Esarhaddon had demanded the allegiance of the eastern mountain tribes – perhaps the same as those which sacked the building in 614 BC.

Above: these little statuettes (average height 13 cm) are very unusual for being carved in the round. From left to right they bring tribute of a lion and an ibex, a gazelle and an ostrich, and a monkey and an antelope, animals suggesting an African or Arabian origin. From Fort Shalmaneser, Room NE 2. Baghdad.

Right: this superb plaque (c. 10 × 10 cm) is one of two from a well in the domestic wing of the Northwest Palace found in 1951; it was lovingly conserved in its damp state until it could reach a laboratory, by the excavator's wife, Agatha Christie Mallowan (better known to the world for her detective stories). The ivory was overlaid with gold leaf and set with carnelian and lapis lazuli (which has mostly dropped out leaving a cement of powdered frit mixed wth calcium carbonate), and the Negro boy's hair curls are rendered with tiny inserted pegs of ivory. British Museum.

Left: although the throne room and other ceremonial rooms in Assur-nasir-apli's palace were decorated with scenes of battle and the chase, most of the inner rooms were lined with ritual scenes: here an eagle-headed genie anoints with a palm spathe the typically Assyrian stylized tree from the bucket he is holding. Like the stone figures at the gates, these beings were conceived as conferring some supernatural protection on the palace and its occupants. Louvre.

Dating and placing the manufacture of the immense quantities of ivory found in the palace storerooms at Nimrud is an extremely difficult task, since no Assyrian king on campaign failed to collect tribute including "ivory beds, ivory thrones, elephant hides, tusks, and precious woods."

Below left: ivory panels backed onto wood form a bedhead, with a characteristic mixture of Egyptian and Mesopotamian motifs (from Fort Shalmaneser, in a stack of ivory furniture in Room SW 7; 84 × 60 cm). Baghdad.

Below: this fan handle was found in the "Burned Palace" near the Nabu Temple, and one of the ladies has suffered from the fire which consumed both buildings when the city was sacked. (Height: 16·7 cm.) Baghdad.

6. The Assyrian and Babylonian Empires

The eastern edge of the site of Assur, looking upstream.

The city of Assur, c. 700 BC. After Andrae.

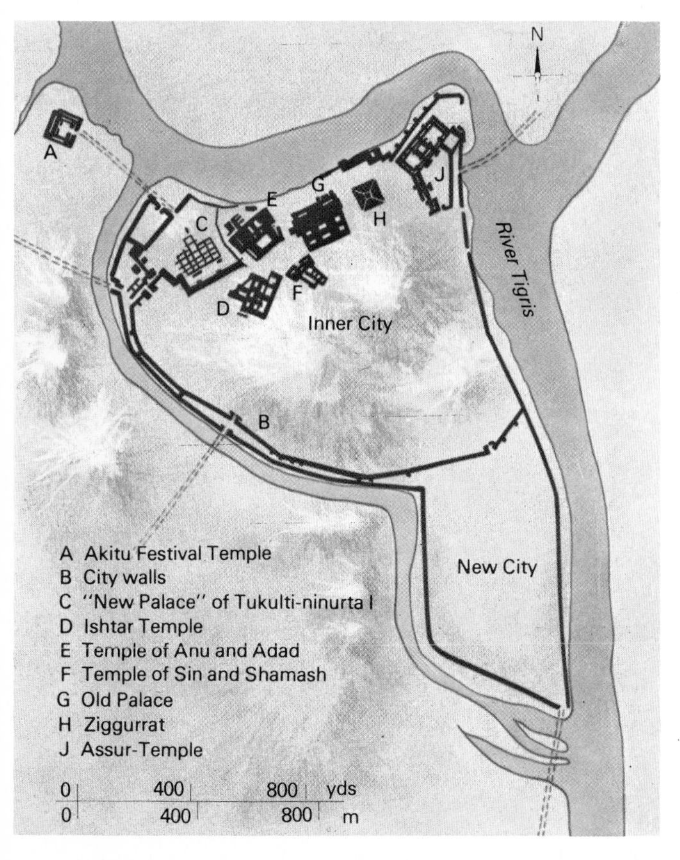

The city of Assur. Qalat Sherqat, the site of ancient Assur, on the west bank of the Tigris where the river cuts through a low range of hills, is not an obvious setting for the capital of a great empire. We have seen Assur as a trading city, occupied and not unimportant during the Early Dynastic and Akkadian periods, and under the kings of the Ur III empire it was the seat of a governor or *ensi*. As far as the evidence goes, its connections throughout the third millennium were with the south, and this must have been because, like Mari on the middle Euphrates, it was in a position to control the passage of boats and rafts down one of the great rivers to the cities of Sumer and Akkad. A treaty tablet recently discovered at Tell Mardikh in Syria proves that Assur was also involved already in a flourishing east–west trade, such as we find during the next phase of its existence, so vividly illustrated by the archives of the merchants of Kanesh.

We know so much in detail about these distant exiles from Assur that it is disconcerting to realize how little we know about their home city. Letters from the parent firms at Assur only rarely discuss anything outside their own commercial affairs, although on occasion a mention is made of "the city" and its representative council of elders – such as when they impose a levy on the Kanesh colony as a contribution towards rebuilding the city-wall of Assur – or we hear of the "prince" who is not accorded the title of

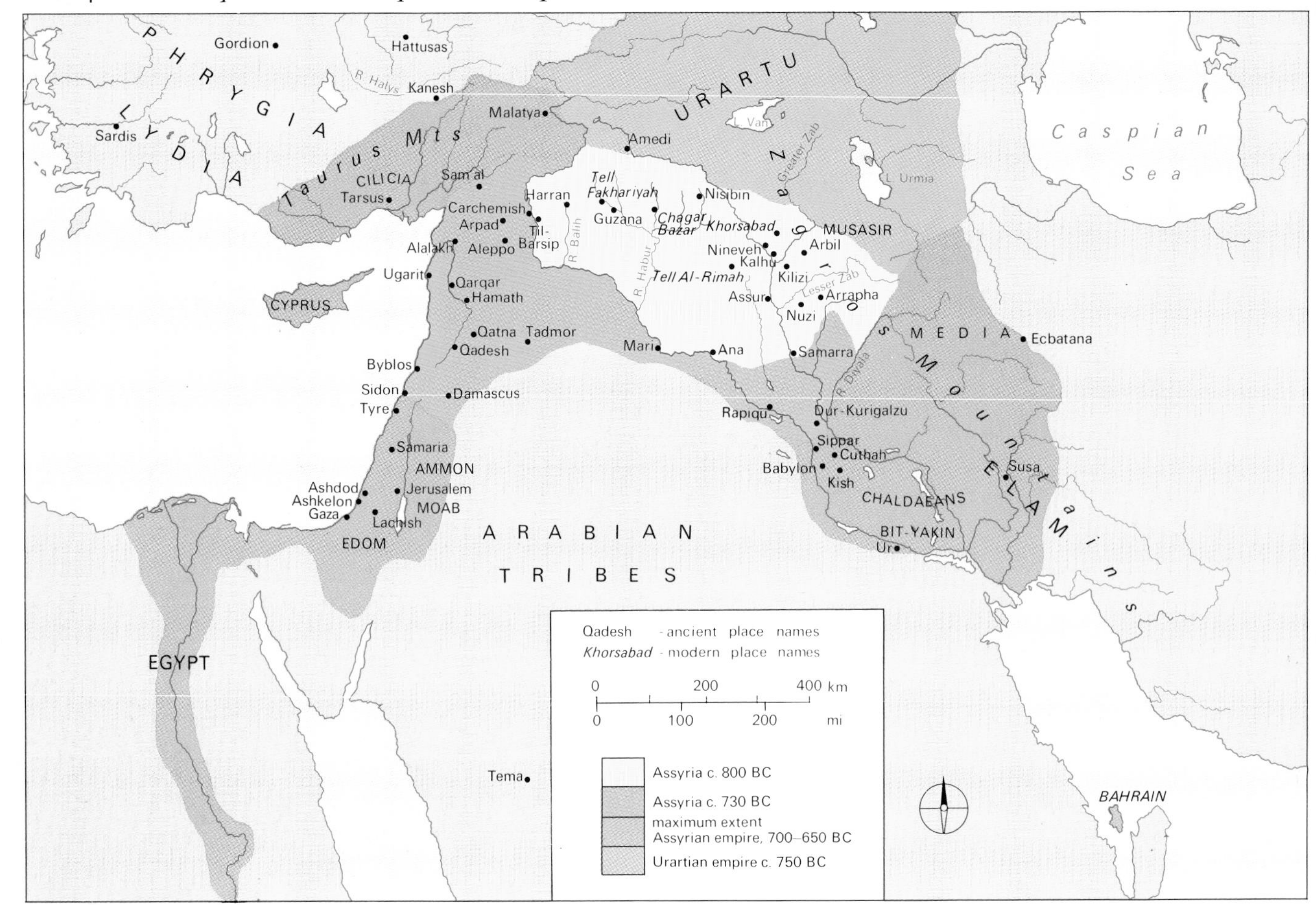

The Assyrian empire.

king by his fellow citizens, and is clearly thought of as the first among equals rather than as an absolute despot. As with Sumer, the earliest phases of Assur's history are illuminated – but also complicated – by the survival of a king list. Despite certain vagaries, such as the barefaced insertion of the ancestors of the usurping Amorite Samsi-Addu, the Assyrian King List records accurately the names of the "princes" also known to us from the Kültepe tablets, and both sources agree satisfactorily with the scarce royal inscriptions of the time. The King List does indeed take us even further back in time, but its information becomes increasingly suspect, and it is hard to say whether the beginning of the list is meant to give the rulers of the city of Assur (who may not have been "Assyrian" at all), or the Assyrian ancestors of the later dynasty: perhaps we should opt for the latter, since the start of the list is summed up as "17 kings who lived in tents," suggesting that at some date the city was captured and adopted by a nomadic tribe. We do not know yet when the very distinctive dialect of the Akkadian language which was spoken at Assur (and hence is known as "Assyrian") came into being, but it is tempting to assume that these nomadic rulers brought it with them, and succeeded in imposing on the ancient trading city both their language and their government.

The interregnum of Samsi-Addu and his son Ishme-Dagan temporarily incorporated Assur into a larger polity, but the scant evidence available suggests that these Amorites made little attempt to control the city's internal affairs: their administrative capital was fixed north of Assur and on the other bank of the river at Ekallate, and if they adopted the Assyrian system of dating, they wrote in Babylonian and not the Assyrian dialect. It is therefore no surprise to find that in due course the old-established families of Assur succeeded in returning to the throne a line of indigenous Assyrian kings, and the city was able once more to run its own affairs and, as far as conditions in the outside world permitted, to pursue its trading activities. The King List gives us an unbroken list of kings' names for this period, but otherwise nothing substantial is known of either the internal or the external history of Assur.

The birth of Assyria. When the veil lifts, and the Kassites emerge as heirs to Babylonia, the Hurrians to the north, we find that Assur has successfully maintained its identity, even though it has been incorporated as a vassal state into the loose Mitannian confederation which also embraced the cities of Arrapha (Kerkuk) and Nuzi, east of the Tigris. However, Mitanni's internal weakness and preoccupation elsewhere soon gave Assur her chance to reassert her independence, and under Assur-uballit I (1365–1330 BC), whom we have already encountered as one of the correspondents of Amenophis IV, this aim was achieved and indeed exceeded. Assur-uballit himself may reasonably be considered the first real "king of Assyria," for it was in his reign that Assur was transformed from a peaceful merchant city-state to the capital of a country called "the land of Assur" and known today as "Assyria." He proved to be the first of a long succession of vigorous and warlike kings, who did not stop at securing the frontiers of an independent Assur, but in emulation of the great powers of the day embarked on a policy of territorial aggrandizement. But however far they marched, the heart of their empire remained the lands first converted into "Assyria" by Assur-uballit I, and before we recount the stages of the formation of the Assyrian empire, it is time we examined the lands from which each campaign was launched.

Assur was a trading city. Its citizens did of course engage in agriculture, but except down on the flats along the river the land around their city was stony and not particularly fertile, and even adequate rainfall was far from guaranteed. Exposed on the west to the first wave of any nomadic movements, threatened by potentially powerful city-states east of the river, and in historical terms even a legitimate target for the ambitions of any Babylonian monarch, the city had to be content with political subordination, or else be prepared to fight. One of the preconditions for military success, whether offensive or merely defensive, is a good commissariat, and since to the south of Assur the terrain is even less welcoming to the farmer, it is obvious that for Assur to become a viable military force its rulers would have to turn their eyes northwards. Here since prehistoric times there lay the important city of Nineveh, and between the two Zab rivers east of the Tigris an equally fertile plain was controlled from Arbil (known to have been conquered by the Ur III kings, and still an important place today). Less well known, but equally significant, was a city called Kilizi (modern Qasr Shemamok), situated between Arbil and Assur in the rolling grassland once described by Layard as "renowned for its fertility" and the "granary of Baghdad." It seems to have been the lasting achievement of Assur-uballit I to incorporate in his new kingdom these prime corn-growing lands which had in the past been Hurrian (or at least under Hurrian domination).

How he did this we cannot guess, since there are virtually no sources for his long reign: in the absence of strong opposition from Mitanni it may have required more administrative than military genius, but however it was, these lands henceforth constitute Assyria *par excellence*, and from now until the final demise of Assyria in 610 BC not one of the three cities we have mentioned left Assyrian hands for any significant length of time, although in the past not one of them is known to have had any special connection with Assur. It is thus for very good reasons that in his second letter to Amenophis IV Assur-uballit I felt himself entitled to add to the title "king of

Button-based glass jar; Middle Assyrian period from Tell Al-Rimah.

Assyria" the words "great king, your brother," which constituted a claim to equality with the pharaoh himself. His international standing also emerges from his dealings with Babylonia: he concluded a marriage alliance by giving his daughter to the Kassite king, and when after his son-in-law's death the Babylonians killed his grandson and attempted to install a usurper, he was strong enough to march to Babylonia and place one of the legitimate line on the throne.

The growth of Assyrian power. Although immediately after Assur-uballit Assyria seems to have passed through a period of what may politely be termed "consolidation," his example was not forgotten, and a generation later there ascended the throne the first of three kings who raised Assyria to the rank of one of the great powers of the day, and foreshadowed her later destiny. Starting from the heartland which they inherited, the kings Adad-nirari I (1307–1275), his son Shalmaneser I (1274–1245) and grandson Tukulti-Ninurta I (1244–1208) carried Assyrian arms as far as Carchemish on the Euphrates, northwards into mountain territory inhabited by Hurrian tribes and already bearing the name of Assyria's later great rival Urartu, and down the lands east of the Tigris to Babylonia, and even to Babylon itself. It is in these three directions that Assyria's military energies would be constantly directed in the ensuing centuries: the immutable facts of her geographical setting imposed on her "the triple series of wars which fill Assyrian annals from the thirteenth century onwards: guerilla wars in the mountains, wars of movement in the Jazirah, and wars of position on the middle Tigris" (Georges Roux).

It would be tedious to follow here in detail the ebb and flow of Assyrian fortunes in each of these theaters of war. Assisted by the temporary preoccupation of the Hittite king, Adad-nirari was able to conquer the entire stretch of northern Mesopotamia that had once been the homeland of the Mitannian kings, and to sack their capital city Washukanni. However, Shalmaneser found it necessary to reimpose Assyrian control over the same area, and whereas his father had allowed the surviving Mitannian king to remain as a vassal, in the old tradition, documents excavated at Tell Fakhariyah on the Syrian frontier with Turkey show the presence there of the Assyrian language and persons with pure Assyrian names, indicating an attempt to install direct Assyrian administration this far west. Business and administrative records found at Tell Al-Rimah, to the west of Nineveh, also reveal that by the reign of Shalmaneser true Assyrian families were resident there, combining their official status as administrators of the district with their private commercial activities. This is a characteristic trait of the whole Middle Assyrian period, that the traditions of commercial liability were adapted to the needs of government administration, much as under the Ur III kings, and the units of government, from small provincial centers to the "ministries" in the capital city, were entrusted to "houses" which are almost surely the direct descendants of the family firms which were organizing the trade with Anatolia some 500 years before.

Southwards the fortunes of Assyria were largely dependent on the energy of the Babylonian king. Assur itself had probably never entirely severed its relations with the southern metropolis, and she undoubtedly felt Babylon to be her cultural superior, with its age-old scribal traditions and expertise in sciences and the pseudo-sciences like omen reading and the performing of rituals, which were equally highly esteemed. Possibly the Kassite kings with their anxiety to be seen as heirs to these old traditions remembered also the days when Hammurapi's rule stretched as far north as Nineveh, and certainly their ambitions clashed with Assyria's in the strip of land between the Tigris and the Zagros hills. Battles were as a rule fought in this area, sometimes near the Diyala river when Assyria was in the ascendant, sometimes near the Zabs in times of Babylonian strength, and a corresponding area of dispute lay south of Mari on the Euphrates. It was during the reign of Tukulti-ninurta I that one of the exceptions to this rule took place.

The Babylonian king Kashtiliash crossed a frontier line agreed between his predecessor and Adad-nirari I, reoccupying Arrapha and the city of Rapiqu on the Euphrates. The Assyrian king retaliated by defeating Kashtiliash and then capturing Babylon itself and reducing virtually the entire country as far as the sea. He then assumed the throne of Babylon himself, and left governors to administer the country. However, this was not a successful venture, and after seven years the country rid itself of Assyrian domination for several centuries to come. Tukulti-Ninurta himself seems to have become estranged from his home city, perhaps because of dissatisfaction with his policies, and built himself a new capital across the river and a little upstream from Assur, naming it Port-Tukulti-

Reconstructed drawing of a wall painting in the new palace of Tukulti-ninurta (surviving portions shown with original colors).

Tiglath-pileser I carved on the natural rock beside his cuneiform inscription on the upper Tigris near Diyarbakir, Turkey.

Ninurta. Here in due course he was murdered by one of his sons in a palace conspiracy.

Assyrian recession. For almost a century Assyria suffered a recession, but she did not experience opposition from the other older powers of the Near East – Egypt, Babylon, Elam and the Hittites – since they were engrossed in their own problems. A momentary blaze of glory attended the reign of Tiglath-pileser I (1115–1077 BC): he restored Assyrian control over all the lands east of the Euphrates, and marched north through the mountain passes to intimidate the unruly inhabitants – even reaching the lands north of Lake Van where he left his image on a rock. His most cherished achievement was probably his march to the Mediterranean, where he received the submission of the major Phoenician cities like Byblos and Sidon, and sailed for a short distance down the seacoast. He even claims to have caught a large fish (perhaps a swordfish), but undoubtedly the most cogent motive for his expedition was neither political nor military, but to fell cedars on Mount Lebanon for the roof of the new temple he was building at Assur to the gods Anu and Adad. However, perhaps the most significant point about this excursion of his to the sea is that he seems to have encountered no opposition from local rulers, showing that not only were the Hittites and the Egyptians preoccupied, but even their erstwhile vassals such as Aleppo have vanished from the scene as political entities. This can confidently be attributed to the arrival of the Aramaeans.

The Aramaeans were not a new force in the days of Tiglath-pileser: already in the reign of Adad-nirari or his son the Hittite king Hattusilis III is forced to explain to Kadashman-Enlil of Babylonia that he had given up sending messengers because of the hostility of the Aramaeans who controlled the land routes. Earlier still, the Kassite king complains bitterly to his Egyptian counterpart of the dangers from Aramaean nomads (called Sutu) who were infesting the desert tracks between their two lands. The seriousness of the threat is indeed apparent from Tiglath-pileser I's own inscriptions: he was forced to cross the Euphrates as many as 28 times in pursuit of the elusive Aramaean nomads, and on one occasion he describes how he marched from as far west as Tadmor (Palmyra) in the desert on the route to Damascus, to Ana on the middle Euphrates, and then downriver as far as the town of Rapiqu on the Babylonian border. The mobility of the nomads, combined with their specialist knowledge and habituation to the inhospitable thirsty land across the river made it virtually impossible to inflict punishment on them or prevent future raids.

Babylonia and Assyria were equally open to incursions on their southwestern flanks, and the only possible effect of such pressure is in the long run the amalgamation of the settled and the nomad populations. Despite his efforts, therefore, it is no surprise to find – from a less angled chronicle text – that by the end of Tiglath-pileser's long reign the Aramaeans had even penetrated to the heart of Assyria, having crossed the Tigris and occupied the districts of Nineveh and Kilizi. They were no doubt impelled by the drought conditions which deny grazing to their animals whilst causing famine in Assyria itself, but pressure of this kind continued during the next reigns, and although Assyria did not suffer from the hostility of her old rivals to the south and west, who were suffering equally under the invasion of the nomads and/or the "Sea Peoples" in the Mediterranean lands, the disorder which followed reduced Assyria to a condition she had not known since she was a minor vassal of the Mitannian empire.

Relief from the Northwest Palace of Assur-nasir-apli at Nimrud, showing the king and his attendants. British Museum.

As invariably happens when the country was thrown into political chaos, our sources for the history of the time dry up, and the events of this dark age can only be reconstructed in retrospect. When the curtain rises once more, we find on the Assyrian stage a new succession of energetic kings, reasserting their authority over lands they considered Assyrian. Assur-dan and Adad-nirari II reestablished a firm hold on the heartlands of Assyria, and Tukulti-ninurta II (890–884 BC), while not expanding the frontier greatly, has left us an invaluable account of a march he made to "beat the bounds" of his kingdom. He marched from the capital Assur down the dry bed of the Wadi Tharthar – suffering torments of thirst on the way – until he rejoined the Tigris at about the level of modern

Samarra. From there he reached the site of the old Kassite capital Dur-Kurigalzu, near modern Baghdad, and crossed to the Euphrates at Sippar. He marched upstream to the confluence of the Habur and Euphrates, and then up the Habur towards the hills and back to his own country from the northwest. The value of this account is that it shows how Assyria's borders were still restricted, and that of the tribes or rulers he encountered en route virtually every one is immediately betrayed by his name as an Aramaean.

Clearly the incursions which had caused Tiglath-pileser so much trouble had intensified, and in due course the fresh wave of nomads had wrested from Assyria much of her former possessions, and were now settled there, or at least in the process of settling. Nor was this process confined to Assyria: Adad-nirari II, Tukulti-ninurta's father, had met strong opposition from a group of Aramaean tribes occupying the lands around Nisibin and Guzana, on the headwaters of the River Habur, but when his grandson Assur-nasir-apli II and great-grandson Shalmaneser III pushed the boundaries of Assyria out to their old limits, they encountered much stiffer Aramaean opposition, centered at first around Amedi (Diyarbakir) and Til-Barsip (Tell Ahmar on the Euphrates), but later organized from Damascus where a strong local dynasty was established. The further west we look the more firmly entrenched we find the Aramaean dynasties, and it is remarkable that in spite of its weakness Assyria had survived the incursions sufficiently to weather the storm and avoid a complete "takeover" such as had happened in the west, or indeed in the Assyrian area at the time of the Amorite incursions 1,000 years before.

Assyria returns to power. Except that the pressure from the nomads was temporarily somewhat relieved, Assyria's strategic position had not much changed. Like their Middle Assyrian forebears, Assur-nasir-apli and Shalmaneser found that the defense of their borders involved them in continuous unrewarding expeditions into the mountains to the north and east, and in long marches across northern Mesopotamia to the Euphrates and beyond. On the other hand, Babylonia was still weak and offered no serious rivalry, and it soon became clear that the old capital of Assur was awkwardly placed to act as the center of government for the new Assyria. Consequently Assur-nasir-apli decided to establish a new capital, and his choice fell upon Kalhu, modern Nimrud, an old town represented by a tell on the east bank of the Tigris between Nineveh and the confluence of the Upper Zab. Here he built a palace on the edge of the mound overlooking the river, and embellished it with unparalleled splendor. The size of the building alone must have made it a considerable achievement, but above the main arched gateways were installed multi-colored designs in glazed bricks, and the walls of the main palace suites were lined with huge slabs of the soft local limestone carved in low relief with the

Top: supper time on one of Assur-nasir-apli's campaigns; the bottom right quarter probably shows a bread oven. British Museum.

Above: detail from the "Black Obelisk" of Shalmaneser III, showing the king retrieving the tribute of Jehu, British Museum.

figures of mythical winged creatures or scenes illustrating the king's own triumphs in war or the hunt for the benefit of his visitors. Perhaps most impressive of all were the giant guardian beasts which flanked the main gateways, and, like their predecessors in Babylonian temples, were intended to ward off any evil influences.

The completion of this project did not go unmarked. The king had a stele carved with a long inscription commemorating the inauguration of his transformed capital. After describing the beauties of his new palace with its seven suites each in a different variety of wood, he records the digging of a canal from the River Zab which brought water across country to supply the gardens of the

View from the acropolis at Van, ancient Turushpa, the capital of the Urartian kings, looking south. In the foreground a cuneiform inscription on the smoothed rock face; below, the mosque and minaret of the medieval city, now deserted.

royal city, in which he planted not only fruit trees and vines, but also a great variety of strange plants which he had gathered in the course of his foreign campaigns. The completion of the palace was celebrated by a huge banquet, whose menu ranged from 14,000 sheep and 10,000 skins of wine to all kinds of spice and large consignments of nuts and dates. Guests at the feast were not only the 16,000 inhabitants of Kalhu and 1,500 royal officials, but "47,074 men and women from the length and breadth of my country" and also "5,000 envoys from the lands of Suhu, Hindana, Patina, Hattu, Tyre, Sidon, Gurgum, Melid, Hubushkia, Kummu and Musasir," making a grand total of 69,574, to all of whom the king dispensed food and drink for ten days, and then sent them home washed, anointed and well contented.

If in the course of this inscription Assur-nasir-apli indulged in a certain amount of preening, it is not without justification. The enumeration of friendly, if not actual subject, states shows how he had built up a ring of protective buffer states and much expanded Assyria's effective borders. In 859 BC he became the first Assyrian king since Tiglath-pileser's successor Assur-bel-kala to reach the Mediterranean, and in his inscriptions he proudly proclaims that he had conquered "from the Tigris to Mount Lebanon and the Great Sea." Nevertheless, a single victorious expedition could not secure permanently the loyalty of the conquered lands, and from his first year Assur-nasir-apli's son Shalmaneser III was engaged in a continuous series of annual campaigns. In spite of not inconsiderable military operations in the mountains to the north, and interventions in the politics of Babylonia and her neighbors, the major effort had again to be devoted to the west. Here Shalmaneser had first to ensure Assyrian control of the area east of the Euphrates, by removing the opposition of Til-Barsip and the ancient city-state of Carchemish. This done, he engaged in a bitter struggle for control of the north Syrian area, which, as in the Amarna Age, remained the key to the trade-rich Phoenician coast and gave access to the much-prized cedar forests on Mount Lebanon and the Amanus range.

His opponents were a hotchpotch of petty states, some of which had preserved the memory, the hieroglyphic script and sometimes even the royal names of the Hittite empire (and are hence referred to as Neo-Hittite), and some of which were similar states ruled by the new Aramaean dynasties largely responsible for that empire's collapse. They were led by Adad-idri of Damascus (Aramaean) and Irhuleni of Hamath (Neo-Hittite), but the alliance included contingents from Israel, Cilicia and even an early Arab tribe. In the battle of Qarqar (853 BC) Shalmaneser inflicted heavy losses on their armies, but since he failed to take Damascus or follow up the victory in other ways, he can hardly have achieved his objective. The same was true of his next major effort in 845 BC when he held a general call-up in Assyria and raised an army of 120,000 men, but once more failed to take Damascus. It was not until the shifting politics of the Syrian area had isolated Damascus under its new king from its former chief allies, Hamath and Israel, that Shalmaneser succeeded in confining their king Hazael in the city of Damascus and receiving his submission. This led to the capitulation of Tyre and Sidon, now the two major trading cities of Phoenicia, and of Jehu "the Israelite." Subsequent campaigns of Shalmaneser in Cilicia and the Taurus mountains show that his authority was respected in north Syria, through which his armies had to pass, but it was not in fact until the reign of his grandson Adad-nirari III that Damascus was entered by an Assyrian army, and although the supremacy of Assyria was

generally acknowledged by the regular payment of tribute, the lands west of the Euphrates were still far from incorporated in an Assyrian empire.

Urartu and Assyria. In her western campaigns Assyria had advanced consistently against determined opposition from local rulers, because the small size of their kingdoms made it easy for her to pick them off one by one. The temporary coalition of Damascus and Hamath had shown what could be achieved by joining forces, but local rivalries were too intense for this to last, and most states took the easy way out and sided with the conquerors. In the north the situation was quite different. Here during the 9th century BC there emerged a vigorous kingdom called Urartu (Biblical Ararat), which welded together the mountain populations into a military force to match Assyria. The name Urartu is already attested as one of the predominantly Hurrian principalities encountered by Shalmaneser I in the 13th century, and again by Adad-nirari II, but its preeminence seems to date only from the middle of the 9th century. The kings of Urartu enjoyed the advantages of a mountain state – difficult approaches, with impregnable fortresses – combined with plenty of lush grassland which served for agriculture but in particular for the breeding of horses, in which they excelled. With their capital at most times on the eastern shore of Lake Van, they controlled the heads of the valleys leading down to the plains of Mesopotamia, where Assyria was unchallenged, and even in the days of Sennacherib the "border of Urartu" was acknowledged by the Assyrians themselves to be within 60 miles of Nineveh.

It seems that at least a tacit recognition must have existed between the two powers under which, except on rare occasions, the mountain barrier was respected as a demarcation of the two empires. However, Urartu during the 8th century BC expanded not only to the north, where the cities of Erebuni and Karmir Blur have been revealed by excavators in Soviet Armenia, but to the east and west. At the height of their expansion they certainly controlled westwards as far as the Euphrates at Malatya (Melid) and pushed down south past Lake Urmia into the Iranian plateau, thus forming a semicircle which hemmed in Assyrian ambitions and threatened to cut off her access to the Mediterranean. In his early years Shalmaneser III had marched twice to Lake Van itself, but that his opponent Arame of Urartu was by no means defeated appears from later campaigns in the north which avoided the Urartian homeland proper. Records for the early 8th century in Assyria are very scarce, which usually implies that the kings had no military triumphs to put on record, and since we know that there were confrontations with Urartu during these years, it is very likely that the Assyrians had the worst of them. This is certainly the case in the 760s and 750s: King Argistis of Urartu records victories over the Assyrians, and his son Sarduris III refers to a defeat of Assur-nirari V. This Assyrian king has left us fragments of a treaty he concluded with the Aramaean king of Arpad, Mati'el, but a few years later the same Mati'el reappears as one of the allies of Sarduris, and we may deduce that Assyrian prestige in the area was at a low ebb.

On his campaigns in the north Shalmaneser visited the tunnel where the Tigris flows for two miles underground (see *above*), and carved his inscription next to the figure of Tiglath-pileser I.

On his bronze gates found at Balawat (*opposite*) he shows a sculptor carving his own relief in the rock, while soldiers wade with torches exploring the tunnel. British Museum.

The situation at home was not much better. It is true that as far as we can tell Assyrian territory proper was never seriously at risk, but Assur-nirari V stayed at home for most of his reign, and in the time of his predecessor the land had suffered from plague and rebellion. Finally in 745 BC a revolution at the capital city of Kalhu threw up a new king who must be acknowledged as the creator of the Assyria which became the mistress of an empire on a scale the world had never before known. Tiglath-pileser III may have taken his name in direct imitation of his illustrious ancestor, and the mode of his accession coupled with his consistent failure to cite his genealogy has led scholars to surmise that he did not come from the direct royal line, although in one inscription he does specifically claim to be the son of Adad-nirari III. Either way, any irregularities in his accession were no doubt soon overshadowed by his spectacular achievements as king. Unquestionably the success of his foreign policy was the result of widespread reform within the country, although details are lacking. In a system inherited from Middle Assyrian days the government of provinces had always been entrusted to old-established Assyrian families, who no doubt administered the province as a profit-making concern and might even pass the office on from father to son. Inevitably with a weak monarch the governors were tempted to arrogate to themselves excessive power, and this is indeed what had happened during the first half of the 8th century BC, from the reign of Adad-nirari III onwards. Of the dangers of this system Tiglath-pileser was obviously well aware, and he removed them in one blow by breaking up the traditional but unwieldy provinces into smaller but more managable units which he placed under high officers of state.

The campaigns of Tiglath-pileser. With this reform completed, and no doubt equally radical innovations in both the army and the administrative system, Tiglath-pileser was ready to undertake the restoration of Assyria's fortunes abroad. In this field too he was an innovator: he cast aside the age-old practice of leaving local rulers as vassals to administer their own territory and expecting military assistance and tribute as the main tokens of their submission, and instead his inscriptions continuously tell us that he "appointed an official as governor over them" or "incorporated that land into Assyrian territory." This he was able to do as a result of his reorganized provincial system, and the vindication of his policy of direct rule was at once apparent. By the end of his reign he could claim to have destroyed entirely any territorial ambitions of Urartu in the west, and he had incorporated into Assyria large stretches of northern Syria up as far as the sea. A local ruler was left in charge of the important – but much reduced – state of Hamath, but after a stubborn resistance Damascus had fallen to the Assyrian armies for the last time, and was also made a part of Assyria. In his campaigns Tiglath-pileser penetrated as far down the coast as Gaza,

The valley of the Lesser Habur, north Iraq, scene of one of Tiglath-pileser's battles on the Urartian border.

and although he stopped short of annexing the cities of Phoenicia and Palestine, they inevitably paid him tribute and acknowledged his supremacy. We have an interesting letter sent to the king from an official appointed by him to supervise the activities of the Phoenician cities; it is on a cuneiform tablet found at Kalhu (Nimrud), and reports on his relations with the people of Tyre and Sidon, and on his efforts to exact taxes from them. He has also instituted an early form of political boycott against Assyria's current enemies, since he controls the trade in the valuable cedars of Mount Lebanon, and reports that he has instructed the Phoenicians to "bring down the wood, and conduct your business with it, but do not sell it to the Egyptians or the Palestinians, or I shall not allow you up into the mountain."

That Tiglath-pileser's motives for conquest were not simply those of a megalomaniac shows quite clearly in his dealings with Babylon. Over the years the conditions in Babylonia seem to have gone from bad to worse: Chaldaean tribes from the desert had apportioned the open country between them, and only isolated cities like Babylon and Cuthah in the north seem to have perpetuated the ancient traditions of the land. One of Tiglath-pileser's first actions was to march down the Tigris and attack the unruly tribes which infested the lower reaches of the river, for which he gained the gratitude of the city dwellers. He was content, however, to leave the kingship of Babylon in the hands of its existing incumbent, Nabu-nasir, and it was not until his death that fresh trouble drew Tiglath-pileser back south. The son of Nabu-nasir had been killed in a coup, and an effort was made to install a Chaldaean usurper called Ukin-zer. Although the Assyrians were able to flush him out of Babylon, he took refuge in the capital of his own dynasty, Shapia, which lay somewhere further to the south, and was obviously well fortified, since he was able to outlast a siege. In the meantime, Babylon was left without a king, and in 729 and 728 BC Tiglath-pileser decided to perform the traditional ritual of "taking the hands of Bel" himself, and thereby proclaimed himself the first Assyrian "king of Babylon" since the ill-fated attempt of Tukulti-ninurta I some 500 years before. Only on this occasion the Assyrian was evidently welcome to the urban population, as a strong deliverer from the destructive tribesmen who were threatening their very existence.

Sargon II. The success of Tiglath-pileser's "new Assyria" inevitably dictated the policies of the kings who followed. Although the old client-king relationship may have been preferred wherever feasible, it became increasingly apparent that the only trustworthy vassal was a dead one, and like the Romans, the Assyrian kings were forced to abolish the local dynasties and progressively annex the conquered territories, ruling them with the efficient civil and military organization made available to them by Tiglath-pileser's reforms. Of his own son, Shalmaneser V,

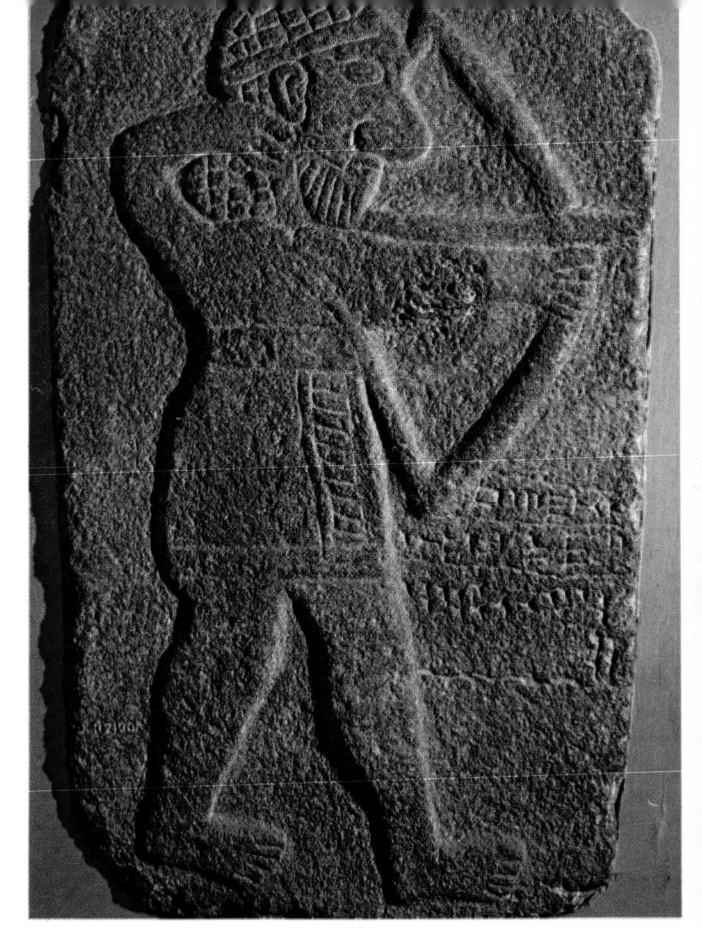

Relief from the palace of Kapara, an Aramaean ruler of Guzana (Tell Halaf), showing in crude style an archer (9th century BC?). British Museum.

almost nothing is known except that during his short reign he began a protracted siege of the Israelite capital, Samaria. It was however only after his death, in 722 BC, that the city fell, and the new king Sargon immediately gave proof of his adherence to the new policies by annexing the land of Samaria and – again following Tiglath-pileser's example – deporting a large body of the population to other parts of the empire. This event is recorded by the Bible as well as by the official Assyrian annalists, and we learn from it that the Israelites were resettled in Gozan (= Guzana, modern Tell Halaf), in Media and in Halah. The first two places are immediately understandable: Guzana was in a fertile area where the expansion of agriculture into lands deserted since the Aramaean incursions was extremely profitable, and Media was almost certainly an area whose own population had been deported, exchanges of this kind with the other end of the empire being quite common. The mention of Halah is more puzzling, since this was a district in the very center of Assyria, close to Nineveh, but the explanation is that it was precisely here, at the foot of the first range of hills bordering the Assyrian plains, that the new king planned to build himself a new capital to be called Dur-Sharruken ("Fort Sargon"). Since the days of Assur-nasir-apli II the kings had lived at his city of Kalhu, and Sargon himself used, and indeed restored, the old Northwest Palace near the ziggurrat. Why he should have elected to move is not known: it may have been for

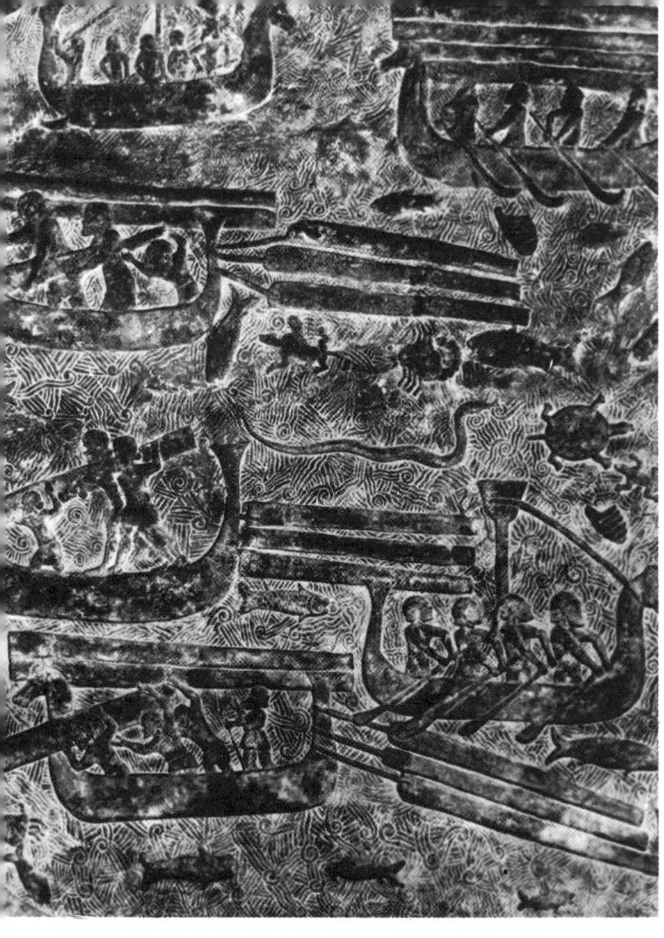

Above: one of the great winged bulls from Sargon's palace at Khorsabad, brought home by Botta to the Louvre. Note the artistic convention which gives the animal five legs!

Above left: relief from the palace of Sargon at Khorsabad: sailors manhandling timber onto their boats, a scene off the Phoenician coast. Louvre.

Below left: some 500 miles further east: the deported populations haul the timber to be used for the roofing of Sargon's new capital at Khorsabad, where this relief was found. Louvre.

personal reasons, since there are no very obvious geographical or strategic grounds for the change, and it is certain from the loving tones in which he describes the work that it was a project near to his heart.

With a proper concern to appear a just ruler, he relates how the existing occupants of the site were either given the full price in silver for their "compulsorily purchased" property, or offered fields elsewhere in compensation. Then began the work of building, for which he made use of deported prisoners of war – no doubt among them the Israelites from Samaria – and levies from the provinces. Two major projects had to be completed: the great fortification wall, planned to be 16,283 cubits in length – a figure somehow mysteriously related to the writing of Sargon's own name – and with eight gateways, and on the west side of the enclosed area a huge platform on which stood the king's own palace complete with temples and subsidiary residences for members of the royal family and high officials of state. The undertaking took some ten years to complete: the first foundations were laid as early as 717 BC, but it was not until 707 BC that the "gods of Dur-Sharruken entered their temples," and Sargon himself, together with "the princes of all countries, my provincial governors, the overseers and supervisors, nobles and eunuchs, and the elders of Assyria took up residence in my palace and held a festival." However, despite all the lavish effort, Dur-Sharruken was not fated to be a success. The population, by Sargon's own account, was a motley collection of deportees from all countries, and had to be assigned special Assyrian officials "to teach them how to reverence god and king;" it seems very unlikely that more than a fraction of the vast projected city was ever inhabited for any length of time, and it certainly never functioned as the thriving metropolis Sargon must have dreamed of. Whether it would have been a different story if he had lived – as with Assur-nasir-apli's Kalhu – we cannot tell; but as it turned out this magnificent creation, which through Botta's discoveries first revealed to the modern world the glories of ancient Assyria, was ironically enough abandoned on the death of its creator almost before it had been completed.

Like Tiglath-pileser, Sargon is reticent about his ancestry, and it is quite likely that both kings adopted a throne name at their accession. With his choice of Sargon, the new king proclaimed the scope of his ambition, and despite his early death in battle, he almost lived up to the name. Assyria under Sargon stretched from Palestine in the southwest to the principalities in the Taurus and even Malatya (Melid) on the Anatolian plateau, eastwards into the Iranian highlands and into traditionally Elamite territory further south. One event in particular must have given Sargon special satisfaction, and that was his encounter with Urartu, the only power of the day that could rival Assyria in military reputation and potential. Since Tiglath-pileser's defeat of Sarduris in the west the two empires seem to have observed a truce, and it was not until Sargon's time that there came another serious confrontation, characteristically not on their mutual border but sparked off in the east where the two powers jostled each other and competed for the allegiance of those kings who still clung to some sort of independence. The critical area seems to have been the Iranian plateau south of Lake Urmia, which was occupied by a population known to the Assyrians as Mannaeans. Here in 716 BC Sargon had been obliged to mount an expedition in support of an Assyrian vassal, and the next year too he had crossed the Zagros ranges to secure the borders of this state and even to raid across the Urartian frontier. In 714 BC, therefore, he decided to punish the two states of Andia and Zikirtu, which had been harassing his vassal. He reached the area from the south, and after a royal welcome from his faithful vassals, who had "heaped up supplies of flour and wine for the feeding of my troops, like my eunuchs, the governors of the provinces of Assyria," he proceeded to exact vengeance on Zikirtu and Andia.

At this stage, however, an unforeseen factor interrupted his plans: the king of Urartu himself sent a message to say that he had come to his vassal's aid and to challenge Sargon to battle. Despite his enemy's advantageous position on a mountain, and the tired condition of his own army, Sargon attacked and routed the Urartian forces, and King Rusas "to save his life abandoned his chariot and mounting a mare fled in full view of his army." The genuineness of this victory is confirmed by later events. Sargon gave up his original plan, which was to march against Andia and Zikirtu, and advanced unopposed through Urartu proper. He seems to have made his way northwards to the shores of Lake Urmia, and then up its west side, and in the description of his campaign, which is cast in the form of a letter to the national god, Assur, he paints a uniquely vivid picture of the country he passed through. First came a province where the "inhabitants had no peers throughout Urartu for their skill in horses," and to whom all the horses in the land were brought to be broken in and trained for battle – to "advance, to wheel and to retreat." Then he ravaged the town of Ulhu, which was remarkable for its system of irrigation which Rusas had himself devised, and which must have been like the *qanat* system still in use today, whereby water from the foot of the hills is led out underground by tunnels reached by deep well-shafts sunk at intervals, to settlements far out in the plain. These marvelous irrigation systems he entirely destroyed, and indeed wherever he went he describes the sacking of the fortresses and cutting down of the trees, whilst he allowed his troops to open the granaries and wine stores and enjoy the traditional rewards of the victor.

Nevertheless, although at the end of the campaign he could claim "430 towns in seven provinces" conquered, he never penetrated to the center of the country, and even the heavily fortified cities he captured were evidently of lesser importance. This appears vividly from the remainder of his campaign, for on his return march Sargon decided to teach a lesson to the king of Musasir, a small mountain state uncomfortably sandwiched between Assyria and Urartu. Somewhat unwisely their king Urzana had omitted to send a mission to congratulate Sargon on his triumphs, and on his way home Sargon took a small task force over difficult mountain terrain and sacked the city of Musasir. Urzana and his family were taken captive, Sargon occupied the royal palace, and the treasures of palace and temple were taken as booty to Assyria.

Sargon's success against Urartu, unplanned though it was, came at an opportune moment. One of the most troublesome areas of the Near Eastern world during the first decade of Sargon's reign was the agglomeration of petty states in the Taurus mountains. They were in a difficult situation, with the Urartians to their east, the Assyrians pushing up against them from the south, and now to their west the rising power of the Phrygians. The complexity of the politics is reflected in Sargon's inscriptions. From them we learn of Pisiris, the vassal ruler of Carchemish, who in 717 BC concluded a rebellious

Above: rock relief at Ivriz, near Ereğli in Turkey: the god of vegetation receives the adoration of King Warpalawas, one of the Neo-Hittite kings mentioned in Sargon's correspondence with Midas.

Right: site of a dam built by Sennacherib on the River Khosr just northeast of Nineveh to divert its waters into an artificial swamp.

alliance with the Phrygian king, none other than the Midas of Classical legend. This attempt to revive the glories of the great days of the Hittite empire was short-lived, and Carchemish was taken and finally absorbed as a new province in the Assyrian empire.

However, unrest continued in the Taurus, and after several attempts to preserve the existing local dynasties Sargon eventually gave up the struggle and annexed most of these small states, even as far across the Taurus as Niğde in Turkey. Thinking, perhaps, that he had settled the area for a while, he turned his attention to Babylonia, and it must have been while he was there that the Assyrian governor of Que (Classical Cilicia) wrote to him, to report on a surprising turn of events: Midas of Phrygia had handed over to him the members of a secret embassy from one of the ostensible Assyrian vassal kings in the Cilician area to the king of Urartu. With this act, Midas had evidently sued for friendly relations with Assyria, and in Sargon's reply, a copy of which was preserved in the Kalhu archives, he greets the news with jubilation, that "in the midst of battle the Phrygian has become our ally." This is eloquent witness of the fact that the Assyrians were not bloodthirsty savages with insatiable territorial greed, but, like the Romans, harassed on all sides and unable to display any weakness for fear of repercussions.

Sargon's death is something of a mystery. The only direct reference to it is the factual statement that the king "went against Eshpai, the Kulummaean, he was killed, and the camp of the king of Assyria . . . [broken]." We do not know who or where Eshpai and the Kulummaeans were, and although Sargon's son and successor Sennacherib does make veiled allusions to the event, it is only to deplore the offense which must have been committed against the gods by his father, since this was the only possible explanation for such a disaster. However, the enemy, who were probably only a northern tribe caught up in a general movement, like the Cimmerians who are first mentioned in letters to Sargon describing a defeat suffered at their hands by Urartu, did not follow up their victory, and Assyria rallied immediately under Sennacherib, who had already gained experience as a kind of military viceroy along the northern borders.

Sennacherib and the fall of Babylon. In fact Sargon had left Assyria so strong and well governed that for his first two years Sennacherib was able to devote his energies to the rebuilding of Nineveh, which he had selected as his capital city. Although always of major importance, this ancient foundation had never been the seat of the Assyrian kings, but now Sennacherib marked out a vast area north and south of the old city mound (today known as Kouyunjik), and had it enclosed by a massive brick wall faced with ashlar masonry and pierced by huge towered gateways. To the west extra protection was afforded by the River Tigris, and special water-gates were built on this side, while another diverted watercourse flowed at the foot of the north wall of the new city. The vulnerable part of the defenses was felt to be the east side, and here, beyond an old wadi bed, another massive line of fortifications was built. On the ancient mound in the center an artificial terrace was prepared, and on it a new royal palace erected with the labor of prisoners of war. The walls of the palace were lined with sculptured slabs of stone illustrating Sennacherib's campaigns in a new and more lively artistic idiom, in which isolated incidents were replaced by scenes portraying a continuous story, and the battles and sieges take place against a background of mountain or marsh. Nor did the artists omit to record domestic events, in particular the building of the palace itself, with realistic scenes of huge bull-figures being loaded onto rafts or dragged into position on rollers, the whole operation directed by the king in person.

So great a city also needed a reliable water supply, both pure water for drinking and in particular for irrigation. It seems to have been a constant preoccupation of Sennacherib's throughout his reign, and he tapped sources of water from an arc of hills enclosing Nineveh to the north, leaving a record of his activities in sculptures and inscriptions at the head of each major canal. In one case his canal ran across a seasonal wadi, and his engineers solved this with a broad paved aqueduct with specially designed boat-shaped piers, while elsewhere the canals had to be carved out of the solid rock, complete with sluices and escape channels.

Sennacherib's first military campaign as king was against Babylonia, where an anti-Assyrian coalition was under the leadership of a certain Marduk-apla-iddina. This man, who was sheikh of the Chaldaean tribe of Bit-Iakin, had seized the kingship of Babylon immediately after Sargon's accession to the Assyrian throne in 722 BC, and had been left in control of the south for ten years. Then in 710–708 BC Sargon had spent two years in Babylonia, and after defeating an alliance which included the Elamite king, had pardoned Marduk-apla-iddina and left him as ruler of the southern "Sea-Land" while he himself "took the hands of Bel" and so assumed the direct rule of Babylon. This arrangement rather surprisingly worked, but apparently Marduk-apla-iddina's loyalty to Sargon did not extend to his son, and immediately after Sennacherib's accession a new revolt was planned. Possibly nothing would have come of it, had Sennacherib shown a personal interest in Babylonian affairs, but for two years he did nothing to assert his authority, and this may have been a fatal mistake, since from now on the politics of Babylonia are one of the major headaches of the Assyrian kings.

The problem was not an easy one: on the one hand Babylonia stood for traditional Mesopotamian civilization, with the ancient cities and scribal schools of Babylon, Nippur and so on, and the Assyrians acknowledged Babylonian culture and the chief Babylonian deity, Marduk; but on the other hand outside the towns the country was overrun by Chaldaean tribes with little or no political cohesion, and small sympathy with the urban populations. Control of the southern part of the area, the "Sea-Land," was normally safely in the hands of the Chaldaeans, and if Assyria wished to keep order here

Above: Sennacherib's rock reliefs at Bavian mark the head of his canal to Nineveh; note fallen sculptures in foreground.

Opposite: rock relief at Maltai, north of Nineveh, perhaps carved by Sennacherib to commemorate an irrigation project. The king (right) follows behind the gods, mounted on animals.

herself, it was essential first to rule the north, from the capital, Babylon. But to hold the kingship of Babylon involved the ritual of "taking the hands of Bel" (i.e. of the statue of Marduk in the main temple called Esagila), and this required the physical presence of the king at at least one annual ceremony, which was inconvenient for an Assyrian king whose attentions might easily be claimed elsewhere in his vast domain. This may at least in part explain Sennacherib's reluctance to take the title himself, and must account for the various attempts to find a suitable substitute to occupy the throne of Babylon during the next half-century.

The complexity of the situation is emphasized by the fact that it was not Marduk-apla-iddina but a local Babylonian nominee who first risked Assyrian displeasure and occupied the throne. This must have forced Marduk-apla-iddina's hand, and in 703 BC he moved up from his base in the Sea-Land, where he was still acknowledged as a king, and seized the kingship. Within the year Sennacherib responded to the threat and moved to reassert his authority; he marched down the Tigris, and after defeating an Elamite army at the north Babylonian city of Cuthah, forced the withdrawal of Marduk-apla-iddina from Babylon: he had brought the Elamites in as his allies, and as on a previous occasion was able to leave them to bear the brunt of the battle. It is interesting to learn from the Bible that he had also made advances across the Arabian desert to the cities of Palestine, including King Hezekiah of Judah – in an effort to create a diversion which would draw the Assyrian army off into the far west.

After Marduk-apla-iddina's withdrawal Sennacherib placed on the Babylonian throne a Babylonian-born noble called Bel-ibni. This did not prove successful, and in 700 BC, during a fresh campaign against Marduk-apla-iddina in which he was finally forced to flee to Elam, Bel-ibni was replaced by Sennacherib's own son, Assur-nadin-shumi, who ruled as king of Babylon until 694 BC. Then renewed trouble in the south – although Marduk-apla-iddina was probably dead, his sons and other family remained active – brought Sennacherib back there with a major expedition assisted with ships brought from the Mediterranean by the skill of trained sailors from Tyre, Sidon and Cyprus (Yadnana). Unfortunately no sooner had the flotilla passed down the Euphrates on its way to the marshlands, than the new Elamite king, called Hallushu, raided the city of Sippar and contrived to capture Assur-nadin-shumi, who was carried off to his death in Elam. A new king, of Babylonian origin, was installed, and reigned for as long as 18 months, but he was defeated near Nippur by the Assyrian army on its long-overdue return from the marshes.

Even now Sennacherib did not take the throne of Babylon himself, and he seems to have shelved the problem since a Chaldaean sheikh stepped into the gap. This state of affairs obviously could not last, and in 691 BC Sennacherib met the combined forces of a new Babylon-Elam alliance on the east bank of the Tigris at the place called Halule, where a major battle ensued: the Assyrian annalist describes it in gory detail – "I [Sennacherib] slit their throats like sheep and cut off their precious lives like a thread; I made their blood stream across the wide earth like the floods from a seasonal rainstorm; my fleet steeds plunged into their gore like a river, and the wheels of my battle chariot were bathed in their blood and dung." Despite the undoubted savagery of the fighting no conclusive result seems to have been reached, but a couple of years later the Elamite king suffered a stroke, and the Babylonian Mushezib-Marduk thus lost his chief ally. Sennacherib took his chance, and after a long siege the city of Babylon fell; the Assyrian king's patience was apparently exhausted, and his soldiery was allowed to sack the famous city, while the statue of Marduk itself was removed from the temple of Esagila and brought to Assur.

The burden of empire. During the last century and a half of the Assyrian empire no one would have denied the superiority of the Assyrian armies, and yet to maintain this reputation continuous fighting was needed. No minor power would venture into opposition to Assyrian might on its own, nor would a major power voluntarily have provoked a confrontation. Inevitably then, the main trouble spots were in the south, where the Chaldaean tribes found support for their aspirations in the age-old reputation of Babylon and the present strength of Elam, and in the far west, where the proximity of Egypt was a constant enticement to the Palestinian princelings to forget the speed with which the Assyrian could come down. However, Sennacherib succeeded in cowing most of the far southwestern states by a demonstration of force early in his reign: most, like Byblos, Ashdod, Ammon, Edom and Moab, proffered their submission before tasting the Assyrian arms, but in Ekron (called by the Assyrians Anqarruna) an anti-Assyrian party unseated the Assyrian protégé and sent him for custody to the king of Judah, Hezekiah. Unwisely Hezekiah relied for support on the king of Egypt – the proverbial "broken reed" – and although he did not actually have to open the gates of Jerusalem to the Assyrian king, he lost his territory to the pro-Assyrian local rulers, and eventually found himself obliged to send after Sennacherib to Lachish with his submission and tribute, since he had already started back for Assyria.

As a result of Sennacherib's soldiering, his son Esarhaddon (Assur-ahhe-iddina) had little trouble in the Levant area, and what trouble he had was soon disposed of. The ruler of a small Cilician state, King Sanduarri, made common cause with the new king of Sidon, Abdi-milkutti, and revolted, but Esarhaddon "trapped him like a bird in his mountain," and "in a single year [676 BC] cut off the heads of Abdi-milkutti in Teshrit [7th month] and of Sanduarri in Addar [12th month]." The stimulus for this revolt may well have been provided by Egypt, and this was certainly the case when Tyre revolted a year later. Tyre itself was safe from direct assault and was not

Above: Neo-Hittite reliefs from Kara Tepe in Cilicia, from the palace of Sanduarri; he is banqueting to the accompaniment of musicians, a coarse imitation of Assyrian scenes.

Opposite: Assyrian siege engines attacking the towers and walls of the city of Lachish, as the defenders hurl down firebrands; campaign of 700 BC (palace of Sennacherib, Kouyunjik). British Museum.

susceptible to being starved out by a long siege, since it lay on an island just off the coast, and this may have led Esarhaddon to strike at the root of the trouble and march against the pharaoh himself. After two relatively unspectacular campaigns in 675 and 674 BC Esarhaddon led his troops against the offending Tirhakah in 671 BC and the whole country fell before the Assyrians and was placed under Assyrian administration. Naturally enough a further campaign was soon needed, and it was in 669 BC on the route back to Egypt that Esarhaddon fell sick and died.

While Esarhaddon's activities in the west, and in particular his invasion of Egypt, were spectacular and successful, with hindsight we may doubt whether they were entirely wise. Trouble was looming in the north of a kind which was hard to combat. Early in his reign Esarhaddon was obliged to repulse the Cimmerians in the Taurus, far to the west, where they had reemerged after passing through the eastern highlands of Urartu, the old rival, with whom a peace was patched up in face of the common threat. In the east the situation was more dangerous still, and nourished the germs of Assyria's final demise. Following his predecessors' policies, Esarhaddon did not attempt to expand Assyrian borders eastwards; some of the petty Zagros states were administered directly by a provincial governor, but for preference a local ruler was left in control, and tied to Assyria by oaths of loyalty in the form of a "vassal treaty." As it happens, several copies of the actual treaties with these eastern princelings have survived, found dashed to pieces against the king's own throne in the Temple of Nabu, god of writing, at Kalhu (Nimrud). However, despite the strings of horrific curses which accompanied these treaties, such traditional means were no longer suited to cope with the new factor on the scene, the eruption from Central Asia of groups – like the Cimmerians and the Scythians – who moved with great speed and in large numbers.

Esarhaddon's inscriptions make great play of his victorious forays deep into the great salt deserts of the Iranian plateau, but a more realistic picture is afforded by a very different document, containing the text of a question put by the king before the sun god Shamash, for his answer through a liver omen: in one of the first links between cuneiform sources and Classical literature, the king uneasily solicits advice about the overtures made to him by a certain Bartatua, none other than the Protothyes of Herodotus – "Shamash, great lord, please make a favorable answer to the question I put to you: Will Bartatua, king of the Scythians, who has now sent his messengers to Esarhaddon, king of Assyria, about the king's daughter – when Esarhaddon, king of Assyria, has given him his daughter in marriage, will Bartatua, king of the Scythians, truthfully speak honest words of peace with Esarhaddon, king of Assyria, and keep the treaty of Esarhaddon, king of Assyria, and act in every way well towards Esarhaddon, king of Assyria? Stand in this sheep, O Shamash, and place in it a favorable sign for me."

Problems of succession. The Assyrian kings fit the traditional image of the Oriental despot in one respect: they had an extensive harem, with branches in different capitals such as Assur or Nineveh, and not unnaturally, they also had a fair number of sons. While at any one time one queen was generally accepted as the chief consort –

and like Esarhaddon's mother Naqia, might be an important personality – it was never a foregone conclusion that the eldest son of this wife would inherit the throne. Esarhaddon himself was, to quote his own words, "the little brother of my elder brothers," but was chosen by Sennacherib as heir apparent and officially inducted into the crown prince's palace. It is hardly surprising that after the assassination of his father he had to put down a rebellion by his jealous brothers before taking over power, but his own experience led him to spare no pains in his attempts to regulate the succession after his own death. His preferred son was Assur-ban-apli, but evidently Shamash-shum-ukin was felt to have an equal claim on the monarchy. His solution of this dilemma was to appoint Assur-ban-apli as heir apparent to the Assyrian throne, and to reserve for Shamash-shum-ukin the equally prestigious title of "king of Babylon," although it was made quite plain where the real power was to reside. To reinforce this decision Esarhaddon assembled his subjects and vassal kings and made them swear that "when Esarhaddon, king of Assyria, dies," they would "install Assur-ban-apli, the crown prince, on the royal throne to exercise the kingship and lordship of Assyria" over them. They also swore to see Shamash-shum-ukin safely set up in Babylon, and this was the occasion when the great treaty tablets we have already mentioned were written out.

In one sense, these elaborate precautions paid off: the

The battle with the Elamites at the River Ulai by Susa: detail. Realistic scenes of this kind first appear in the reign of Sennacherib (palace of Assur-ban-apli, Kouyunjik). British Museum.

transfer of power at his death went smoothly, and each brother was duly acknowledged as ruler of the realm allotted to him. But for Shamash-shum-ukin the situation was bound to rankle, and he counted among his subjects the actual and spiritual descendants of Marduk-apla-iddina, who had caused such ceaseless trouble in Babylonia for Sargon and Sennacherib. Eventually in 652 BC Shamash-shum-ukin declared his rebellion, in alliance with the king of Elam to the east, and the Arabs of the desert in the west. However, neither of his main allies proved quite satisfactory, and even with the infusion of Assyrian military traditions, the Babylonian armies were still no match for Assyrian troops. The end of the revolt came in 648 BC, when Babylon finally succumbed to famine after a two-year siege, and Shamash-shum-ukin cast himself into the flames of his own palace. After him the lists give a mysterious person called Kandalanu as king of Babylon, and it seems now most likely that this was a throne-name adopted by Assur-ban-apli, who therefore reverted to direct rule as the most trouble-free cure for this persistent headache.

Assyria's scholar-king. Assur-ban-apli's scribes have left us admirable accounts of his military successes, but no doubt for him, as well as for us, his greatest triumph was not with the sword but the stylus. The library collected in Nineveh by Assur-ban-apli earns him a place among the great enlightened patrons of letters, and this is a claim he would certainly have cherished. He tells us of his early training that "I solve complex mathematical reciprocals and products with no apparent solution, and I read abstruse tablets whose Sumerian is obscure and whose Akkadian is hard to construe." Although he then proceeds to describe his prowess in other fields, such as javelin throwing, and may not indeed have achieved a very high grade of scribal craft, to judge from some of the tablets written by his scholars for him, this does not undermine the fact that the finely written tablets excavated from the mound of Kouyunjik by Layard, Rassam and George Smith have brought Assyriologists the literary masterpieces of ancient Mesopotamia – the Epic of Gilgamesh and the Epic of Creation, to name but two – and provided not only the great range of cuneiform literature but also the means to decipher it, in the shape of the lexical compendia of Akkadian and Sumerian words and synonyms which now constitute the backbone of the lexicography of the two languages.

There is ample evidence that it is Assur-ban-apli himself who deserves the credit for all this. His was a deliberate attempt to assemble a corpus of cuneiform literature, and his scribes were enjoined to seek out compositions and compile them where necessary into mammoth series. We have a letter written by the king himself giving instructions for the collection of different religious and omen texts from the private and temple libraries of Borsippa, and in another letter one of his subjects reports that he is bringing from Babylon "an old tablet made by Hammurapi."

Decline and fall. It is hardly a coincidence that Assyria's greatest library should have been collected by her last great king. In both the political and the cultural worlds newer forces were gaining ground, and Assur-ban-apli's library can be seen as an attempt to enshrine the ancient cuneiform traditions which were fast giving way before the more vigorous influence of the Aramaean language and its alphabetic script. If the cultural decline could be sensed, the speed of Assyria's political demise could hardly have been foreseen. Assur-ban-apli's own reign was by no means inglorious: although he experienced the usual harassment from Arabs in the desert, and was even forced to withdraw altogether from his father's conquests in Egypt, he achieved an effective settlement of the Babylonian problem, he frequently defeated and finally almost entirely abolished the Elamite kings, and he successfully dealt with further Cimmerian threats on the far northwestern borders in response to appeals from Gyges, king of Lydia.

However, these events belong to the first part of his reign, and the silence of the later years is ominous. Assur-ban-apli himself died some time between 631 and 627 BC, and although his later years may have been troubled, it is only after his death that the scale of the trouble becomes apparent. Within less than a quarter of a century Assyria was crippled by internal strife, and in Babylonia from 626 BC onwards a sheikh called Nabopolassar gradually imposed his rule over the entire south. With a quick succession of Assyrian kings, and without detailed historical sources, the precise course of events still eludes us, but the main events are clear: in 614 BC the city of Assur was breached and sacked by a Median army in collaboration with the Babylonians, and in 612 BC Nineveh itself was taken, and the "exceeding great city of three days' journey" of Jonah met its fate at the hands of the Median-Babylonian alliance. The loss of Nineveh was decisive: in the words of the prophet Nahum, Assyria's "crowned are as the locusts, and her captains as the great grasshoppers which camp in the hedges in the cold day, but when the sun ariseth they flee away, and their place is not known where they are." As he foretells, her people were "scattered upon the mountains," and even though an Assyrian court under King Assur-uballit reconvened in Harran near the Euphrates, it was only a gesture. The rule of this last king of Assyria evaporated in 605 BC as a mere side-effect of greater events, when at the battle of Carchemish the Egyptian army – now on the Assyrian side – suffered a severe reverse at the hands of a Babylonian army led by Nabopolassar's son, Nebuchadnezzar.

The new order. The fall of the Assyrian empire was hardly sudden, but its total disappearance as a political entity must have been a trifle unexpected. Previous empires had collapsed, witness the great Hittite kingdom, but their creators had survived in one form or another, whereas Assyria vanishes without trace. One reason for this is the absorption of Assyria into an Aramaic world whose frontiers were not political, but ironically this first "Mistress of the World" also fell a victim to the efficiency of her own imperial administration. For the gradual process of absorption which had begun with the lands between the Tigris and Euphrates, and had then been extended under Tiglath-pileser III and his successors to the entire Near East from Egypt to the Caspian, had eradicated the majority of local dynasties and left in their places Assyrian governors and Assyrian military garrisons which without indigenous support depended entirely on the central administration for their coordination. The consequence was that the collapse of the Assyrian empire left a power vacuum into which were sucked Egypt, Babylon and the rising star of Media. With the destruction of Nineveh the old Assyrian heartlands were parceled out among them, and for many centuries the lands between Persia and the Mediterranean were an unregarded marching ground for the armies of Cyrus, Alexander and their successors. For the present, however, the mantle of the Assyrian kings passed to the new dynasty at Babylon. Its founder, Nabopolassar, had died here in 605 BC after a reign of 21 years, and was succeeded by his son Nebuchadnezzar, who cut short his military follow-up of the Carchemish victory in the west, to return to the capital and ensure his succession.

Nebuchadnezzar's reign lasted for 43 years, and its glory raised Babylon in the eyes of his contemporaries to be the equal of Assyria. Yet Nebuchadnezzar himself, though he had shown himself a competent general, was by no means a world conqueror after the Assyrian pattern. These years give an impression of unnatural calm, as though western Asia rested in the eye of a hurricane. In the southwest, it is true, the continuing antagonism of Egypt led to a number of military engagements, but these were hardly more than scraps: like the Assyrians before him, Nebuchadnezzar had trouble with the desert Arabs, and with Tyre – safe on its island until Alexander comes on the cene; but perhaps the most important sideshow, and certainly the best documented, was provided by the little state of Judah.

Here in 597 BC the city of Jerusalem fell to the Babylonian armies, and its king was taken captive with his court, and yet only 11 years later, in 586 BC after a second revolt, Nebuchadnezzar's own nominee as king, Zedekiah, was blinded at Riblah and carried off together with much of the rebel city's population to exile by the waters of Babylon. Apart from this we hear next to nothing of military exploits: in part this is because the Assyrian style of annalistic inscriptions was not used by the Babylonian kings, but it is also true that with the help of military and administrative traditions inherited from the Assyrians, Nebuchadnezzar was able to maintain his empire without recourse to annual major campaigns. For his northern and eastern frontiers were sealed by the advancing Median empire, which penetrated Anatolia as far west as the River Halys: here, after an inconclusive battle in 585 BC, a border was set between Cyaxares the Mede and the Lydian king Alyattes who controlled the west, with a Babylonian and a Cilician called in as arbitrators, as we learn from Herodotus.

Babylon. Nebuchadnezzar's claim to be a great king must be based rather on his peaceful achievements, and this means on the capital which he built. Although since the days of Hammurapi Babylon had been recognized as the chief city of the south, and the throne of Babylon had carried with it great prestige, the city itself had not been the metropolis of an empire, and Nabopolassar had had little leisure during his struggle for supremacy to devote to ambitious building schemes. Now however his son set out to make of Babylon the greatest city the world had known. In his own inscriptions he relates in loving detail the progress of his new capital, of its double defensive wall, along which Herodotus reports that a four-horse chariot could be driven, of its temples and palaces.

His pride is justified not only by the reality exposed by Koldewey's excavations, but by the reputation his Babylon gained among its contemporaries. Herodotus accords it a long and essentially accurate description, while the Greek world endowed Nebuchadnezzar with immortal fame as the builder of one of the seven wonders of the world, the Hanging Gardens which he built for a homesick princess from the eastern hills. It is sad that little survives today from which the visitor to Babylon can recreate past glories. All the major works were of baked brick, an enormous outlay, but ironically this very fact has guaranteed the city's destruction, since it has served for many centuries as a quarry for the finest building material available. With the splendid files of bulls and dragons in colored glazed brick along the Processional Way, parts at least of the city must have been spectacular indeed, but now the low ruin mounds broken only by the jagged silhouettes of the rooms of the palace have little appeal alongside the narrative reliefs of the Assyrian kings.

The last years of Mesopotamian hegemony. The principles which guided the choice of the king during the Neo-Babylonian empire are obscure. True, Nebuchadnezzar himself followed his father and was himself succeeded by his son, but this son proved incapable and after two years he was replaced not by another son, but by his brother-in-law, a distinguished but elderly gentleman called Nergal-shar-usur (Neriglissar). He seems to have ruled with some success for the remainder of his natural life, some four years, but his son, who succeeded him in 556 BC, lasted only a few months.

Opposite: the Babylon of Nebuchadnezzar, looking over the Ishtar Gate with the ziggurrat of Marduk back right. After Unger.

Now the throne for no very apparent reason passed to another senior statesman called Nabu-naid (Nabonidus), but although he was probably the very Babylonian who negotiated the peace between Lydia and Media in 585 BC, it soon became clear that he was not the vigorous monarch needed by his country at this juncture. For whereas all around him the political scenes were shifting, and a new order was on the horizon, Nabonidus' interests, to judge from his own inscriptions, were centered on the restoration of the ancient shrines of Sumer and Akkad, and we read at length of the academic care with which omens were consulted and the temple foundations reexcavated and identified as far back as Sargon and Naram-Sin of Akkad. The contrast shows nowhere more clearly than in Nabonidus' own words:

"At the beginning of my reign the gods showed me a dream: in it there stood together Marduk, great lord, and Sin [the moon god], light of heaven and earth. And Marduk said to me, 'Nabonidus, king of Babylon, bring bricks on your own horse and chariot and build the temple Ehulhul that Sin, great lord, may take up his abode therein.' I replied reverently to Marduk, chief of the gods, 'That temple which you tell me to build is surrounded by the barbarian [i.e. Median], and his forces are all-powerful.' But Marduk said to me, 'The barbarian of whom you speak, he and his land and the kings who march at his side will not exist.' And indeed, after three years his young vassal Cyrus, king of Anshan, routed him, and with his small force scattered the hordes of the barbarians, and took back Astyages, king of the Medes, in bondage to his land."

One of the glazed brick lions (sacred to Ishtar) from the Processional Way leading to the Ishtar Gate at Babylon. Louvre.

Perhaps because his mother, who died in 547 BC at the age of 104, was a devotee of the god Sin, Nabonidus also showed him special devotion. This in part took the form of rebuilding his temple at Harran at a time when the "young vassal" of Astyages was mopping up the rest of western Asia, but more critically it also led to an estrangement between Nabonidus and the Babylonians. Whether the quarrel was only with the powerful priestly clique jealous for the position of Marduk, or with the entire population, is unclear, but in the sixth year of his reign Nabonidus left the government of Babylonia in the hands of his son Bel-shar-usur (Belshazzar), and for ten years lived in voluntary seclusion in the oasis of Tema in the middle of the Arabian desert, not even returning to Babylonia for the funeral obsequies of his mother. When, in 539 BC Nabonidus did eventually return to his capital, the writing was already on the wall. After his defeat of Croesus of Lydia Cyrus now logically had to add the ancient center of civilization to his empire. The last days of Babylonian independence are described curtly by the local chronicler: "On the 14th day of the 7th month Sippar was taken without a battle, and Nabonidus fled. On the 16th day Ugbaru, governor of Gutium, and the army of Cyrus entered Babylon without a battle. Nabonidus was captured in Babylon after his withdrawal. . . . On the 3rd day of the 8th month Cyrus entered Babylon."

It is symptomatic of the expansion of world horizons that this event is reported in Classical and Biblical tradition. That the capture of the great fortified city took place in the absence of Cyrus and without resistance is explained by the account of Herodotus: "Cyrus posted his army where the river enters the city, and another detachment where the stream leaves it, and instructed his troops to make their entry into the city along the Euphrates channel when they saw it was fordable." He himself marched upstream to divert the river into a lake, and so his army was able to enter the city along the Euphrates bed. "Because of the great size of the city – so the inhabitants tell – those in the outer parts were overcome while in the center they were still unawares, for all this time they were dancing and carousing at a festival which was under way, until they discovered the facts only too plainly." Fittingly Babylon fell by default. Whether or not Belshazzar's Feast was the decadent revel portrayed by the Prophet Daniel, after more than 2,000 years of world primacy Mesopotamian civilization had shot its bolt. Political and cultural initiatives now came from outside the Near East. Mesopotamia was absorbed into the Persian and then the Hellenistic worlds, and the cuneiform traditions soon faded away into faint echoes in the Bible and the collections of Greek antiquarians.

Further Reading

Adams, R. McC., *The Uruk Countryside* (Chicago, Ill., 1972).

Bittel, K., *Hattusha: The Capital of the Hittites* (New York, 1970).

Cambridge Ancient History, vols. 1–3 (Cambridge, 1970–73).

Gelb, I. J., *A Study of Writing* (London, 1952).

Grayson, A. K., *Assyrian Royal Inscriptions* (Wiesbaden, 1972).

Gurney, O. R., *The Hittites* (2nd ed., Harmondsworth, 1954).

Hinz, W., *The Lost World of Elam* (London 1972).

Kramer, S. N., *The Sumerians* (Chicago, Ill., 1963).

Laessøe, J., *People of Ancient Assyria* (London, 1963)

Layard, A. H., *Nineveh and its Remains* (London, 1849).

——*Nineveh and Babylon* (London, 1853).

Lloyd, S., *Foundations in the Dust* (Harmondsworth, 1947).

——*The Art of the Ancient Near East* (London, 1961).

——*Mounds of the Ancient Near East* (Edinburgh, 1963).

Moortgat, A., *The Art of Ancient Mesopotamia* (London, 1969).

Neugebauer, O., *The Exact Sciences in Antiquity* New York, 1962).

Oates, D., *Studies in the Ancient History of Northern Iraq* London, 1968).

Oppenheim, A. L., *Ancient Mesopotamia* (Chicago, Ill., 1965).

——*Letters from Mesopotamia* (Chicago, Ill., 1968).

Piotrovsky, B. B., *Urartu,* tr. J. Hogarth (London, 1969).

Pritchard, J. B., *Ancient Near Eastern Texts relating to the Old Testament* (3rd ed., Princeton, N. J., 1969).

——*The Ancient Near East in Pictures* (Princeton, N. J., 1969).

Roux, G., *Ancient Iraq* (London, 1964).

Strommenger, E., and M. Hirmer, *The Art of Mesopotamia* (London, 1964).

Waterfield, G., *Layard of Nineveh* (London, 1963).

Woolley, C. L., *Excavations at Ur: A Record of Twelve Years' Work* (London, 1954).

Acknowledgments

Unless otherwise stated, all the illustrations on a given page are credited to the same source.

W. Andrae (ed.), *Coloured Ceramics from Ashur* (1925) 118 (top)
Ashmolean Museum, Oxford 72
Dick Barnard, London 18, 64, 75 (center), 87 (bottom), 135
Bildarchiv Foto Marburg, Marburg 13 (bottom), 32 (bottom left)
British Museum, London 16, 27 (bottom), 27 (top left), 28, 29 (top right), 31 (top), 32 (bottom right), 46, 47 (left), 48 (bottom right), 50 (bottom), 51 (top), 52 (bottom), 56, 95 (top), 99 (right)
British School of Archaeology, Iraq 28 (top left)
Elsevier Archives, Amsterdam 11 (bottom), 21 (top), 35 (bottom), 41, 96, 100, 122, 125 (top left)
Forhistorisk Museum, Moesgärd 90
Foto Scala, Florence Jacket, 24, 26, 29 (bottom), 30 (bottom left), 31 (bottom right), 45, 48 (top), 48 (bottom left), 49 (bottom), 51 (bottom), 54, 67, 74, 78, 79 (top), 80, 81, 91, 93, 113 (top), 114, 125 (top right), 125 (bottom), 136
Roger Gorringe, London 47 (right), 84 (top), 110 (top right), 115 (bottom)
Robert Harding Associates, London 9, 13 (top), 33, 34, 36, 38, 39, 40, 42, 52 (top), 52 (center), 60, 83 (bottom), 85 (right), 85 (top left), 86, 87 (top), 88 (top), 108 (bottom)
David Hawkins, London 58 (bottom), 105, 118 (bottom), 123 (top)
Hirmer Verlag, Munich 20, 53, 70 (bottom), 71, 97 (right), 103 (bottom)
Michael Holford Library, Loughton 15, 17, 21 (bottom), 27 (top right), 30 (top), 32 (top), 50 (top), 61, 75 (top), 79 (bottom), 95 (bottom), 99 (left), 101 (top), 113 (bottom), 119, 120, 124, 130, 132
Kadirli Adana, Turkey 131
Lovell Johns, Oxford 10, 68, 83 (top), 92, 116
David Oates, Cambridge 63 (bottom), 65, 110 (bottom), 111 (top), 112, 117, 127 (right), 128, 129
Oriental Institute, Cambridge 110 (top right)
Oriental Institute, University of Chicago 70 (top)
Picturepoint, London 22, 30 (bottom right), 57, 97 (left), 101 (bottom), 103 (top), 111 (bottom)
Nicholas Postgate 11 (top), 55 (top), 59, 62, 63 (top), 76 (bottom), 94, 106, 115 (top), 121, 123 (bottom), 127 (left)
Michael Roaf 82, 88 (bottom), 89 (top right and bottom)
Ronald Sheridan's Photo-Library, London 73, 76 (top), 98
R. F. S. Staar, *Nuzi*, vol. 2 (1937) 102
Staatliche Museum, Berlin 12
Maurizio Tosi, Naples 75 (bottom)
University of Newcastle-upon-Tyne, University Library and Department of Archaeology 55 (bottom)
University of Rome, Italian Archaeological Mission in Syria, courtesy of Paulo Matthiae 31 (bottom left)
University of Pennsylvania Museum, Philadelphia 2, 19
Sir Mortimer Wheeler 84 (bottom), 85 (bottom left)

The publishers have attempted to observe the legal requirements with respect to the rights of the suppliers of photographic materials. Nevertheless, persons who have claims are invited to apply to the Publishers.

Glossary

Abdi-milkutti King of **Sidon.** His exact dates are not known, but he was beheaded in 676 BC after revolting against Esarhaddon and trying to escape to Cyprus.

Abu Habbah Modern name of site of ancient **Sippar.**

Abu Salabikh Site of a hitherto unidentified Sumerian city about 14 miles northwest of Nippur.

Abu Shahrain Modern name of site of ancient **Eridu.**

Adab City in central Sumer on the ancient Euphrates, now the site of Bismayah.

Adad Chief weather-god of the Mesopotamian pantheon, also worshiped in Syria and Palestine (as Hadad). He came especially into prominence in the first millennium BC with the arrival of Aramaean tribes.

Adad-idri Assyrian rendering of the Aramaic name Hadad-ezer, who was the chief opponent of Shalmaneser III c. 850 BC, and is mentioned in the Bible as Ben-Hadad, king of Damascus.

Adad-nirari Name of three kings of **Assyria**, especially Adad-nirari I (1307–1275 BC).

Adapa Mythical "wise man" from the city of **Eridu** and son of the god **Ea.** He is the hero of a poem in which he "broke the wing of the south wind" but, with his father's advice, visited heaven and obtained pardon.

Aka King of Kish and son of **En-mebaragesi.** The Sumerian epic tale of "Gilgamesh and Aka" relates how the army of Kish led by Aka was defied by **Gilgamesh** of Uruk.

Akkad Name of the capital city of the Dynasty of Akkad which was founded by **Sargon.** Its exact site has never been identified, but it was probably not far from Kish. From this dynasty onwards southern Mesopotamia was called the land of "Sumer and Akkad."

Akkad, Dynasty of Founded by **Sargon** (original form of name: Sharrum-ken), 2334–2279 BC, who was succeeded by his two sons Rimush, 2278–2270 BC, and Manishtushu, 2269–2255 BC, and his grandson **Naram-Sin,** 2254–2218 BC. The dynasty survived for another 64 years in very reduced circumstances.

The god Adad

Akkadian Semitic language spoken in Mesopotamia as far back as our evidence reaches and almost certainly earlier. First well attested as the "Old Akkadian" dialect spoken by the Akkad Dynasty, it is represented later in the south by **Babylonian**, which becomes the literary language of the whole Near East, and in the north by the distinct **Assyrian** dialect.

Alalakh City and small state in the second millennium BC on the Orontes on the route from Aleppo to Ugarit; its modern name is Tell Açana and it was excavated by Sir Leonard **Woolley** before and after World War II.

Aleppo Major city in northern Syria, capital of the state of Yamhad in the early second millennium BC and later very important to the Hittite empire under its modern name Halpa.

Alexander the Great Son of Philip of Macedon; conquered Mesopotamia after the battle of Gaugamela in which he defeated Darius III in 331 BC, and later died at Babylon (323 BC) after his eastern conquests.

Al-Hiba Modern name of site of ancient **Lagash**.

Alluvium Silty soil deposited by the rivers in southern Mesopotamia, forming a deep and potentially fertile flood-plain.

Alyattes King of Lydia who met the advancing Medes under **Astyages** at the battle of the River Halys which can be dated by an eclipse to 585 BC.

Amanus Mts Range of mountains projecting south to the Levant coast from the Taurus and so lying across the routes to Cilicia from Syria. Famous for its cedars.

Amarna Age Period illuminated for us by the correspondence from the palace of King Akhenaten at the site of El-Amarna in Egypt (c. 1400 BC).

Amar-Sin (or Amar-Suen) Name of the third king of the 3rd Dynasty of **Ur**.

Amenophis Name of four kings of the 18th Dynasty in Egypt. In particular, Amenophis III (1417–1379 BC) and his son Amenophis IV (Akhenaten, 1379–1362 BC), both of whom were concerned in the "Amarna" correspondence.

Amorites Nomadic tribes from the Arabian Desert, first attested during the Akkad Dynasty. During the Ur III period and subsequent disruptions they established local dynasties throughout western Asia. Their language, known only from their personal names, is of the West Semitic group.

An, Anum Sumerian and Akkadian names of the sky-god (in Sumerian *an* means "sky"). He was worshiped especially at **Uruk**, but not of great importance in historical times.

Andrae, Walter (1875–1956) German archaeologist who directed the excavations at **Assur** from 1903 to 1914. After the Great War

Apotropaic figurine

worked in the Near Eastern Department of the Berlin Museum, becoming its director in 1928.

Apotropaic figurine Magical statuette of an animal or supernatural being, used to ward off evil influences; especially buried in the foundations of buildings and under thresholds.

Aqar-Quf Modern name of site of ancient Dur-Kurigalzu near modern Baghdad, briefly the capital of the **Kassite** kings.

Arabs First attested in the inscriptions of Shalmaneser III (858–824 BC) and encountered throughout the next two centuries as camel-riding nomads in the Arabian Desert.

Aramaeans Nomadic tribes which flooded into the settled areas of the Near East c. 1000 BC, founding local dynasties. Although politically absorbed by the Assyrian empire, their language, Aramaic, became the lingua franca of the area and survives to this day. Parts of the Bible are written in Aramaic.

Arame King of **Urartu** who fought with Adad-idri of Damascus against Shalmaneser III of Assyria.

Argistis Name of two kings of **Urartu.**

Arnuwandas Name of three kings of the **Hittites**.

Winged disk of the god Assur

Artatama Name of a king of **Mitanni**, subsequently defeated by his rival **Tushratta.**

Assur Name of the capital city of **Assyria** (and its god), today the site of Qalat Sherqat.

Assur-ban-apli Last major king of **Assyria**.

Assur-bel-kala (1074–1057 BC) Son of Tiglath-pileser I and king of Assyria.

Assur-dan Name of three Assyrian kings, especially Assur-dan I (1179–1134 BC).

Assur-nadin-shumi Name of the eldest son of **Sennacherib**: appointed king of Babylon in 699 BC, and captured and killed by the Elamites in 694 BC.

Assur-nasir-apli Name of two Assyrian kings, especially Assur-nasir-apli II (883–859 BC).

Assur-nirari Name of five kings of Assyria, especially Assur-nirari V (754–745 BC), who concluded a treaty with **Mati'el** of Arpad.

Assur-uballit Name of two Assyrian kings, especially Assur-uballit I, virtual founder of the Assyrian empire (1365–1330 BC).

Assyria "The Land of **Assur**." The north Mesopotamian area with the cities of Assur, Nineveh and Kalhu (Nimrud). Later used for the entire Assyrian empire.

The list of Assyrian kings in the Neo-Assyrian period is given below (dates follow J. A. Brinkman in A. L. Oppenheim, *Ancient Mesopotamia*, pp. 335–47):

Assur-dan II	934–912
Adad-nirari II	911–891
Tukulti-ninurta II	890–884
Assur-nasir-apli II	883–859
Shalmaneser III	858–824
Shamshi-adad V	823–811
Adad-nirari III	810–783
Shalmaneser IV	782–773
Assur-dan III	772–755
Assur-nirari V	754–745
Tiglath-pileser III	744–727
Shalmaneser V	726–722
Sargon II	721–705
Sennacherib	704–681
Esarhaddon	680–669
Assur-ban-apli	668–627
Assur-etelli-ilani	626–624?
Sin-shum-lishir	?
Sin-shar-ishkun	? –612
Assur-uballit II	611–609

Assyrian Dialect of **Akkadian** first attested at Assur c. 1900 BC, and surviving until the collapse of the Assyrian empire as the vernacular of north Mesopotamia.

Astyages King of Media and son of Cyaxares; dispossessed by the youthful **Cyrus** (c. 550 BC), who was according to legend his daughter's son.

Awan, Dynasty of Line of kings ruling Elam in the Early Dynastic III period and briefly credited with the kingship of Sumer. The exact location of their capital Awan is unknown.

Babylon City which first came to prominence as the seat of the 1st Dynasty of Babylon of which Hammurapi was the most important member, and which came to an end in 1595 BC. It remained capital of the south ("Babylonia") until the foundation of Seleucia on the Tigris by the successor of **Alexander**.

Babylonian Dialect of **Akkadian** used in the south and standardized about the time of Hammurapi; conventionally the spoken language is divided into Old (to 1595 BC), Middle (to c. 1000 BC) and Late Babylonian phases.

Baghdad Capital city of modern Iraq, founded on the Tigris in 762 AD by the Caliph Mansur and capital of the Abbasid Caliphate.

Bahrain Island in the Arabian Gulf off the coast of Arabia; it served as a staging post on the sea voyage down the Gulf to the Indus valley, and is identified with ancient **Dilmun**.

Bartatua Akkadian rendering of the name of the Scythian king who is mentioned (as father of King Madyas who was present at the sack of Nineveh) by **Herodotus** as Protothyes.

Bau Chief goddess of the city of **Girsu** and wife of Ningirsu.

Bedouin Modern Arab tribes leading a nomadic life in the Arabian Desert.

Bel "Lord"; a name of **Marduk**, chief god of Babylon.

Bel-ibni Babylonian noble appointed by **Sennacherib** to rule Babylon after the defeat of Marduk-apla-iddina; he lasted only two years (702–700 BC).

Bel-shar-usur (or Belshazzar) Son of **Nabonidus** and effective king of Babylon for the years when his father was living at Tema (c. 550–540 BC). Famed from the Bible as Belshazzar, at whose feast the writing was seen on the wall, foreshadowing the conquest of Cyrus (Book of Daniel).

Bell, Gertrude M. Lowthian (1868–1926) British traveler and scholar, also a keen alpinist. After important political services in the creation of the new state of Iraq, she remained in the country and established its Department of Antiquities.

Birs Nimrud Modern name of the site of ancient **Borsippa.**

Bismayah Site of ancient **Adab.**

Bit-Yakin "The House of Yakin"; name of a major **Chaldaean** tribal group in south Babylonia, to which **Marduk-apla-iddina** belonged.

Borsippa City close to Babylon, on the west of the Euphrates, and the home of the god **Nabu**. Modern name Birs Nimrud; excavated by **Rawlinson** and the German Babylon expedition.

Botta, Paul-Emile (1802–70) First discoverer of Assyrian sculptures at Khorsabad, having been appointed French vice-consul in Mosul for this reason in 1842; later made consul at Jerusalem (1848) and Tripoli (1855).

Breasted, J. H. (1865–1935) Egyptologist and ancient historian of repute, from 1919 till his death the Director of the Oriental Institute of the University of Chicago, and chief instigator of its excavation program in the Near East.

Buckingham, James Silk (1786–1855) English traveler and author of a series of books on his Near Eastern journeys, during which he traveled mostly disguised as an Egyptian gentleman; later a Member of Parliament (1832–37).

Budge, Sir Ernest Alfred Wallis (1857–1934) British Orientalist who was a member and later the Keeper of the Department of Egyptian and Assyrian Antiquities (1893–1924). Published many works on Egyptian, Syriac and Ethiopic subjects.

Burnaburiash Name of two **Kassite** kings, especially Burnaburiash II (1375–1347 BC).

Canning, Sir Stratford (1786–1880; later 1st Viscount Stratford de Redcliffe) British Ambassador to the Sublime Porte (i.e. the Sultan of Turkey) from 1825 to 1829 and again 1841 to 1857. During the second period he assisted **Layard** with funds and backing for his excavations in Assyria.

Carchemish (ancient Kargamish, modern Jerablus) Important city on the Euphrates on the present Turkish-Syrian frontier. Known in the Mari texts, the Hittite sources, and as the center of a small Neo-Hittite kingdom, from which the sculptures excavated by a British Museum expedition (under Woolley, Hogarth and T. E. Lawrence) date.

Carnelian Red stone of the chalcedony group much favored in Mesopotamia for beads.

Chaldaean Another name for Babylonian and the tribes which inhabited Babylonia in the first millenium BC. The Chaldaean Dynasty was the last Babylonian dynasty.

The list of kings is given below (dates follow J. A. Brinkman in A. L. Oppenheim, *Ancient Mesopotamia*, pp. 335–47):

Nabopolassar	625–605
Nebuchadnezzar II	604–562
Evil-Merodach	561–560
Neriglissar	559–556
Labaši-Marduk	556
Nabonidus	555–539

Chronology Dates before the Amarna Age are in dispute by as much as 100 years because of the "Dark Age" after the 1st Dynasty of Babylon. We follow here the so-called "Middle Chronology" which places the end of the 1st Dynasty in 1595 BC, and the dates given by J. A. Brinkman in A. L. Oppenheim, *Ancient Mesopotamia*, pp. 335–47.

Cilicia That part of Anatolia enclosed on the north by the Taurus range and on the south by the Mediterranean. In Classical times divided into the coastal plain and "Rough Cilicia," the northern hilly part. In the second millennium known as Kizzuwadna, in the first millennium called by the Assyrians Que.

Cimmerians Nomadic horde from Central Asia which preceded the **Scythians** and pressed against the established kingdoms of Urartu, Phrygia and Assyria in the 8th and 7th centuries BC.

City-state Political unit centered on and controlled by a single city.

Cone mosaic Method of wall decoration of the **Uruk** period by which clay cones were thrust into the brickwork so that their colored heads form mosaic patterns.

Croesus King of Lydia, famed in Greek tradition for his wealth, but conquered in his capital Sardis by **Cyrus.**

Cuthah North Babylonian city near Kish, today Tell Ibrahim.

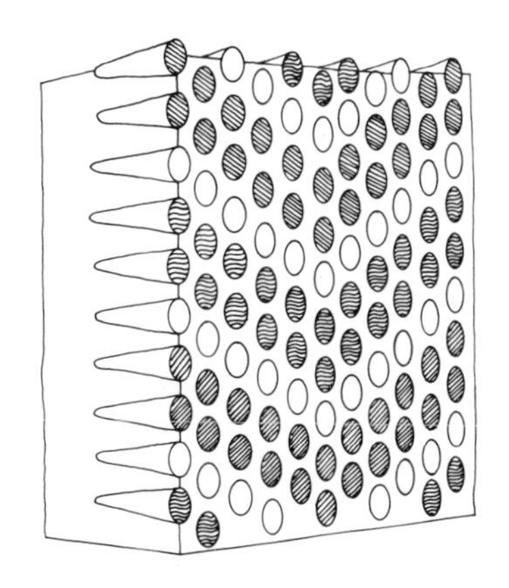

Cone mosaic pattern from Uruk

Cyaxares King of Media who allied with **Nabopolassar** to bring down the Assyrian empire (c. 612 BC). He was succeeded c. 584 BC by his son **Astyages.**

Cylinder seal Seal (usually made of stone but also of shell, frit or other materials) engraved with a design and pierced down the center for suspension. Typical of Mesopotamia from 3000 BC onwards, but gradually replaced by stamp seals during the first millennium BC.

Cyrus I Founder of the Persian empire. He unthroned **Astyages** and conquered **Croesus** of Lydia and **Nabonidus** of Babylon. Died 529 BC and was succeeded by Cambyses.

Darius I (521–486 BC) Succeeded Cambyses on the Persian throne and launched the first Persian invasion of Greece in 490 BC. Author of the Behistun trilingual inscription through which **Rawlinson** deciphered cuneiform.

Delougaz, Pinhas (1901–74) Member of the Diyala expedition responsible for the excavations at Khafajah, and subsequently a professor at the Oriental Institute, University of Chicago.

De Sarzec, Ernest (1837–1901) French excavator of Tello (Girsu); appointed vice-consul at Basra (1877) and later consul at Baghad; created Minister Plenipotentiary in 1899.

Dilmun In Sumerian literature a sort of paradise, but known from economic documents to be a staging post on the sea route to the Indus, and credibly identified with the island of **Bahrain**.

Diodorus Siculus Greek historian (from Sicily) who lived c. 40 BC and wrote a world history in 40 books, of which 15 survive. It includes some details of Mesopotamia, but they are of varying reliability depending on their source.

Dolerite Igneous rock of which the black stone statues of **Gudea** are said to be made.

Drehem Modern name of the site of ancient Puzrish-Dagan, an administrative clearing-house for animals just south of Nippur, founded in the Ur III period.

Dumuzi Sumerian god (known to the Bible as Tammuz). In myths he is the beloved of **Inanna** (Ishtar), but later his worship was a popular (and not official) religion, and he was a fertility god comparable to the dying god Adonis of Greek mythology.

Dur-Kurigalzu City near modern Baghdad founded as his capital by one of the **Kassite** kings called Kurigalzu, modern **Aqar Quf**.

Dur-Sharruken Ancient name "Fort

Sargon" of Sargon II's new capital north of Nineveh, started in 716 BC; the site is now called Khorsabad and was first excavated by **Botta**.

Ea Akkadian name of the god known in Sumerian as Enki. He is city god of **Eridu**, and god of wisdom, magic incantations and the waters under the earth.

Eannatum Name of two of the **ensis** of **Lagash** in the Early Dynastic III period, especially Eannatum I, the author of the Stele of the Vultures.

Early Dynastic period Term coined by H. Frankfort to describe the period between the Uruk and Jamdat Nasr (= **Protoliterate**) periods and the accession of Sargon of Akkad, i.e. c. 3000–2350 BC. It is conventionally divided into:
Early Dynastic I c. 3000–2750 BC
Early Dynastic II c. 2750–2600 BC
Early Dynastic III c. 2600–2350 BC

Ebla City and state in Syria not far south of Aleppo, now **Tell Mardikh;** important in the Akkad period and at the time of Hammurapi.

Elamite Language of the land of Elam (centered around the cities of Susa and Anshan in southwest Iran). It is not related to any other known language, and was the second language of the Behistun inscription (the others were Old Persian and Akkadian).

En Sumerian title of the priestly ruler of Uruk, and of high priests and priestesses at Ur and elsewhere. The title forms part of the names of several gods and many humans.

En-heduanna Daughter of **Sargon of Akkad**, appointed the priestess of the moon-god Nanna and his wife Ningal at Ur, and author of at least one Sumerian poem.

E-ninnu Literally "The Fifty House," the name of the temple of Ningirsu at Girsu, which was rebuilt by Gudea and was the occasion of the composition of his great Cylinder inscriptions.

Enki Sumerian form of the name of the god **Ea**.

Enlil Chief god of the Sumerian pantheon, and city god of **Nippur.** His wife is Ninlil. It was Enlil's position as king of the gods which led Th. **Jacobsen** to suggest that Nippur had once been the center of a political league, and even in historical times it was the religious capital of Sumer.

Enlil-bani King of Isin (1860–1837 BC) who came to the throne after having been placed there as a temporary substitute for the real king, so as to suffer the evil consequences predicted by the omen priests.

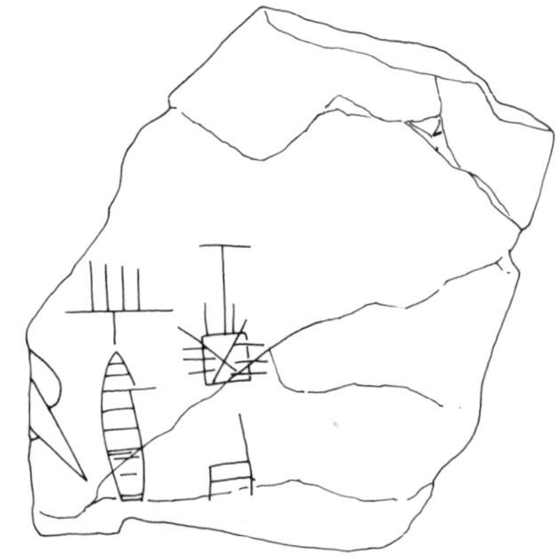

The inscription of En-mebaragesi

En-mebaragesi King of Kish c. 2600 BC, and father of **Aka**. He is at present the earliest of the kings mentioned in the Sumerian King List who is historically attested (by stone bowls bearing his name).

En-meduranki Named in the Sumerian King List as the king of Sippar before the Flood; remembered as the founder of the science of divination, and even mentioned in Greek transcription by the late historian Berossus.

En-merkar King of Uruk and the father of **Lugalbanda**. He was renowned in the Sumerian epic poem "Enmerkar and the Lord of Aratta" which records his trade negotiations with a city in the highlands of Iran.

Ensi Sumerian term for the ruler of a city state; its precise religious and political connotations are still a matter of debate.

En-temena Fifth ruler of the Ur-Nanshe dynasty of **Lagash.**

Epic of Creation Modern title of an Akkadian religious poem in praise of **Marduk**, which was recited in the course of the New Year rituals at Babylon. It relates the rebellion of the underworld gods, led by the personified sea (Tiamat), against the great gods, and how Marduk was eventually sent against her and created the world from her corpse, in recognition of which he was crowned king of the gods.

Equid Animal of the horse family, including horses, donkeys, mules and onagers (wild asses).

Ereshkigal Divine "Queen of the Underworld," wife of Nergal.

Eridu Sumerian city a little southwest of Ur and the first seat of kingship according to the King List. Modern site is called Abu Shahrain.

Esagila Sumerian name of the great Temple of Marduk at Babylon.

Esarhaddon (Assur-aha-iddina) Biblical form of the name of the king of Assyria after Sennacherib (680–669 BC).

Eshnunna City and state in the Diyala region east of modern Baghdad during the third and first half of the second millennium; modern name of site Tell Asmar.

Etruscans Population of central Italy before and during the early centuries of Rome. An eastern Mediterranean origin has often been suggested for their otherwise unknown language.

Extispicy Practice of inspecting the entrails (or *exta*) of slaughtered animals so as to derive from them ominous signs.

Fara Modern name of the site of ancient **Shuruppak**. The term "Fara period" is often applied to the first half of the Early Dynastic III period after the inscriptions found here.

Firman In the Ottoman empire, an official document, including one granting permission (for excavations etc.).

Fox Talbot, W. H. (1800–77). Distinguished British scientist who invented photographic techniques but was also interested in the decipherment of ancient languages.

Frankfort, Henri (1897–1954) Dutch scholar and authority on ancient Near Eastern art and archaeology. Excavated at El-Amarna in Egypt and then in Iraq for the Oriental Institute, University of Chicago. From 1949 held the chair of the History of Pre-Classical Antiquity in the University of London.

Frit Artificial glazed material often used for small ornaments in Mesopotamia.

German Oriental Society (Deutsche Orient-Gesellschaft) Learned society in Berlin responsible for most of the German archaeological work in Mesopotamia.

Gilgamesh Legendary hero of Sumerian and Akkadian literature. He is named in the Sumerian King List as the fifth king of the 1st Dynasty of Uruk, and fixed in time by the synchronism with Aka of Kish, son of **En-mebaragesi**. The "Epic of Gilgamesh" is an Akkadian poem in 12 tablets which weaves the tales about him into the story of his search for eternal life, incorporating a version of the "Flood Story" which is told to him by the "Babylonian Noah," Ut-napishtim, whom he visits.

Gipar Sumerian term for that part of a temple complex reserved for the *en*-priestesses.

Girsu One of the three main cities of the Sumerian city-state of Lagash; modern site known as Tello, excavated by **de Sarzec** and his successors.

Grotefend, Georg Friedrich (1775–1853) German scholar and schoolmaster who proposed in 1802 the correct decipherment of no fewer than 10 of the 37 Old Persian characters in the inscriptions of Darius at Persepolis.

Gudea *Ensi* of Lagash c. 2130 BC, and the subject of many magnificent stone statues. He restored the temple of Ningirsu at Girsu (the **E-ninnu**), and his great Cylinder inscriptions were composed to celebrate this event.

Guti Name of a mountain people who descended into Sumer and Akkad c. 2200 BC at the end of the Akkad Dynasty. Their domination was short-lived, and they are found in the mountain country east of Kerkuk centuries later by the kings of the Middle Assyrian period.

Gyges King of Lydia and contemporary of **Assur-ban-apli**; well known to the Greek historians such as Herodotus.

Halaf (Tell) Important archaeological site on the upper Habur river, excavated by Baron Max von **Oppenheim**. It yielded painted prehistoric pottery now known as "Halaf ware" and a palace belonging to Aramaean rulers of c. 900 BC, when the town was called Guzana.

Hall, H. R. H. (1873–1930) Ancient historian and member of the British Museum Department of Egyptian and Assyrian Antiquities, of which he was Keeper (1924–30). Primarily concerned with Egypt and the Aegean, he was also sent out to work for the museum in 1919 at Ur, Al Ubaid and Eridu.

Hallushu King of Elam (699–693 BC); his full name was Hallushu-Inshushinak and he was the chief ally of **Marduk-apla-iddina** against Sennacherib.

Hamath City on the Orontes in Syria between Aleppo and Damascus (modern Hama), seat of an Aramaean or Neo-Hittite dynasty in the early first millennium BC.

Hammurapi Sixth king of the 1st Dynasty of Babylon (1792–1750 BC); himself an Amorite by extraction, it was during his reign that the writing of the Akkadian language in cuneiform was standardized, and his Code of laws is the supreme example of this.

Hanging Gardens of Babylon One of the Seven Wonders of the World, built (according to Greek authors) by **Nebuchadnezzar II** for a wife pining for her homeland in the Persian mountains. Probably an extravagant "roof-garden"; it is possible that a massive and enigmatic structure in the northeast corner of the palace, including a complex irrigation installation, was the substructure for the Hanging Gardens.

Harem Women's quarters of a Near Eastern palace or household, and its inhabitants.

Hattic Ancient Anatolian language of unknown affinities which is met with in the Boğazköy texts alongside Hittite and Hurrian.

Hattusas Capital of the Hittite empire; now the archaeological site of Boğazköy in central Turkey east of Ankara.

Hattusilis Name of three Hittite kings, especially Hattusilis I (c. 1650 BC) who was the virtual founder of the kingdom, and Hattusilis III (c. 1275), perhaps the last really effective king of the **Hittites**.

Hazael Aramaean king of Damascus (c. 843 BC), who fell out with the city's former allies Hamath and Israel, and features in the Biblical narrative; although besieged by Shalmaneser III in Damascus he retained his throne.

Herodotus (c. 480–425 BC) Greek historian called by Cicero the "father of history." The overall theme of his history is the struggle between the Greeks and the Persian empire, but in its earlier parts especially there are many digressions on the history and character of the countries concerned, including Egypt and Mesopotamia.

Hesiod Early Greek poet (perhaps 8th century BC), who wrote a *Theogony* describing the myths of Uranus ("heaven") and Kronos his son, and their conflict with the sky-gods in terms strongly reminescent of the Hurrian and even Mesopotamian creation stories.

Hezekiah King of Judah (c. 716–687 BC); he connived with **Marduk-apla-iddina** of Babylon and drew on himself the displeasure of Isaiah for his provocation of the Assyrian king. Although Jerusalem itself was not taken, he submitted to **Sennacherib** at Lachish in 700 BC.

Hieroglyphic A hieroglyph is strictly a "holy character" and refers to the traditional picture-writing of Egypt. Because of its similarity to this, the Anatolian picture-writing of c. 1600–600 BC is known as "Hieroglyphic Hittite" although it is now apparent that it was used mainly to write a language related to Hittite called Luwian.

Hilprecht, Hermann Vollrat (1859–1925) German Assyriologist who held the chair of Assyriology at the University of Pennsylvania (1886–1911) and was much concerned in the work at Nippur. He also was involved in the organization of the Imperial Ottoman Museum at Istanbul (1893–1909).

Hincks, Revd. Edward (1792–1866) English scholar who did as much as **Rawlinson** in working out the decipherment of the Akkadian cuneiform inscriptions; one of four decipherers who presented versions of the prism of Tiglath-pileser I to the Royal Asiatic Society in 1857.

Hittites In modern usage, the Indo-European people who ruled central Anatolia c. 1800–1200 BC, and the petty states of the Taurus and north Syrian region in the early first millennium BC (Neo-Hittites). The major kings of the Hittites in their classical period are:

Tudkhalias II	floruit c. 1460
Arnuwandas I	1440
Hattusilis II	1420
Tudkhalias III	1400
Suppiluliumas I	1370
Arnuwandas II	1330
Mursilis II	1329
Muwatallis	1300
Urhi-Teshup	1280
Hattusilis III	1275
Tudkhalias IV	1250
Arnuwandas III	1220
Suppiluliumas II	1200

Hogarth, D. G. (1862–1927) Classical archaeologist with special interest in the eastern Mediterranean and Anatolia. Keeper of the Ashmolean Museum, Oxford, from 1909, and also worked at Carchemish with Leonard **Woolley** (1911–14).

Hrozny, Bedrich (1879–1952) Czech Orientalist, Professor at the University of Prague from 1919. Sent in 1914 to copy Hittite texts from Boğazköy in the Istanbul Museum, he demonstrated in an article published in 1915 that the Hittite language was of the Indo-European group; later he excavated part of the Old Assyrian colony at Kanesh (Kültepe).

Hurrians Population of northern Mesopotamia and the highlands of eastern Anatolia in the third and second millennia BC. There was never any "Hurrian empire" but the states of **Mitanni** and Hanigalbat were largely of Hurrian composition, and Hurrian texts are found from **Nuzi** to Alalakh and Boğazkoy.

Ibal-pi-el Amorite ruler of Eshnunna at the time of Hammurapi of Babylon.

Ibbi-Sin Last king of the 3rd Dynasty of **Ur**. He was carried off to Elam by the Elamite invaders who sacked the city of Ur, but his real downfall was caused by the increasing power of the **Amorites** which disrupted the empire.

Inanna (Akkadian: Ishtar) Sumerian goddess of love and war; city goddess of Uruk, and also Akkad, and beloved of **Dumuzi.**

Indo-European Group of languages to which most modern European languages belong, as well as Latin, Greek and Sanskrit. Hittite is the earliest known member of the group.

Irhuleni Neo-Hittite king of Hamath and ally of Ahab of Israel and Adad-idri of Damascus against Shalmaneser III.

Ishbi-erra First king of the 1st Dynasty of Isin (2017–1985 BC); he had been a high official under **Ibbi-Sin** and surviving letters describe his defection which led to his founding of the new dynasty.

Ishtar Akkadian name of the goddess **Inanna.**

Isin City in central Sumer and seat of two dynasties, that founded by Ishbi-erra and ended by the defeat by Rim-sin of Larsa (2017–1794 BC), and the 2nd Dynasty of Isin which ruled Babylonia after the Kassites (1156–1025 BC). The site's modern name is Ishan al-Bahriyat.

Isputahsus King of Kizzuwadna c. 1500 BC, who concluded an alliance with Telepinus the Hittite king, and whose seal-impression found at Tarsus is the earliest known Hieroglyphic Hittite text.

Jacobsen, Thorkild (1904–) Member of the Chicago Diyala project, and influential Sumerologist. Director of the Chicago Oriental Institute (1946–48) and recently Professor of Assyriology at Harvard.

Jamdat Nasr Site excavated by the Oxford-Chicago expedition to Kish in the 1920s; it yielded a style of painted pottery and early economic tablets which were unique at that time and have given the name of Jamdat Nasr to the last part of the **protoliterate period**, immediately before the **Early Dynastic period**.

Jehu King of Israel (c. 841–814 BC), who founded a new dynasty after Ahab, and submitted to Shalmaneser III.

Kadashman-enlil II (c. 1279–1265 BC) Kassite king contemporary with Adad-nirari I of Assyria and Hattusilis III of the Hittites.

Kalhu Assyrian city chosen by Assur-nasir-apli II as his new capital; it remained the capital of the Assyrian empire until **Sargon** moved to Khorsabad c. 706. Modern name of the site is Nimrud.

Kanesh Name of the Anatolian city in which Assyrian merchants set up their trading colony (c. 1900–1800 BC), modern Kültepe.

Kara Tepe Hilltop fortified site in the mountains north of Adana (Cilicia), and palace of Sanduarri who was beheaded by Esarhaddon in 676 BC. Turkish excavations since 1947 have uncovered sculptured reliefs and in particular a bilingual Phoenician and Hieroglyphic Hittite inscription which enabled the decipherment of the latter script.

Kaska People in northern Anatolia who occasioned continuous trouble to the Hittites in the north and east.

Kassites Race which gained control of Babylonia after the collapse of the 1st Dynasty of Babylon; their closest connections seem to be with the hilly country to the northeast. Their language is neither **Semitic** nor **Indo-European**.

Khorsabad Modern name of the site of ancient Dur-Sharruken, first excavated by **Botta** in 1843.

King Lists 1. Sumerian King List. A composition giving the names of the "kings" of Sumer with the lengths of their reigns from mythological times "before the Flood" down to the 1st Dynasty of Isin, a period of perhaps 1,000 years.

2. Assyrian King List. A similar composition giving the names and lengths of reign of the kings of Assyria from mythical times before 2000 BC down to the Neo-Assyrian period. An invaluable historical source.

Kish Major city in the north of "Sumer and Akkad," seat of the first dynasty after the Flood listed in the Sumerian King List (see also **Aka**, **En-mebaragesi**, **Mesalim**). Modern names of site (two areas) are Uhaimir and Ingharra.

Kizzuwadna Kingdom and land which emerged in **Cilicia** between the Hittite Old Kingdom and the later classical period of the Hittites (cf. **Isputahsus**).

Koldewey, Robert (1854–1923) German architect and archaeologist; after working at **Al-Hiba** and **Zurghul,** Baalbek and other classical sites, he was sent in 1899 to excavate at Babylon for the **German Oriental Society**.

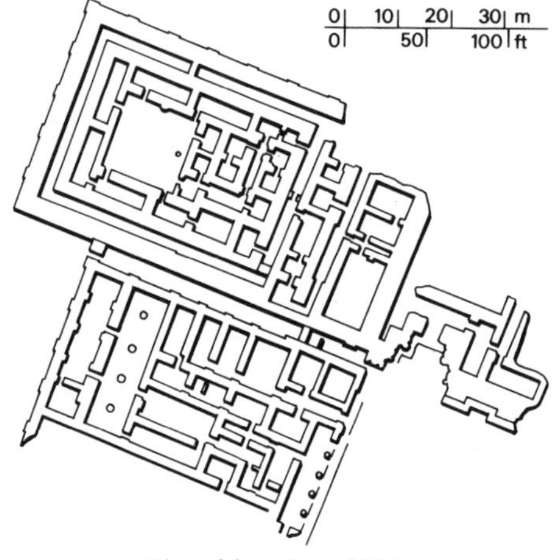

Plan of the palace of Kish

Kouyunjik Main palace mound at **Nineveh**.

Kültepe Modern name of the site of ancient **Kanesh**.

Lagash Sumerian city (modern Al-Hiba) and capital of a city-state which included the major cities of Sirara (Zurghul) and Girsu (Tello). Although it does not feature in the Sumerian King List, it had two important dynasties, that of **Gudea** and the Pre-Sargonic dynasty of **Ur-Nanshe**, whose approximate dates are:

Ur-Nanshe	2494–2465
Akurgal	2464–2455
Eannatum I	2454–2425
Enannatum I	2424–2405
Entemena	2404–2375
Enannatum II	2374–2365
Enentarzi	2364–2359
Lugalanda	2358–2352
Urukagina	2351–2342

(Dates after E. Sollberger and J.-R. Kupper, *Inscriptions royales sumeriennes et akkadiennes.)*

Lamashtu Akkadian term for a female demon with eagle's claws, unkempt hair and a canine head, who is especially malignant towards the new-born child.

Lapis lazuli Blue stone much prized by the Mesopotamians and (at least today) mined only in a remote part of Afghanistan.

Larsa Sumerian city not far east of Uruk, seat of an Amorite dynasty which shared power with Isin after the collapse of the 3rd Dynasty of Ur; modern Senkereh.

Lawrence, T. E. (1888–1935) "Lawrence of Arabia" who participated in the excavations of **Hogarth** and **Woolley** at Carchemish and later put his knowledge of the Near East to use as British adviser to the Arab Revolt.

Layard, Austen Henry(1817–94) Excavator of **Nineveh** and **Nimrud**, and subsequently diplomatic representative of Great Britain in Madrid and Istanbul.

Levee Geographical term for the bank of silty soil deposited each side of a river or canal when it floods.

Lipit-ishtar King of Isin (1934–1924 BC), and promulgator of a law code written in Sumerian which in its surviving portions often foreshadows the provisions of Hammurapi's later, more famous code.

Lloyd, Seton (1902–) Member of the Egypt Exploration Society's team at El-Amarna under **Frankfort**, and subsequently worked with the Diyala expedition at Tell Asmar and Tell Agrab. Later Technical Adviser to the Iraq Department of Antiquities, then Director of the newly founded British Institute of Archaeology at Ankara (1949–61);

Professor of Western Asiatic Archaeology in the University of London (1962–69).

Loftus, William Kennet (1821–58) Appointed in 1849 as a geological member of the Turco-Persian frontier commission, he had the opportunity to investigate several southern sites, including Ur and Warka, and took over the work of Kouyunjik after **Layard**.

Lugal Sumerian word for "king" (literally "big man").

Lugalbanda King of the 1st Dynasty of Uruk and son of **Enmerkar**. According to tradition the father of **Gilgamesh**, and the hero of some Sumerian epic poetry.

Lugalzagesi King of the 3rd Dynasty of Uruk but originally probably from Umma (c. 2340–2316 BC); he defeated Lagash, and claimed hegemony over the lands from the "Lower to the Upper Sea" but was later defeated himself by **Sargon of Akkad**.

Luwian Indo-European language closely related to Hittite and found in the cuneiform Hittite inscriptions from Hattusas; also the language of the "Hieroglyphic Hittite" texts.

Makan Land beyond Dilmun on the Arabian Gulf sea route, perhaps the Makran coast of southeast Iran.

Malatya Modern form of the ancient Melid, a city on the Anatolian plateau on the upper Euphrates, and capital of an Assyrian province.

Mallowan, Sir Max (1904–) British archaeologist who worked first as **Woolley**'s assistant at Ur, then independently at various sites in Syria and Iraq: Arpachiyah, Tell Brak, Chagar Bazar etc.; from 1949 to 1963 director of the excavations of the British School of Archaeology in Iraq at Nimrud. Professor of Western Asiatic Archaeology in the University of London (1947–62).

Mannaeans Population of northwestern Iran during the 8th century BC in an area which was a bone of contention between the Assyrian and Urartian kings.

Marduk City god of Babylon, who later replaced Enlil as chief god of the Mesopotamian pantheon, when Babylon had become the capital of the country. His wife was Sarpanitum, his temple Esagila. See also **Epic of Creation**.

Marduk-apla-iddina (floruit 720–703 BC) Sheikh of the Chaldaean tribe of Bit-Yakin and opponent of the Assyrians in Babylonia. King of Babylon 721–710 and again briefly in 703 BC. He is mentioned in the Bible as Merodachbaladan who sent messengers to Hezekiah to incite him to revolt against Sennacherib.

The god Marduk

Mari City on the right bank of the Euphrates, now Tell Hariri just west of the modern Iraqi-Syrian frontier; seat of an important Akkadian dynasty in the Early Dynastic III period, and of Amorite dynasties at the time of Hammurapi (see also **Yasmah-adad, Zimri-Lim**).

Mariannu Akkadian form of a Hurrian(?) word for a class of warrior.

Mati'el Aramaean king of Arpad at the time of Assur-nirari V of Assyria with whom he made a treaty (c. 750 BC).

Medes People of Iranian (Indo-European) stock who established themselves in western Iran towards the beginning of the first millennium BC, south of the **Mannaeans**. Their capital was Ecbatana (modern Hamadan), and although they are first mentioned by Shalmaneser III, their rise to power coincides with the decline of Assyria. Under **Cyaxares** they combined with Nabopolassar to sack Nineveh, but his successor **Astyages** was toppled by **Cyrus I**.

Meluhha Furthest stage of the Arabian Gulf trade route, beyond Dilmun and Makan; possibly the Indus cities.

Mesalim Although not mentioned by the Sumerian King List, known as the "King of Kish" not only by his own inscriptions found at Adab, but also mentioned by Entemena of Lagash as having delimited the frontier between Lagash and its great rival Umma.

Mesanepada King of the 1st Dynasty of Ur, whose inscription is known from the Royal Cemetery at Ur, and whose son A-anepada built the Ninhursag Temple at Ubaid.

Midas King of Phrygia and contemporary of **Sargon II** (c. 710 BC).

"Middle Chronology" See **Chronology.**

Mina Weight in the Mesopotamian system of about 1 lb or half a kilogram. Normally 60 shekels = 1 mina, and 60 minas = 1 talent.

Mitanni Name of the empire which flourished c. 1550–1400 BC in north Mesopotamia and Syria and extended its domination as far east as Nuzi and Assur. Its populace was largely Hurrian, but there seems to have been an Indo-European (or more precisely Indic) strain among the ruling class, although the degree of their influence is very much a matter of dispute.

Mohenjo-Daro With Harappa, one of the two major sites of the Indus Valley civilization in Pakistan.

Mursilis Name of two Hittite kings: Mursilis I (c. 1620 BC) and Mursilis II (c. 1330 BC).

Mushezib-marduk Chaldaean sheikh who seized the kingship of Babylon after the battle of Halule (691 BC) but was defeated in 689 BC when the city was taken by Sennacherib's army.

Muwatallis Hittite king, c. 1300 BC.

Nabonidus (or Nabu-naid) Last king of the Chaldaean Dynasty (555–539 BC), known to the Classical tradition as Nabonidus, and the father of **Bel-shar-usur**.

Nabopolassar Biblical form of the Babylonian name Nabu-apla-usur, the upstart who usurped the Babylonian throne in 626 BC and died in 605 BC leaving the empire to his son **Nebuchadnezzar II**

Nabu City god of Borsippa near Babylon; he was the son of **Marduk** and god of scribal craft.

Nabu-nasir King of Babylon (747–734 BC), assisted in the retention of his throne by Tiglath-pileser III of Assyria.

Naditum Class of priestess in Babylonian temples at the time of Hammurapi, living a kind of celibate life in a "cloister."

Nahum Biblical prophet who declared the downfall of Nineveh.

Nammahani Ruler (*ensi*) of Lagash, son-in-law of Ur-Bau (c. 2113–2111 BC); he was defeated by Ur-Nammu of Ur.

Naqia, wife of Sennacherib

Nanna Sumerian moon-god (Akkadian: Sin), chief god of Ur and husband of Ningal.

Nanshe City deity of Sirara in the state of Lagash, and the patron goddess of fish.

Naqia Aramaic name of the wife of Sennacherib and mother of Esarhaddon, known in Akkadian as Zakutu, also meaning "pure."

Naram-Sin Grandson of **Sargon of Akkad** and the other great conqueror of his dynasty (2254–2218 BC); also the name of a king of Eshnunna contemporary with **Samsi-Addu**.

Nebuchadnezzar II Biblical form of the name Nabu-kudurri-usur, the second king of the Chaldaean Dynasty (604–562 BC), son of **Nabopolassar** and the builder of Babylon.

Neo-Babylonian Term applied conventionally to the linguistic and historical period from c. 1000 to 532 BC.

Neo-Hittite Term applied to the small states in north Syria and the Taurus region in the early first millennium BC.

Nergal City god of Cuthah and the husband of Ereshkigal, god of plague and of the underworld.

Nergal-shar-usur King of Babylon (559–556 BC); his name is rendered Neriglissar in the Bible.

Niebuhr, Carsten (1733–1815) Engineer in the employ of the king of Denmark, who was a member of an expedition to explore Arabia Felix in the 1770s. He became the only survivor and made his way back to Europe through Iran, where he made the first reliable copies of the cuneiform inscriptions at Persepolis.

Nimrud Modern name of the site of ancient **Kalhu**, on the east bank of the Tigris not far south of Nineveh.

Nineveh Capital of **Assyria** from the reign of Sennacherib until its sack in 612 BC; it lies on the east bank of the Tigris opposite modern Mosul, and comprises the two mounds of Kouyunjik and Nebi Yunus, with a large lower town encircled by a wall.

Ningirsu City god of the city of Girsu in the state of Lagash, and husband of **Bau**.

Ningal Sumerian moon-goddess, wife of **Nanna**.

Ninhursag Sumerian goddess of birth; city goddess of Kesh. It was to her that the shrine at Ubaid was dedicated.

Nippur (modern name Nuffar) Central Sumerian city of the god **Enlil**; excavated by American expeditions from Pennsylvania and Chicago.

Nisaba Sumerian goddess of reeds, and hence of the scribal skills (reeds being used as a **stylus**); her city Eresh lost its importance after the Sumerian time and she was supplanted as god of writing by **Nabu**.

Noah Biblical hero of the Flood story, equivalent to the Sumerian Ziusudra and Akkadian Ut-napishtim.

Nuzi Name of a city of Hurrian population forming part of the Mitannian empire, not far east of Assur; called in the Old Akkadian period Gasur, the modern name of the site is Yorghan Tepe, excavated by an American expedition in the 1920s.

Oppenheim, A. Leo (1904–74) Austrian-born scholar who fled Vienna in 1938 and after stretches in Paris and New York joined the Oriental Institute of the University of Chicago in 1947. Editor of the Institute's Assyrian Dictionary for 18 years, and concerned with all facets of Mesopotamian life and letters.

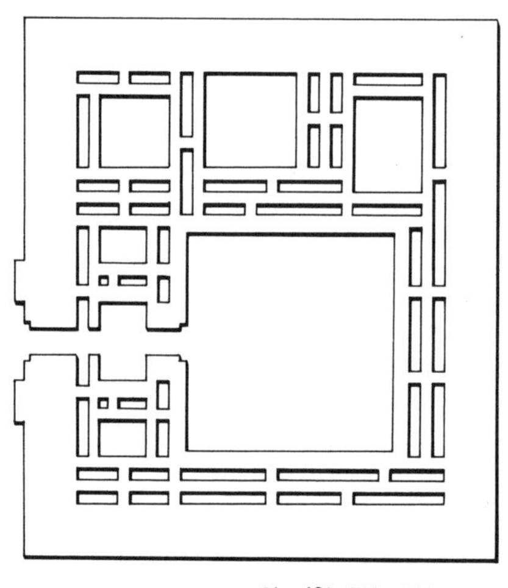

Naram-Sin's palace at Brak

Pottery from Tell Billa in the Nuzi style

Oppenheim, Baron Max von (1860–1946) German archaeologist whose chief contribution to Mesopotamian studies was the excavation of **Tell Halaf** in 1911–13 and 1927–29.

Oppert, Jules French Assyriologist who was a member of the French archaeological expedition to Mesopotamia in 1851–54, and made distinct contributions to the decipherment of cuneiform texts in the early years.

Ottoman Ruling house of the sultans of Turkey which fell shortly after World War I; the Ottomans governed (and often misgoverned) most of the Near East including modern Iraq, Syria, Palestine and Saudi Arabia.

Pantheon Complete assemblage of gods and goddesses in a given religion.

Parrot, André (1901–) French archaeologist, who has worked at Senkereh and Tello but is best known for his excavations at **Mari**; Director of the Louvre in Paris (1968–72).

Pasha Honorific title for governors of provinces (among others) under the Ottoman empire.

Pehlevi Dialect of Persian in use under the Sasanian empire (c. 3rd–7th century AD).

Persian Old Persian is the Iranian dialect in which the great Behistun inscription of Darius was written, using the "Old Persian" alphabet of letters invented for the purpose and imitating cuneiform script.

Phrygia Land in inner Anatolia, its capital Gordion to the west of modern Ankara; powerful especially in the 8th and 7th centuries BC (see also **Midas**).

Pictograph Sign or character in a writing system which is still recognizably a picture.

Pisiris Neo-Hittite king of Carchemish, still a semi-independent state until he was dethroned in 716 BC by **Sargon** for intriguing with the Phrygians.

Place, Victor (1818–75) French consul at Mosul (1851–54) and the excavator of the Palace of Sargon at Khorsabad after P. E. **Botta**.

Protoliterate period Term adopted by the Diyala expedition to designate the end of the Uruk period and the Jamdat Nasr period (which is also termed Uruk III), during which the first written documents appear in Mesopotamia.

Qatna City east of the Orontes in central Syria, center of a state in the second millennium BC; modern Meshrifeh.

Ramesses II Egyptian pharaoh (1290–1224 BC) who undertook major campaigns in the Syrian area but eventually concluded a peace with his main opponents the Hittites.

Rassam, Hormuzd (1826–1910) Christian gentleman of Mosul, and sometime British vice-consul at that city; assistant of A. H. **Layard**, and later sent on a mission by the British government to the mad King Theodore of Abyssinia (1864), by whom he was imprisoned for two years; returned to the archaeological scene in Mesopotamia in 1877.

Ras Shamra Modern name of **Ugarit**.

Rawlinson, Major-General Sir Henry Creswicke (1810–95) Officer of the Indian Army, who copied the Old Persian version of the Behistun inscription while on duty at Kermanshah (1835–37), and subsequently copied the Babylonian version while Resident of the East India Company at Baghdad (1847). He deciphered both versions; later became a Member of Parliament.

Relief Sculpture in which the design is carved to stand out from the surface of the rock, stele or other material.

Rich, Claudius James (1787–1820) Resident of the East India Company at Baghdad from 1807, and collector of Oriental antiquities (including manuscripts); the first to report with any accuracy on the ruins of Babylon and Nineveh.

Rim-sin King of Larsa (1822–1763 BC) who defeated Larsa's great rival Isin, but was later defeated himself by **Hammurapi** of Babylon.

Royal Asiatic Society British society founded in 1823 to promote the study of the languages and culture of the Near and Far East, and publishers of a Journal which carried many of the early contributions towards the decipherment of cuneiform texts.

Rusas Name of two kings of **Urartu**; especially Rusas I, king of Urartu at the time of Sargon's eighth campaign (714 BC).

Sachau, Ernst (1845–1930) German Arabic scholar, professor at the University of Berlin from 1876.

Samsi-addu Amorite form of the name of an older contemporary of Hammurapi, who ruled Assur, Mari and most of north Mesopotamia c. 1795 BC; his name in Akkadian is Shamshi-adad.

Samsu-ditana Last king of 1st Dynasty of Babylon (1625–1595 BC); under him the city of Babylon was sacked by the Hittite King Mursilis on a raid down the Euphrates.

Sanduarri Neo-Hittite king of a small Cilician kingdom who was beheaded in 676 BC by Esarhaddon (see also **Kara Tepe**).

Sanskrit Classical Indian language.

Sarduris Name of at least three kings of **Urartu**.

Sargon of Akkad (2334–2279 BC) Founder of the Dynasty of Akkad; according to tradition he was the son of a priestess found by a gardener floating on the Euphrates in a reed basket, and in his early days the cupbearer to Ur-Zababa, king of Kish.

Sargon (II) of Assyria (721–705 BC) Father of **Sennacherib**, and the builder of Khorsabad.

Saushtatar King of **Mitanni,** c. 1450 BC; we have documentary evidence that his empire stretched from Nuzi east of Assur to Alalakh in the west.

Scythians Nomadic people of Central Asian origin who followed the Cimmerians into northwestern Iran around the beginning of the 7th century BC, and were later known to the Greeks on the north shores of the Black Sea.

Sea Peoples People of uncertain ethnic affinity who invaded the lands of Anatolia, Syria and Palestine c. 1200 BC on the collapse of the Hittite empire, but were successfully opposed by the Egyptians.

Seisachtheia Greek term for a decree absolving the population of debts or other economic or social burdens.

Seleucid Dynasty founded after Alexander's death by one of his generals, Seleucus, which ruled Mesopotamia c. 311–95 BC.

Sargon II sacks Musasir

Semitic Group of languages which includes Arabic, Aramaic, Amorite and Akkadian, as well as Hebrew, Phoenician, Ethiopic and other Arabian languages.

Senkereh Modern name of the ancient site of **Larsa**.

Sennacherib Biblical form of the name of Sin-ahhe-eriba, king of **Assyria** (704–681 BC), son of Sargon and father of Esarhaddon.

Sethos I Egyptian pharaoh of the 19th Dynasty (1308–1290 BC).

Shalmaneser Biblical form of the name Shulmanu-ashared, borne by five kings of **Assyria**, in particular Shalmaneser I (1274–1245 BC), son of Adad-nirari I, and Shalmaneser III (858–824 BC), son of Assur-nasir-apli II.

Shamash Akkadian sun-god, worshiped especially at the cities of **Larsa** and **Sippar**; Sumerian form: Utu.

Shamash-shum-ukin Brother of **Assur-ban-apli**; given the kingship of Babylon after the death of his father Esarhaddon, but he later revolted against his brother's suzerainty (in 652 BC) and threw himself into the flames of his own palace when Babylon was taken in 648 BC.

Shamshi-adad Name of five kings of Assyria, especially Shamshi-adad I who is known in Amorite as **Samsi-addu**.

Shar-kali-sharri (2217–2193 BC) Fifth, and last significant, king of the **Akkad Dynasty**.

Sharri-kusukh (also called Piyasilis) Appointed king of Carchemish under his father Suppiluliumas I, and remained after the great king's death under his brother Mursilis II.

Sheikh Traditional, and usually hereditary, head of a tribe.

Shemshara Modern form of the name of the

city of Shusharra, now represented by a mound in the Rania plain, northeast Iraq, which was excavated in 1956 in advance of a new dam on the Lesser Zab by a Danish expedition; the tell yielded correspondence of Old Babylonian date between the local chieftain and **Samsi-addu** his ally.

Shulgi Second king of the 3rd Dynasty of Ur (2094–2047 BC).

Shuruppak Sumerian city on the old Euphrates in central Sumer, home of the Sumerian "Noah" Ziusudra and one of the five cities which held the kingship before the Flood; modern name **Fara**.

Shu-sin Fourth king of the 3rd Dynasty of Ur (2037–2029 BC).

Sidon Major Phoenician port on the Lebanese coast north of Tyre.

Sin Akkadian name of the moon-god **Nanna**.

Sippar City on the Euphrates north of Babylon, seat of one of the five dynasties of kings "before the Flood"; modern **Abu Habbah**.

Sirara City in the state of Lagash, on the canal flowing southeast from the capital, and abode of the goddess **Nanshe**; modern name **Zurghul.**

Smith, George (1840–76) Engraver by training, he was taken on to work on the Kouyunjik tablets by the British Museum for his evident interest and flair; after his discovery of the "Flood Tablet" he went out to excavate at Nineveh (1873), but on a later expedition succumbed to the summer climate in Aleppo.

The god Shamash

Society of Biblical Archaeology Founded in 1870 by the efforts of Dr Samuel Birch (Keeper of Oriental Antiquities at the British Museum) to investigate the "Archaeology, Chronology, Geography and History of Assyria, Arabia, Egypt, Palestine and neighbouring countries"; it published Transactions and Proceedings, but after 50 years it was merged with the older **Royal Asiatic Society.**

Stater Greek coin also used in Mesopotamia during the Seleucid age.

Stele Upright stone generally shaped and carved with an inscription and/or representation, very often bearing the figure of the king.

Strabo (c. 64 BC–21 AD) Greek writer, born in Cappadocia, author of a work on geography which includes information about Mesopotamia.

Stratigraphy Accumulation of levels on an archaeological site, the correct interpretation of which should reveal its history.

Stylus Writing implement; in the cuneiform system, the pointed reed (or substitute for it) with which the wedge-shaped impressions were made in the clay.

Sud City god of **Shuruppak**.

Sumu-abum First king of the 1st Dynasty of Babylon (1894–1881 BC).

Suppiluliumas I Hittite king and principal restorer of Hittite fortunes both in Anatolia and in Syria; c. 1380–1330 BC.

Susa One of the ancient capital cities of Elam, in the Khuzistan district of southwestern Iran; favored as a residence by the Achaemenid kings of Persia.

Susiana Plain around **Susa**; geographically an outlier of the Mesopotamian plain.

Sutu Nomadic tribes occupying the desert between Mesopotamia, Syria and Palestine from the time of Hammurapi down to the 13th century BC, when they were overwhelmed by the Aramaean incursions.

Syllabary Writing system in which each character stands not for a single vowel or consonant ("alphabet") but for a whole syllable (e.g. *ba*, *ab* or *bab*).

Taurus Mts Major range of mountains separating the central Anatolian plateau from the lower lands of Cilicia and Syria.

Taylor, Col. British Political Agent in Turkish Arabia and Resident of the East India Company at Baghdad after **Rich**, until 1843

Scribe using a stylus

when **Rawlinson**, whose original work at Behistun he assisted, succeeded him.

Taylor, J. G. British vice-consul at Basrah, who excavated for the British Museum at Ur and Eridu (1853–54).

Telepinus King of the Hittite Old Kingdom (*fl.* 1525 BC).

Tell Arabic word for a hill, often used to describe the mounds representing archaeological sites.

Tell Asmar Modern name of the site of ancient **Eshnunna**, excavated in the 1930s by the Chicago Diyala expedition.

Tell Harmal Modern name of a mound just east of modern Baghdad; it was excavated in the late 1940s by the Iraq Department of Antiquities who discovered a town of the Old Babylonian period with many cuneiform tablets; its ancient name was Shaduppum.

Tell Mardikh Site not far south of Aleppo excavated in the 1960s and 1970s by an Italian expedition and now known to be the ancient **Ebla**; c. 15,000 cuneiform tablets of the Old Akkadian period were found there in 1975.

Tello Modern name of site of ancient **Girsu**, excavated by French expeditions under de Sarzec, Cros, de Genouillac and Parrot.

Theocracy Political entity ruled in theory by a god, and therefore usually in practice by the temples and their priests.

Thompson, Reginald Campbell (1876–1941) Assyriologist who excavated at Nineveh in Iraq and worked for many years in the British Museum; later Reader in Assyriology at the University of Oxford.

Tiamat In Mesopotamian mythology, the personified sea, a force of evil hostile to the great gods (see also **Epic of Creation**).

Tiglath-pileser Biblical form of the name Tukulti-apil-esharra, borne by three kings of **Assyria**, especially Tiglath-pileser I (1115–1077 BC) and Tiglath-pileser III (744–727 BC).

Tirhakah Biblical form of the name of the Egyptian pharaoh Taharqa, of the Nubian 25th Dynasty (c. 689–664 BC).

Tudkhalias Name of four kings of the **Hittites**, especially Tudkhalias III, the father of Suppiluliumas.

Tukulti-ninurta I King of Assyria (1244–1208 BC) son of Shalmaneser I.

Tukulti-ninurta II King of Assyria (890–884 BC), father of Assur-nasir-apli II.

Tushratta King of **Mitanni** (c. 1380–1350 BC); the author of letters in Hurrian and Akkadian from the Amarna archive; his daughter Tadu-hepa was married to Amenophis III in a traditional means of cementing an alliance.

Tuthmosis Name of four Egyptian pharaohs of the 18th Dynasty, especially Tuthmosis III (1490–1438 BC) and Tuthmosis IV (1412–1402 BC).

Tyre Major Phoenician city on the Lebanese coast, not far south of Sidon; until Alexander took the city by building a causeway from the mainland, it was on an island and usually secure from siege.

Ubaid Tell Al-Ubaid, a small mound some 3 miles north of Ur, where **Hall** and **Woolley** excavated a sanctuary of the Early Dynastic III period dedicated to Ninhursag. Here too were found painted pottery of the prehistoric period of a style which is now known as Ubaid (also spelled Obeid).

Ugarit North Syrian seaport (modern Ras Shamra), the capital of a small second-millennium kingdom; it has been excavated since 1933 by a French expedition under C. F. Schaeffer, yielding cuneiform texts in Akkadian, Sumerian, Hittite and Hurrian, and "Ugaritic" texts in an early West Semitic language, written in a local cuneiform script and in an early form of the alphabet.

Umma South Sumerian city(-state) not far northwest of Lagash, whose bitter rival it was; modern Tell Jokha.

Ur Major Sumerian city on the southern Euphrates, city of the moon-god Nanna (Sin) and his spouse Ningal; modern name of the site El-Muqayyar. Three Dynasties of Ur are recognized by the Sumerian King List, the most important being the 1st (time of Royal Cemetery, c. 2500–2400) and the 3rd, whose kings are listed below:

Ur-Nammu	2112–2095 BC
Shulgi	2094–2047 BC
Amar-suen	2046–2038 BC
Shu-sin	2037–2029 BC
Ibbi-sin	2028–2004 BC

Urartu (Biblical Ararat) Kingdom in the region of Lake Van, corresponding to the later Armenia. First mentioned in the time of Shalmaneser I, it became a serious rival to Assyria in the reign of Shalmaneser III, and disappeared at much the same time as the Assyrian empire. The main Urartian kings and their Assyrian contemporaries are:

Aramu	c.850	Shalmaneser III
Sarduris I		
Ispuinis		Shamshi-adad V
Menuas	c.800	Adad-nirari III
Argistis I		Assur-dan III
Sarduris II	c.750	Assur-nirari V
Rusas I		Sargon II
Argistis II	c.700	Sennacherib
Rusas II		Esarhaddon
Sarduris III	c.650	Assur-ban-apli

Ur-Nammu First king of the 3rd Dynasty of Ur (2112–2095 BC), and father of Shulgi.

Ur-Nanshe Founder of a dynasty at **Lagash** in the Early Dynastic III period.

Uruk (Biblical Erech, Sumerian Unug, Akkadian Uruk, modern Arabic name Warka). Major Sumerian city on the old Euphrates not far northeast of Ur. After the discovery here of temples, works of art and the earliest known inscriptions, the period before the early Dynastic is usually known as the Uruk period. Uruk was also the home of important dynasties in the Early Dynastic period (see also **Enmerkar**, **Gilgamesh**, **Lugalbanda**), and remained of importance into the Parthian period.

Ur-zababa King of the 4th Dynasty of Kish (see also **Sargon of Akkad**).

Utu-hegal King of Uruk after the Akkad period (2123–2113 BC), who drove the Gutians out of southern Sumer but was himself defeated by **Ur-Nammu**.

Wadi Arabic term for a seasonal watercourse.

Warka Modern name of the site of ancient **Uruk**.

Wheeler, Sir (R. E.) Mortimer (1890–1976) Doyen of British archaeology, having worked principally on Roman sites in Britain, in Brittany and on the Indian subcontinent; Professor of the Archaeology of the Roman Provinces at the University of London (1948–55); protagonist of high standards of stratigraphic excavation.

Woolley, Sir (C.) Leonard (1880–1960) Perhaps the best known of British Near Eastern archaeologists, noted particularly for his work at Ur (1922–34). His most startling discoveries were made in the Royal Cemetery which yielded incomparable treasures of early Sumerian civilization. He began life as a field archaeologist in Egypt, but in 1912 succeeded Campbell **Thompson** as director of the excavations at Carchemish (1912–14, 1919). In later years he dug at al Mina and Alalakh in northern Syria.

Yamhad Name of the kingom of **Aleppo** in the early second millennium BC.

Yarim-lim Amorite king of **Yamhad** (Aleppo) who sheltered **Zimri-Lim** during his exile from Mari, and helped him subsequently to regain his throne.

Yasmah-adad Ruler of **Mari** under his father **Samsi-addu** (c. 1795 BC); after the death of Samsi-addu the city of Mari was soon retaken by **Zimri-Lim**.

Zagros Mts Major mountain chain separating the Iranian plateau on the east from the Mesopotamian plains on the west.

The ziggurrat at Assur on a seal impression

Ziggurrat (also *zikkurrat*) Anglicized form of the Akkadian word for a stepped "temple-tower," built in rectangular stages diminishing in size towards the summit on which there was sometimes a small shrine.

Zimri-Lim Amorite king of **Mari**, son of Yahdun-lim, who fled west from Samsi-addu but returned after his death, only to be defeated finally by **Hammurapi** c. 1763 BC.

Ziusudra Sumerian name of the "Noah" figure, who survived the Flood by building a boat after he had received a warning from the god Enki/Ea.

Zurghul Modern name of the site of ancient **Sirara**.

Index

Page numbers in *italics* refer to illustrations or their captions.